LOUISIANA STATE UNIVERSITY STUDIES

Humanities Series

DONALD E. STANFORD, Editor

———

Number Thirteen

Studies in German Literature

1963

LOUISIANA STATE UNIVERSITY STUDIES

MAX GOODRICH, General Editor

The Louisiana State University Studies was established to publish the results of research by faculty members, staff, and graduate students of the University. Manuscripts of exceptional merit from sources other than aforementioned are considered for publication provided they deal with subjects of particular interest in Louisiana.

The Studies originally appeared as a unified series consisting of forty-two numbers, published between the years 1931 and 1941. In 1951 the Studies was reactivated, and is now being issued in the following series: Social Sciences, Humanities, Biological Sciences, Physical Sciences, and Coastal Studies. Other series may be established as the need arises.

The Studies in each series will be numbered only serially, without volume designation.

Requests for exchanges should be addressed to the Gift and Exchange Division, Louisiana State University Library, Baton Rouge. All other communications should be addressed to the Louisiana State University Press, Baton Rouge.

STUDIES IN
GERMAN LITERATURE

Edited by

CARL HAMMER, JR.

LOUISIANA STATE UNIVERSITY PRESS

BATON ROUGE

MCMLXIII

To John T. Krumpelmann

Foreword

AT THE TIME of origin of the plan for a collection of studies to be presented to John T. Krumpelmann on his retirement from teaching at Louisiana State University in 1962, Dr. John A. Thompson, Chairman of the Department of Foreign Languages, requested the following persons to serve as a "Festschrift" committee under the chairmanship of the editor: Professors Wyatt Pickens, Bohdan Plaskacz, Kenneth Wilson-Jones, and Waldo McNeir (now Professor of English at the University of Oregon). Dr. McNeir, then Humanities Series editor of the "Louisiana State University Studies," arranged for inclusion of the prospective volume as a number in the series.

Invitations extended to friends of Professor Krumpelmann, including fellow-students at Harvard, former colleagues and pupils, as well as associates in professional organizations, met with a gratifying response. The untimely death of Professor Walther Fischer of the University of Marburg unfortunately prevented his contributing a promised essay. Luckily, however, Professor Horst Oppel, Director of Marburg's "Englisches Seminar," who edited the *Festschrift für Walther Fischer* (containing articles by Professors Krumpelmann and McNeir—the latter a recent Fulbright lecturer at Marburg), has furnished an important study of early German times in Louisiana. Professor Oppel visited our university in 1958 as a guest-speaker.

Sincere thanks are owed to all—contributors, committee members, and others—who have furthered the endeavor resulting in this book. Finally, a word of appreciation should be expressed to the departmental secretary Mrs. Margaret Beste for her efficient typing assistance.

Preface

Greetings from the Federal Republic of Germany

PROFESSOR JOHN T. KRUMPELMANN retired at the end of the 1962 academic year, after a distinguished career. As Consul-General of the Federal Republic of Germany in New Orleans, I consider it indeed a pleasure and a privilege to honor his accomplishments on behalf of my government and myself.

John T. Krumpelmann is known in the academic world as an outstanding scholar in the field of German philology and literature. It is not, however, the purpose of this contribution to point out his scholarly achievements. They are well known, and many of his colleagues who are more qualified for this task will do that. As the official representative of the Federal Republic of Germany, I should like to emphasize the excellent services which John T. Krumpelmann has rendered to German-American relations. It certainly cannot be said that he has done political work in the usual sense of the word. But by teaching the German language and literature and by calling the attention of his American compatriots to the German cultural achievements, Professor Krumpelmann has accomplished more for the understanding of my country in the United States of America than many ordinary politicians could do.

Professor Krumpelmann's career, however, did not consist exclusively in work with his university and his students. It was not merely a small academic circle to whom he taught German language and literature and to whom he gave a true picture of

Germany and German culture; he did his best to bring Germany close to a very broad public: in Baton Rouge, in the state of Louisiana, and, in the course of his long career, in the United States generally. He has succeeded well in his endeavors.

It seems appropriate here to recall his impressive list of publications which indicates a variety of interests. Bearing in mind Professor Krumpelmann's services for the mutual understanding of Germany and America, I find that his publications in the field of comparative literature appeal especially to me. I should like to mention in particular his translation of German poetry into English.

So it is with a feeling of deep gratitude that I express to him the very best thanks of the German government for the work he has done. I am sure that for a personality like Professor Krumpelmann retirement from his academic office does not mean complete retirement and that he will continue his activities, for in so doing, he will help foster the friendly relations which now already exist between the German and the American people. It is in this sense that I am looking forward to many more years of co-operation in the cultural field between Professor Krumpelmann and the German Consulate General in New Orleans—a co-operation which has proved so fruitful in the past.

HANS MARMANN
Consul-General
of the Federal Republic of Germany

Contents

John T. Krumpelmann
by
Carl Hammer, Jr.

AN ENTHUSIASM FOR interpreting literary relationships across the boundaries of language seems to have been predestined by inheritance for the one to whom this volume is dedicated. The circumstances of his early life combined with the broad experience of his academic career to foster an innate capacity for sensing international belletristic exchanges, above all, those obtaining between America and Germany.

John Theodore Krumpelmann was born August 8, 1892, in New Orleans—ever the meeting place of diverse cultures—as the son of John and Marie Louise Bernard Krumpelmann. There his paternal grandfather, a native of Germany, had settled; there his father was elected to the Louisiana legislature around the turn of the century. His mother, as her name indicates, was descended from an old Louisiana-French family. It is therefore not surprising that their son displays both German thoroughness and Gallic *esprit* and possesses a sympathetic understanding of Louisiana's great cultural heritage from France, as well as an exceptional acquaintance with the significant, but too little-known contributions of the German element to the development of New Orleans and the Pelican State in general.

After attending public and parochial schools of his native city, he entered Tulane University in 1911. He received the degrees of Bachelor of Arts there in 1915 and Master of Arts the following year; his graduate subjects were German, English, and Greek. During the sessions of 1914–16 he was first an assistant, then a teaching fellow, in German at Tulane. (He often cites, as proof of his "uphill progress," his having begun as a teacher of German in September, 1914.)

The young "Magister" next spent a year at Harvard studying Germanic philology and obtaining a second Master's degree, awarded in 1917. A year's teaching at Lehigh University was followed by service as a second lieutenant in the U. S. Infantry (Company Intelligence Officer), 1918–19. Thereupon he was Instructor in German at the University of North Carolina, 1919–21, and, on a part-time basis, at Harvard, 1921–24, simultaneously pursuing studies toward the doctorate, with a dissertation concerning Bayard Taylor's role as a literary mediator between Germany and the United States. Having received his doctoral diploma in June, 1924, he went to Europe for fifteen months as a Parker Traveling Fellow (of Harvard) and studied at the universities of Munich and Berlin. (In the fall of 1924 he made the acquaintance of Marie Hansen Taylor, widow of Bayard Taylor, then in her ninety-sixth year; this was probably her last visit from an American, since she died a few months later.)

Upon his return to America, Dr. Krumpelmann was Assistant Professor of German at the University of North Carolina, 1925–27, and then Associate Professor of German at St. Stephen's College (Columbia University), 1927–33. During the summers of 1926, 1927, and 1930, he served as Director of Foreign Travel, successively for New York University, the University of North Carolina, and the School of Foreign Travel (state of New York) —a position involving the arranging and conducting of European tours with residence, for study, in Munich. In 1933 he was Lecturer in German at the Institut für Ausländer, University of Berlin.

Meanwhile, in 1929, he had married Miss Catherine Dalton, of London, England. Well-known in cultural and social circles of Baton Rouge, Mrs. Krumpelmann has endeared herself to many as a gracious hostess.

Dr. Krumpelmann became Professor of German at Marshall College in 1934 and spent four years there in that capacity, being likewise Dean of Men from 1936 to 1938. In the latter year he returned to the Deep South to join the faculty of Louisiana State University, serving as Assistant Professor of German until 1942; as Associate Professor, 1942–48; and as Professor of German since 1948. He officiated as Acting Head of the Department of German in 1949 and 1953 and as Acting Chairman of the Department of Foreign Languages in the spring and summer of 1961. In the course of his twenty-four years at this institution, our senior colleague has ably filled numerous important committee assignments, frequently as chairman.

Students of Professor Krumpelmann (many of them now prominent in the educational world) unanimously testify to the inspiration they received from his teaching and from the personal interest that he always took in the problems of his pupils. A humanist in the fullest sense, he has consistently treated the sphere of language and literature as a humanistic study. If any course offered by the German staff at Louisiana State University has become a "classic," it is his seminar in German-American literary relations. Besides imparting German instruction on the various levels, he introduced the study of Russian at this university during World War II. As part of his intensive training in preparation for teaching the language, he spent the summer of 1944 at Cornell University studying advanced Russian. For more than a dozen years thereafter he conducted Russian classes, occasionally through the fourth semester.

From March, 1945, until September, 1947, Dr. Krumpelmann was on leave in Europe as Attaché of the U. S. Department of State in charge of exploitation of the archives of the German Foreign Office. In the summer of 1949 he attended the International Goethe Bicentennial Convocation at Frankfurt am Main as the initiator of official participation therein by the United States and as the delegate of the South-Central Modern Language Association and Louisiana State University. He was one of ten American university professors of German who, in the spring of 1954, were guests of the Federal Republic of Germany on a thirty-day study tour of German educational and cultural institutions. For the academic year 1954–55, he received a Fulbright appointment as lecturer (on German-American literary influences) at the University of Frankfurt. In January, 1956, he was a recipient of the Schiller Sesquicentennial Medal, presented by the German Consul in New Orleans acting for his government, in recognition of "efforts on behalf of promoting cultural relations between the United States and Germany."

Dr. Krumpelmann is a member of the Modern Language Association of America, the South-Central Modern Language Association, the American Association of Teachers of German, the American Association of Teachers of Slavic and East European Languages, and the Louisiana Foreign Language Teachers' Association, besides holding honorary membership in the International Mark Twain Society and Delta Phi Alpha (national honor fraternity for German). He is one of the founders and a former president of the LSU Philological Club. The South-Central Modern Language Association, however, has claimed his most active participation. A charter member, he served for some sixteen years as Associate Editor (for German) of the *South-Central Bulletin,* as Acting Editor in the spring of 1952, and as Business Manager in 1952–53. Upon his election as President of the Association for 1959–60, he took the lead in initiating a fourth number of the bulletin as an annual scholarly issue containing studies by South-Central Modern Language Association members.

For John Krumpelmann writing and research indeed constitute a labor of love. His impressive list of publications indicates a variety of interests; yet even a casual glance reveals a predilection for the realm of comparative literature. Thus we find Lessing and Kleist linked with Shakespeare; Schiller with Pope; and, conversely, George Eliot with Theodor Storm, to cite some Anglo-German literary parallels. More extensive is the array of investigations in the German-American category. Here one encounters among Germans: Goethe, Schiller, Duke Bernhard of Saxe-Weimar, Sealsfield (Karl Postl), Gerstäcker, and Storm; among Americans: Bayard Taylor, Longfellow, Hawthorne, Irving, Mark Twain, and—as one displaying twentieth-century affinities with Goethe—Marcus Cook Connelly. (Three articles deal with echoes of *Faust* in American literature.) A book now in progress concerns young southern scholars in Germany in the era of Goethe. Numerous contributions to *American Speech* and other journals attest his preoccupation with American lexicography, especially its German facet. Of his translations of four German dramas (three in their respective original meters), one by Hans Sachs represents the era of the Renaissance and Reformation; another, by Gryphius, the Baroque period; and two, those of Schiller and Kleist, that great age of the *Hochklassik* and the early phase of the Romantic movement in Germany. *The Broken Jug,* his rendition of Kleist's famous comedy, *Der zerbrochene Krug,* was successfully performed in 1950 by the Louisiana State University Players' Guild. His version of Schiller's *Jungfrau,* entitled *The Maiden of Orleans,* appeared in print as an offering to the Schiller Bicentennial of 1959. Finally, mention should be made of two articles in which he has conclusively shown that Schiller virtually raised Joan of Arc to sainthood more than a century before the Church beatified and, later, canonized her.

We have spoken of the teacher, the scholar, and the man of affairs in the academic world; let us now consider the personality of the gentleman who forms the subject of these pages. The unusual esteem and popularity that he enjoys among his fellowmen reflect his liking for people and his sympathetic, warmly human attitude. Adroitly sociable, a witty *causeur,* and a gifted storyteller, he enlivens any company in which he happens to be. Those of us who for long years have had the privilege of daily association with John, know him as a loyal, sincere friend and a valued counselor.

Perhaps the term "retirement" has never been more relative than in the case of our honored colleague at the end of nearly a quarter of a century of outstanding service to Louisiana State University. To him it means increased opportunity for the realization of long-cherished plans for further research, publication, lecturing, and travel. One is reminded of the words which Conrad Ferdinand Meyer wrote to Gottfried Keller on the occasion of the latter's seventieth birthday: "Ihnen ist wahrhaftig nichts zu wünschen als die Beharrung in Ihrem Wesen. Weil Sie die Erde lieben, wird die Erde Sie auch so lange als möglich festhalten."

The friends of John Krumpelmann, in like manner, unite in the wish that he may long continue his present active existence, and that the world, of which he has proved such an exemplary citizen, may reward his affection for it with many productive years to come.

Studies in German Literature

Charles Timothy Brooks's
Mary Stuart

by
Arthur Burkhard

SCHILLER'S BICENTENNIAL HAS been much celebrated, not only in German-speaking countries[1] but also in the Anglo-Saxon world.[2] English and American scholars have delivered and published commemorative lectures;[3] Schiller's life and accomplishment have been reappraised;[4] his poems[5] and plays[6] have been translated anew; some of his more important dramas have been produced in England and America by amateurs and professional companies, sometimes in the original German, more frequently in new or refurbished English versions.[7] *Maria Stuart* appears to have been an especial favorite both as to actual performances[8] and to renewed attempts to make Schiller's rhetorical tirades more acceptable to contemporary, non-Teutonic ears.[9] It seems an opportune moment, therefore, to call attention to an English translation of this play, completed more than a hundred years ago, conspicuously neglected during all of this time and passed over in a casual reference even by its author's most recent biographer.[10]

In his somewhat subjective monograph, Camillo von Klenze appears less interested in the author of this neglected translation, Charles Timothy Brooks, than in the genteel tradition which he couples with the name of Brooks as the second part of his title. Throughout, he seems more concerned with pre-

senting ideas of his own, relevant and irrelevant, than with the
by no means negligible accomplishment of Brooks, distinguished not so much as an independent poet but rather as an
industrious and workman-like translator from the German. In
the library of the university in which von Klenze served for
years as a professor (Brown University, Providence, Rhode
Island), reposes the manuscript of Brooks's translation of *Mary
Stuart,* as a part of the Harris Collection, where it is catalogued
as p 76-BR 777 m 1839. The manuscript was, as an enclosed
card indicates, "Presented by Mrs. H. L. Stevens," with whom,
or with one of whose relatives, von Klenze seems to have made
contact without fully exploiting his information. The present
writer was fortunate enough to receive encouragement from
another one of Brooks's direct descendants and, with the additional helpful co-operation of officials of the John Hay Library
of Brown University and the Houghton and Widener Libraries
of Harvard University, has been able to inspect the manuscript
under most advantageous conditions.[11]

The manuscript—consisting of three folders, uniformly eight
by thirteen inches in size, composed of stout unruled paper with
deckled edge, loosely stitched together with needle and thread,
written in a clearly legible hand in ink with the numbers in the
upper right hand corners of its 185 pages still visible except
where the edges, ragged and yellow, are crumbling off—is complete, except for the last page, torn at the top, where the first
line is partly mutilated. On this final page, with its missing
number later supplied in pencil, is written in the author's hand,
"Finis, Thursday evening 6 o'c(lock) Nov 7, 18X9." The third
digit is rather indistinct; comparison with the numerals in the
various page numbers could make it either three or five, but as
November 7, 1859, was a Monday, November 7, 1839, a Thursday, and Brooks presumably did not enter the wrong day of the
week, we are forced to accept the almost incredible fact that this
mature and competently composed manuscript was the work of
a young man, only twenty-six years of age.

The manuscript is prepared with care and apparently written
throughout by the same hand; sometimes with a fine pen with

regular letters now no longer always distinct, at other times with a broader pen with confident strokes that make the letters stand out, still bold and black. Some of the pages have no revisions; e.g., the two successive pages 83 and 84 and the later page 125; others, for example, page 58 have been much revised.

That the manuscript was inspected by contemporaries is shown by a penciled note on page 71. In the translator's lines, "No, You! Your evidence/The powerful and consequential Lord's/Could hurl me to the earth," the word "consequential" has a penciled ring around it, accompanied by this comment, "Americanism, is it not? Certainly not English" RWE. It is tempting to suppose that RWE is Ralph Waldo Emerson, whom Brooks knew and whose critical judgment he esteemed.

Further evidence of the care with which the manuscript was composed is furnished by the fact that there is only one minor omission: on page 181, in the brief interchange between Elizabeth and Davison (III, 14) one speech of Davison's, consisting of three words, was lost in the transcription.[12] Nor are there any longer gross errors, of which von Klenze culls many from early translations by Brooks. The most glaring is, perhaps, the inexcusably careless misinterpretation of Elizabeth's two lines (II, 9), "Verjüngte sich nicht dieser Talbot selbst/Als er auf ihren Reiz zu reden kam" as meaning, "Did not this very Talbot when his speech/Turned on her beauty, make her young again!"[13]

Among the more unfortunate features of the translation are the frequent and altogether unnecessary inversions which tend to discourage a modern reader at the very outset: thus, on pages 2 and 3 of Brooks's manuscript, one is subjected to, "E'en thus at Stirling feasted she her spouse/And drank from gold, herself and paramour," and not much later, "Durst the rude creature to your face say that?" (12); "Give ear and learn how Heaven deliverance sends" (18); "This wretched one no God came near to save" (57); "Has with the course of justice naught to do" (65); "He is of royal blood, that am not I" (83). These unhappy inversions continue, indeed persist, to the very end. For Schiller's simple question in fairly normal word order, "Wen rief er gegen mich nicht auf," Brooks poses the unlovely query,

"Whom did he not against me summon forth?" (99); similarly for Schiller's colloquial assertion, "Durch Drohung nur verschafft' ich mir den Eintritt," the abnormal arrangement, "Only by threats did I admission gain" (178). Such unpleasant inversions bring ruin to a rhetorical climax: "Aye, go thy way, thou false dissembling queen!/As thou dost cheat the world, so cheat I thee/'Tis right, a noble act thee to betray!" (67). Such a rendering does justice neither to Schiller's polished periods, nor to Mortimer's exalted state. It is equally sad to hear Elizabeth's question to Leicester end on a stilted and artificial note: "These, then, Lord Leicester, are the witching charms/No man can look on with impunity,/Charms in whose light no other woman may,/Unless to be annihilated, stand?" (102).

To be sure, Brooks is not alone in using this all too easy inversion of conventional speech, nor is he unique among translators of his and even later times in a somewhat over-poetic preciosity of diction.[14] One observes this tendency even in the rendering of simple, prosaic stage directions: *Unterbricht ihn lebhaft* becomes "interrupts him with spirit" (9); *er hält inne,* "he suppresses emotion" (24); *Mortimer forschend ansehend,* "casting a searching glance at Mortimer" (62); *nachlässig hinwerfend,* "dropping her words in a negligent way" (85); *zurückfahrend mit Ahnung,* "starting back with misgiving" (91); *Page geht zögernd ab,* "Page retires reluctantly" (127). Longer and similarly straightforward stage directions receive similar careful formulation: "At first stands mute and stiff with amazement, but soon collects himself and his eye follows Leicester with a glance of the most profound contempt" (123). Equally evocative is "he approaches her in a suppliant posture, she turns her back upon him, he stands in despair, then says with a resolute tone" (149).

There is, of course, no reason why Brooks should not be allowed to render, *Mortimer allein* (II, 6) as "Mortimer, solus"; in fact, as countless of his revisions show, he deliberately prefers the choice and archaic to the colloquial and commonplace to achieve what he considers proper poetic diction. The word "near"; for example, in the question, "Is no one near?" is

crossed out and above it is inserted, "nigh" (121). The effect of
the resultant translation is, therefore, if somewhat precious, yet
not without a singular and inimitable archaic flavor: "Not
publicly nor privily shall black/And bloody murder touch your
life" (27); "mummed up and masked in every sort and shape"
(53); in both cases a conscious manipulation of alliterative effects (publicly, privily; black, bloody; mummed, masked).
Everywhere heightened elegance and, now and then a Shake-
sperian reminiscence, "Thought over every thing and written
down/upon the tablets of my memory" (60); "Where I at last
can quite disburden me/Of long constraint" or, on the same
page (74), " 'Tis known full well that you above all men/Have
long enjoyed her preference."

In more extended discourse the archaic and alliterative effects
become accumulative: "And better far beseems me now to
wear/The mourning crape than to array myself/In all the stateliness of bridal robes/For from the groaning clouds a fearful
bolt/Shall burst full soon upon my heart and house" (48). Here
again, wilful alliteration (fearful, full; heart, house) together
with the rhythmic impact of the polysyllabic "stateliness," even
more finely savored in "unrelentingly," as here: "Benignant
Princess! Was it possible/To mock thee with such brazen inso-
lence,/So unrelentingly to sport with thee!" (120). Brooks is,
of course, fully conscious of the fact that prudent use of repetition can make dramatic appeal: "A fine device!/So finely
pointed! Only, what a pity—/So finely sharpened that the point
broke off!" (120); "Haply that there yet/Is time! Not even the
shadow of a doubt/Or foul reproach shall sully our fair fame"
(180). It would be inexcusable prejudice, however, to disregard
the fact that modern ears listen with distaste to archaic whimsy:
Melvil reveals himself to Mary (V, 7) with all too many thy's,
thee's, and thou's, together with their contracted and outmoded
concomitant verbal forms: "If thou so earnestly desirest this,/
Then learn, O Queen, that for thy comfort, God/May even
deign to work a miracle!/Here is no priest, sayst thou, no holy
Church/Nor body of the Lord? Thou err'st! Here is/A priest, a
God here meets thee face to face."

Anyone sensitized to stylistic finesse, especially those who have undertaken translation, will appreciate the untiring attempts Brooks makes to improve his version by discriminating revision. For Elizabeth's, "Verhüte Gott, dass wir den Ruhm befleckten" (II, 3), Brooks crosses out his earlier rendering, "God grant, we ne'er may forfeit our renown" and substitutes the more closely literal but equally elegant, "Nay, God forbid, our honor should be stained!" (54). To the prosaic, "My nephew who returned not long ago," Brooks prefers, "My nephew who but lately has returned" (60). To avoid the inversion, "The next new moon shall all thy terrors end," Brooks later inserts, "shall set thy fears at rest" (67). The rhythmically clumsy formulation, "It has been granted earlier than you dreamed," is smoothed over in, "You little dreamed 't would be fulfilled so soon" (91); the halting line, "I'll cast myself before the feet of her" is helped to an independent existence, "I'll cast myself submissive at her feet" (96); "And graciously I here vouchsafe to you/The solace of the royal countenance," gains by alliterative collocation, "The sight and solace of my countenance" (98). Brooks begins lamely enough Elizabeth's demand of Davison (V, 14), "The sentence, Sir, which in your hand I placed," but he redeems himself immediately with, "Which I yesterday/Consigned to you in trust" (180). What a pungent climax polysyllables impart to Leicester's reply to Burleigh: "—Es ist an diesem Hofe/Niemand, durch dessen Mund Graf Leicester sich/Erlauben und verbieten lassen kann!" (IV, 6); after crossing out five or six inferior versions, Brooks finally triumphs: "—There is not at this court/The man through whom Earl Leicester shall receive/Permission, prohibition or command!" (128).

Everywhere Brooks demonstrates how polysyllables help reproduce the rhythmic flow of the original: "Illustrious Queen, this is a day of joy!/Would it were such to all, would Heaven this isle/Held not one mourning, anguish-burdened heart!" (51); frequently, elsewhere, Brooks evolves a similar hyphenated *epitheton ornans,* "You fancy you know all things, nothing can /Elude your argus-eyed sagacity" (132). He is never at a loss for an appropriate yet unacademic polysyllable, "And mystery still veils the perpetrator" (119); "—Speak, shameless one,/And by denying, aggravate your guilt!" (129). Leicester's feigned excuse, "Doch redlich war die Absicht, es geschah,/Die Feindin zu erforschen, zu verderben" (IV, 6) is expanded into rotundity by the happy insertion of "irrevocably": "Yet honest was my aim, nor did it fail/At least to prove the malice of thy foe/and seal, irrevocably seal her doom!" For Elizabeth's contemptuous but conventional reply, *Elende Ausflucht!* Brooks substitutes a forceful polysyllabic juxtaposition, "What pitiful and petty subterfuge!" Leicester's account of Mortimer's arrest receives double improvement: a former version, "—his own mouth/This very moment has revealed it to me;/I had him seized at once and in despair" is made more forceful and compact "—his own mouth/Revealed it to me scarce a moment since;/I bade the guard arrest him on the spot" (153). The earlier rendering, "Should not discharge such gloomy offices," is elevated into a more virile masculine-ending line, "Should not be charged with such unhappy tasks" (136). Elizabeth's threat to Davison (V, 14), "Wehe dir, wenn Unglück/Aus dieser eigenmächt'gen Tat erfolgt" receives fulsome but idiomatic expansion, "Woe unto thee, if mischief shall ensue/From this presumptuous, arbitrary act" (182). When Schiller varies from the iambic pentameter to an occasional hexameter, Brooks becomes the perfect sedulous ape, imitating the rhythmic cadence of his master's voice: "Erst mit dem Tode kommt der Ueberfluss zurück" (V, 3), "And now at length with death comes affluence again" (157).

Many of the revisions cultivate an alliterative effect, for example: "Consider what you say", "Weigh well the words you speak" (155); "What I, poor plundered one, had left me still", "What I, poor plundered captive still possessed" (161); " 'Twas woman's frailty only made thee err", "From woman's frailty all thy faults arose" (170). Schiller's repetition of words is retained: Mary's entreaty to Elizabeth, "Nicht/An diesem traur'gen Ort geschähe jetzt/Die unglückselig traurige Begegnung" (III, 4), "Not in this dismal place would have occurred/Our dismal, our distressing interview" (99). Brooks does not hesitate to intrude

alliteration, even when nonexistent in the text: Kennedy's an-
guished cry to Melvil, "O Melvil! Melvil! Mussten wir's erle-
ben/Den Anbruch dieses Tags zu sehn!" (V, 1), "O Melvil!
Melvil! Could we not have died/Before the dawning of this dismal day!" (152-53). If Brooks here exceeds Schiller, and perhaps good taste, with a superfluity (died, dawning, dismal,
day), on another occasion, having duplicated but two of
Schiller's alliterations, instead of all three, he soon compen-
sates, not to say overcompensates for the omission: "—Sie
geht dahin, ein schon verklärter Geist,/Und mir bleibt die
Verzweiflung der Verdammten" (V, 10), "—She passes up, a
spirit glorified,/For me remains damnation and despair" (175).
For Schiller's *verklärter, Verzweiflung, Verdammten*, Brooks
has only "damnation" and "despair"; but the lines are amply
solidified by the repetition of "passes", "up", "spirit", and
"despair"!

Here and everywhere, Brooks identifies himself with Schiller's
original, manifesting, however, as befits an expert translator,
less close adherence to its literal sense than a faithful appreciation of its poetic spirit. Not infrequently we find him expand-
ing, sometimes in order to be more idiomatic, at other times to
clarify or reinforce, most often perhaps, because he cannot curb
the infernal facility of his inspired pen. Okelly's fearful proph-
ecy, "Und ich und Ihr, wir alle sind des Todes" (III, 8), is made
more fulsome but becomes unmistakably idiomatic, "And you
and I and all the rest of us/Are dead now, every mother's son"
(114); Aubespine's evasive response, *Ein Rasender gewisslich*
(IV, 1), becomes more expansive but also more affirmative, "A
madman, past all question, Earl" (115); Elizabeth's compact
indictment of Mary, "O, sie ist eine abgefeimte Bübin" (IV, 5),
is resolved into its various vindictive component parts", "O
she's an artful, arrant knavish woman" (127); Kent's factual
report, "Der Auflauf wächst, das Volk ist länger nicht/Zu bänd'-
gen" (IV, 9) receives alliterative reinforcement, "The tumult
waxes fierce, the people's wild/Impatience is no longer to be
tamed" (138); Aubespine's simple overture to Burleigh, "My-
lord, mein treues Herz/Teilt die gerechte Freude dieser Insel"

(IV, 2) is converted into an unctuous diplomatic approach, "My lord, my faithful bosom shares the joy/And righteous exultation of this isle" (116). Similarly, Leicester's apprehensive anxiety, "Ich bin entdeckt, ich bin durchschaut—Wie kam/Der Unglückselige auf meine Spuren!/Weh mir, wenn er Beweise hat" (IV, 4) is rendered into nervous alliterative, idiomatic English which reveals close identification with the speaker's emotional state, "I am detected, read and riddled through—/How came the miserable, meddling wretch/Upon my track! Woe's me, if he has proofs!" (120).

The tendency to expansion will at times make three lines in translation for an original two, especially in moments of emotional stress as in Shrewsbury's demand that Davison return the document of death, "Gebt, werter Sir, die Sachen liegen anders,/Die Untersuchung muss erneuert werden" (V, 14), "Return it, worthy Sir, affairs have now/Assumed a new and quite a different face,/Investigation must be straight renewed" (181). Nowhere is there betrayal of the original sense even when three lines of text yield four in translation, as in the following two excerpts both of which are in the most commonplace prose and present a difficult challenge lest the rendering sound banal: Mary's question to Melvil, "Wie steht's um Didier, meinen alten Kämmerer?/Doch der Getreue schläft wohl lange schon/Den ew'gen Schlaf, denn er war hoch an Jahren" (V, 6), "And how fares Didier, my old chamberlain?/But sure that trusty servant long ere this/Has laid him down to his eternal sleep/For he was old, I think, and full of years" (160). Or Mary's concern for the welfare of her servants, "Ich bitte, meine Diener ungekränkt/Nach Schottland zu entlassen oder Frankreich,/Wohin sie selber wünschen und begehren" (V, 8), "I pray, moreover, that my servants may/Be suffered, unmolested to depart/To France or Scotland whither they themselves/Wish and desire earnestly to go" (171). Expansion sometimes serves the purpose of clarification: of Elizabeth's acid appraisal of Mary at their encounter, addressed to her entourage, "Wie, Mylords?/Wer war es denn, der eine Tiefgebeugte/Mir angekündigt? Eine Stolze find' ich,/Vom Unglück keineswegs ge-

schmeidigt" (III, 4), Brooks allows not one syllable to escape,
"—How, my Lords?/Who was it then who spoke to me of one/
Bowed down so low? I see before me here/A haughty woman
whom misfortune has/In no wise softened" (96). One feels in-
clined to sanction increase of three lines to five when it is a
question of rendering Mortimer's adolescent infatuation: "Wie
dich der edle königliche Zorn/Umglänzte, deine Reize mir ver-
klärte!/Du bist das schönste Weib auf dieser Erde!" (III, 6),
"That noble kingly indignation, how/It kindled up thy countenance and gleamed/From eye and brow and cheek and every
feature/And in my sight transfigured all your charms!/Thou
art the loveliest woman this earth holds!" (105–106).

One must admire the power of emotional projection of this
kindly Protestant divine[15] as he identifies himself with the ardor
of the impassioned Catholic convert, Mortimer, and allows himself to enumerate Mary's several feminine charms, elaborating
on the single word *Reize,* which had sufficed for Schiller. Nor
can even he who in similar translations from German drama
remained pedantically insistent on adhering line for line to the
author's text,[16] withhold charity when Brooks adds an extra line
to Mary's wish for a final blessing from the Church: "All
earthly matters I have settled now/And hope to leave the world
in peace with man,/No human being's debtor—There is now,/
Melvil, but one thing that forbids the soul/To lift itself on free
and joyful wing/Above the troubles and the woes of time"
(V, 7). Nor does it appear overindulgent to excuse twelve lines
for Schiller's original nine in order to enable Kennedy to do
justice to the composure of Mary at sight of the scaffold (V, 1):
" 'Tis not, Sir,/By slow degrees we sunder Nature's ties/And
tear ourselves away from earthly life—/With one strong, sudden
effort, instantly/Even in the twinkling of an eye, the soul/Its
scattered strength collecting, must exchange/Time for Eternity,
and God was pleased/to grant my Lady at that moment power/
with manly soul to spurn the hopes of earth/And calmly trust-
ful to lay hold on Heaven/No sign of pallid fear, no word of
sorrow/Disgraced my Queen—" (153–54).

On the other hand, it is not unkindly to observe, that the

eight lines of English, with which Brooks lets Leicester steel himself, are less in tune with our time than Schiller's seven lines of German (V, 10): "—Abandoned wretch, it boots thee now no more,/with woman's tenderness to melt away/In these soft sympathies. The joy of love/No longer sheds its sunlight on thy path,/With brazen harness be thy breast now clad!/Thy brow be hard and cold as flinty rock!/Would'st thou not lose the meed of thy vile crime,/Boldly must thou maintain it to the end!" (175). Despite some excellencies, like the fortunate substitution of "the meed of thy vile crime" for "the prize of infamy" in translation of *Preis der Schandtat,* its general effect is that of poetic diction belonging to an age long past.

Brooks makes a valiant effort to duplicate Schiller's rhymes. He brings the first three acts to a successful rhyming close: (I) "And rest assured, old Paulet's faithful arm/Shall neither let her do, nor suffer harm"; (II) "And let the meaning be that from pure love/My heart allows what it cannot approve"; (III) "I stay. I am resolved her life to save,/Or make my bed beside her in the grave." He also ends several scenes with a satisfactory rhyming couplet: (III, 5) "When from her height of pride I hurled her, he/Stood close beside, his presence strengthened me" (105); (III, 6) "—To what saint, what altar fly?/Here brutal force, within the murder cry" (112). On occasion, Brooks reproduces also rhymes occurring not at the close of scenes or acts but in moments of emotional fervor: Mortimer's announcement of his audacious plans for the liberation of Mary (III, 6), "Let life and all its hope be set at stake,/You must be free and ere the morning break" (107); Mortimer's still rasher threat to possess Mary (III, 6), "I'll have thee, doubt not that, and yet so true/As God's in Heaven, I swear I'll have thee, too" (109). Elsewhere, however, although his skill in rhyming is abundantly attested here, and in the printed excerpt of Joan of Arc,[17] Brooks seems not to deem it worth his while to reproduce all the rhymes with which Schiller in the third act surfeits us.

Like many another translator, whether from fatigue, haste, momentary loss of interest, or undue failure in revision, Brooks, now and again, writes inferior lines: Mortimer's insistence with

Leicester, "Mit einer kühnen Tat müsst Ihr doch enden,/ Warum wollt Ihr nicht gleich damit beginnen?" (II, 8), produces this lame result in Brooks, "You must then end with a bold stroke at last;/Why not begin with a bold stroke at once?" (81); nor do the closing lines of this scene reproduce the force of the original, as Mortimer takes contemptuous leave of Leicester, "Bringt Ihr die selbst! Zum Werkzeug ihrer Rettung/Bot ich mich an, nicht Euch zum Liebesboten", "Bear them yourself! 'Twas as the instrument/Of her deliverance I lent my hand/ And not for carrying your love messages!" (82).

It has been left to the last to extol some of the excellencies which distinguish Brooks's translation. Hardly is he under way, when he produces lines like, "—he would quail/With trembling hand take his confession back" (41); "This is the thought that weighs upon our Queen—/O that this artful, mischief-making woman/Had only died before she set her foot/On England's shore!—To that I say Amen!" (41–42); " 'Tis true, this choice is forced upon her now/By stern, unchangeable necessity" (43); "The weightiest points already are adjusted/And France has given her assent thereto" (46); all four of these felicitous phrases within the space of as many pages before we have more than entered the second act. Elizabeth, for example, commends Mortimer in these well-chosen words (II, 5), "You showed a daring soul and for your years/Rare self-control. He who has learned so soon/And learned so well that difficult of arts,/Deception, has proved him worthy ere his time/And cut the years of his probation short" (64, 65). Mortimer's caustic observation on Leicester's behavior reads as well in English as in German, "—Wie kleine Schritte/geht ein so grosser Lord an diesem Hof" (II, 8), "—What narrow paths/So great a Lord at such a Court must tread" (73); so also, Leicester's expression of relief, "Ich muss des langen Unmuts mich entladen", "I must roll off this long-borne load of woe" (74); or Mary's reproach to Paulet, "O warum hat man mich nicht vorbereitet!" (III, 2), "Oh, why, why was I not forewarned of this!" (91).

High points in the translation are reached in the fifth and sixth scenes of the fourth act. Here, as an example, the colloquy between Elizabeth and Burleigh (IV, 5): (Elizabeth) "Thus to entrap me! Make such game of me!/The traitor! In triumphal pomp and state/To show me up before his paramour!/Burleigh, was ever woman so deceived?" (Burleigh) "How he prevailed, I cannot comprehend/What power, what magic arts enabled him/With such consummate skill to overreach/The wisdom of my Queen." (Elizabeth) "—O, I shall die/For shame! How must he secretly have mocked/My weakness! When I thought to humble her,/I was myself the butt of her contempt!" (125). Or, again, Elizabeth's threat in the same scene, "High as he stood, so deep be now his fall,/Great as his glory be his ignominy!/Once an example of my weakness, now/Let him be made a standing monument/Of my stern energy and strength of will" (126).

The sixth scene of the fourth act has so many apt renditions that a mere recital, without critical comment, serves to impress. Leicester, on entering brusquely, "I'll see the man who has the impudence/To bar me from the chamber of my queen" (128); to Elizabeth's interjection, "Your hope is vain to cheat my ear with words", Leicester makes this fluent reply, "Let babblers and back-biters cheat thy ear/With empty, juggling words, but I will speak/Straight to thy heart, And what I have made bold/To do, relying on your favor, that/Before thy heart alone I now would seek/To justify—no other law I own,/I bow to no tribunal other than/The free affection of Elizabeth!" (129). In answer to Elizabeth's accusation, "Can you deny that you were secretly/In understanding with the Queen of Scots,/Received her likeness and held out to her/The hope and promise of deliverance?" (131), Leicester makes a firm attempt at justification, "The rank I occupy, the confidence/Our good Queen honors me withal, must strike/Each doubt of my good meaning to the ground" (131–32). Finally, Leicester's retort to Burleigh, "My Lord! You love to prate before you act,/And are yourself the bell that tells your deeds" (132); Leicester's acquiescence in the death of Mary, "—much as I revolt/From measures of extreme severity,/I see and feel the welfare of the Queen/Demands this bloody offering" (135), followed a little later by his unwilling acceptance of the office of executioner, "Still, to give full assurance of my zeal/And satisfy my queen, I lay aside/The privilege my dignity confers/And take upon myself the odious charge" (136).

The emotional pitch does not diminish nor the pace slacken, as we approach the end. Kent's prosaic report on the attitude of the London populace, "Der Pöbel glaubt's und wütet. Nur das Haupt/Der Stuart, das noch heute fällt, kann ihn/Beruhigen" (IV, 7), receives literal and elevated transfer, "The multitude believe it and their rage/O'erleaps all bounds. The Stuart's head alone/Which falls this very day can quiet them." Davison's frightened request for clarification from Elizabeth, "Vergönne mir in dieser grossen Sache/Dein blindes Werkzeug willenlos zu sein" (IV, 11), gets its full impact of meaning, "O grant me in this great and solemn cause/To be thy blind and passive instrument" (148). Mary's confession to Melvil remains moving in the English transcription (V, 7), "With envious hatred has my heart been filled,/And thoughts of vengeance rankled in my breast./ I hope forgiveness of my sins from God,/And yet could not forgive my adversary" (168). And finally, Shrewsbury's belated but unfortunately unsuccessful plea for delay,"/Doch dieser Wahnsinn selbst/Beweiset desto mehr, O Königin!/Lass Dich beschwören, übereile nichts,/Befiehl, dass man von neuem untersuche," (V, 14), retains a heartfelt and simple sincerity, "Yet this madness of itself/Proves much/it proves so much the more, O Queen!/Let me entreat thee, act not hastily,/Command a new investigation" (180).

Brooks's sense of rhythm, his poetic insight, his power of emotional identification, his adroit manipulation of polysyllables help to enliven lines which in the modern version have a humdrum monosyllabic beat which only courtesy could term iambic pentameter. For the unrhythmic succession of monosyllables, "Me now, to raise me up from my deep fall!" Brooks makes a minor but important variation: "To raise me up who am so deeply fallen!" For the mechanical transliteration, "At your feet as you now lie here at mine," Brooks introduces "prostrate" to accentuate both "your" and "mine," "Prostrate at your feet, as you lie at mine"; for the prosaic assertion, "Lady Mary, you are in your place," Brooks archly avers, "Nay, Lady Mary, 'tis your proper place!" For the false beat in the halting line, "When you look at me with that icy glance," Brooks happily substitutes "behold": "When you behold me with that icy look."

To a disinterested outsider, it seems that Brooks's rendering is better than either the oldest or the newest translation of Schiller's lines from this same scene. For Schiller's "—Wie, Mylords?/Wer war es denn, der eine Tiefgebeugte/Mir ange-kündigt? Eine Stolze find' ich,/Vom Unglück keineswegs ge-schmeidigt," we read, in the version of Mellish adapted by Bent-ley, "—How, my Lords?/Which of you had announced to me a prisoner/Bowed down by woe? I see a haughty one/In no way humbled by calamity"; in the recent translation of Passage, "—What's this, my Lords?/Who was it then that told me of a woman/In deep humility? I find a proud one/No wise subdued by adverse fortune." Who shall say that Brooks is merely a second best, when he renders the lines, on page 26: "How, my Lords?/Who was it then that spoke to me of one/Bowed down so low? I see before me here/A haughty woman whom misfor-tune has/In no wise softened."

It would have been an act of commendable piety to print this unpublished translation in its entirety, in recognition of Brooks's achievement and in celebration of Schiller's bicenten-nial, and eminently timely, had the date turned out to be 1859, as was assumed until investigation of the calendar proved the assumption wrong. Since conditions do not permit publication in full, the writer offers these excerpts as a tribute not only to Brooks but also to that other translator to whom this volume is dedicated.

Die deutsche Siedlung in Louisiana im Spiegel des Amerika-Romans der Goethezeit: Heinrich Zschokkes *Prinzessin von Wolfenbüttel*

by
Horst Oppel

DIE DEUTSCHE SIEDLUNG am unteren Mississippi, die in der Kolonialzeit als "Côte des Allemands," seit 1812 als "German Coast" bezeichnet worden ist, spielt in der Geschichte der deutschen Auswanderung nach Nordamerika zweifellos eine untergeordnete Rolle. Handelt es sich doch dabei um eine kleine, überdies gänzlich isolierte Gruppe bäuerlicher Siedler, die nur für kurze Zeit ihre Selbständigkeit zu wahren vermochte, um dann fast spurlos im französischen Volkstum aufzugehen.

Die Erschliessung Louisianas hat bekanntlich seit 1717 zu den Aufgaben der Compagnie des Indes gehört, die eine grosszügig angelegte Werbeaktion nicht nur in Frankreich, sondern auch in den eroberten Teilen Südwestdeutschlands und in der Schweiz durchführte. Eine planmässige Übersiedlung deutscher Auswanderer hat 1720 der französische Finanzminister John Law, ein geborener Schotte, betrieben. Über die Anzahl der in Deutschland angeworbenen Louisiana-Auswanderer besitzen wir jetzt verlässliche Angaben. Nach Ausweis der in Pariser Archiven befindlichen Dokumente lässt sich auf höchstens 2600 Deutsche schliessen, die der Werbung Folge leisteten.[1] Von ihnen hat wiederum nur der kleinere Teil die neue Welt gesehen, da bereits die lange Wartezeit in französischen Häfen und die Ungunst der Schiffsreise erhebliche Verluste durch Krankeit und Seuche verursachten. Da man in Neu-Biloxi, das als Auffanglager gedacht war, keinerlei Vorkehrungen getroffen hatte, mussten die klimatischen Bedingungen und der Mangel an Nahrungsmitteln neue Opfer fordern.[2] Die Überlebenden wurden von Laws Agenten Elias Stultheus zum Arkansas gebracht, wo sie in der Nähe der Einmündung des Flusses in den Mississippi zu Rodungsarbeiten eingesetzt wurden. Nach dem Bankerott Laws verlangten die enttäuschten Siedler von Gouverneur Bienville ihren Rücktransport nach Europa, konnten aber dann doch überredet werden, oberhalb von New Orleans kleine Landzuteilungen anzunehmen. Zu ihnen stiess ein neues Kontingent von etwa 330 Auswanderern, die unter dem Befehl des ebenso umsichtigen wie unternehmungslustigen Karl Friedrich auf dem Schiff ''Le Portefaix'' am 4.6.1721 in Neu-Biloxi eingetroffen waren.

Die Lage der deutschen Siedlung dürfte auf dem rechten Ufer des Flusses zwischen den beiden nach Nordosten gerichteten Krümmungen von Bonnet Carré und Norco zu suchen sein, also in dem Flussabschnitt unterhalb von Lucy bis oberhalb von Hahnville.[3] Nach den Ouacha-Indianern, die das Gelände kultiviert hatten, wurde der etwa 8 km südwestlich der Siedlung gelegene See als ''Lac des Ouachas'' (später ''Lac des Allemands'') und die Siedlung selbst zunächst ''Aux Ouachas ou le village des Allemands'' genannt. Eine Zählung von 1722 hält die Namen der drei deutschen Dörfer fest: ''Mariedal'' (= Marienthal) mit 82, ''Wen'' (= Hoffen) mit 94, ''Ansbourg'' (= Augsburg) mit 70 Einwohnern.[4] Angaben über Namen, Herkunft, Alter und Religion der Siedler, des weiteren über die Grösse ihrer Besitzungen, die Ernteerträge und den Viehbestand vermittelt die Zählung vom 12.11.1724.[5] In den folgenden Jahren hat sich die Siedlung auf die linke Flusseite ausgedehnt. Bien-

ville mag, als er die Deutschen ansiedelte, auf eine Sicherung
der Lebensmittelversorgung von New Orleans bedacht gewesen
sein.[6] Neben der Belieferung des städtischen Marktes haben
sich die deutschen Siedler auf den Anbau von Tabak und
Indigo verlegt. Überschwemmungen (wie im Jahre 1734) und
Gefährdung durch Choctaw-Indianer (1748) haben die wirtschaftliche Entwicklung beeinträchtigt und teilweise zur Ab-
wanderung geführt. Zu der Zeit, als die französische Herrschaft
zu Ende ging (1763), war die deutschstämmige Bevölkerung in
ihrem Siedlungsgebiet weitgehend mit neuen Einwanderern
aus Frankreich und Kanada durchsetzt. Vor allem Akadier
hatten sich an der Côte des Allemands niedergelassen. Die
Französierung des deutschen Bevölkerungselementes dürfte
verhältnismässig rasch vor sich gegangen sein.[7] Dieser Assimilie-
rungsprozess wurde noch dadurch erheblich gefördert, dass es
nie deutsche Lehrer oder Priester im Mississippidelta gegeben
hat.[8] Die deutsche Volksgruppe war zu klein und war überdies
zu radikal von allen Bindungen an das Mutterland abgelöst,
um eine dem Pennsylvaniendeutsch vergleichbare deutsch-
französische Mundart ausbilden zu können.[9] Mit dem Ende der
Kolonialzeit war das deutsche Element zu einem Bestandteil
der Louisiana-Franzosen geworden.[10]

Die deutsche Siedlung am unteren Mississippi vom Beginn
des 18. Jahrhunderts ist zu einer Zeit, als in Europa die verschiedenen Spielarten des "Amerika-Romans" in Mode waren,
zu literarischen Ehren gelangt. Von einer Gruppe französischer
und deutscher Auswanderer, die in Louisiana ein neues Leben
beginnt, berichtet Heinrich Zschokke in seiner *Prinzessin von
Wolfenbüttel* (1804). Dieses Werk, das 1820 dramatisiert und
1829 in eine Oper umgearbeitet wurde, bedeutet in seiner
Urfassung wohl den "grössten Treffer," den der "exotische
Roman" der Goethezeit erzielte.[11]

Heinrich Zschokke, am 22.3.1771 in Magdeburg geboren und
am 27.6.1848 in Aarau gestorben, wurde nach seiner Übersiedlung in die Schweiz (1796) zum Wortführer des aufkommenden
europäischen Liberalismus. Er hat sich selbst in erster Linie als
Lehrer und Erzieher zur Toleranz und zum kosmopolitischen

Denken verstanden. Historische und erbauliche Schriften
machen nicht nur im Umfang den Hauptteil seines literarischen
Schaffens aus, sondern sind auch von ihm als eigentlicher Ertrag
seines Lebens betrachtet worden.[12] Wie seine Autobiographie
Eine Selbstschau (1842) bereits mit dem für den ersten Teil
gewählten Untertitel *Das Schicksal und der Mensch* andeutet,
ist er es niemals müde geworden, unter dem schwer auf ihm
lastenden Eindruck persönlicher und zeitgeschichtlicher Wirren die Frage nach dem Sinn des menschlichen Lebens und den
ordnenden Kräften des Daseins zu stellen. Aus der Altersper-
spektive der Selbstschau legt er in der Erinnerung noch einmal
den Weg zurück, der ihn von den Kindheits-und Jugendjah-
ren in Magdeburg zum Wanderleben des Schauspielers und
Theaterdichters, zum Studenten der Theologie in Frankfurt an
der Oder, schliesslich zum Wahlschweizer werden liess, der als
Leiter des Seminars von Reichenau seine pädagogische Berufung und als Republikaner inmitten der Katastrophe der Revo-
lutionskriege seine politische Artung entdeckte. Von seinen
literarischen Neigungen und Verdiensten ist in der Autobiographie auffallend wenig die Rede. In dem Kapitel "Schriftstel-
lerisches Streben" wird das "Pult des Schriftstellers" als "eine
Lehrkanzel" ausgegeben, "um welche sich die unsichtbare Ge-
meinde von Tausenden horchend sammelt."[13] Zwar räumt
Zschokke ein, dass er im Zustand der Übermüdung durch "erns-
tere Arbeiten und Anstrengungen" sich zuweilen den Über-
gang in "das fröhliche Feenreich der Fantasie" gestattet und
"Blumen in einer idealen Welt" gebrochen habe. Aber sofort
fügt er einschränkend hinzu: "Was ich in solchen Stunden,
Tagen und Wochen dichtend vollbrachte, hatte für mich keinen Wert, als das Vergügen seines Entstehens. Vollendetes zu
liefern gebrach's mir an Lust, an Zeit, an Beharrlichkeit, am
Bewusstsein des Mangels höherer Weihe."[14] Zur Wirkungs-
geschichte seiner schöngeistigen Schriften wird nur vermerkt,
dass die freundliche Aufnahme der Erzählung *Das Goldmacher-
dorf* (1817) und ihre Verbreitung in Frankreich, Italien und
Russland den Autor erfreute.[15] Der Amerika-Roman *Die Prinzessin von Wolfenbüttel* wird in der Autobiographie nicht mit

einem einzigen Worte erwähnt. Er gehörte für Zschokke zu den
leichten Produkten einer überströmenden "Gemüthsseligkeit,"
die ihn wenigstens vorübergehend "mit der abstossenden Wirklichkeit zu versöhnen pflegte." [16]

Die Distanzierung, mit der der spätere Zschokke dem literarischen Erfolg seiner frühen Schriften begegnet, wird zu einem
guten Teile von dem Umstand bestimmt, dass er allen Anlass
hatte, dem künstlerischen Geschmack seines Zeitalters zu miss-
trauen. Musste er doch erleben, wie sein Räuberroman *Abällino, der grosse Bandit* (1793) dem "unbärtigen Dichterling" un-
verdiente Ehre eintrug und in dramatischer Gestalt (1795) "mit
Geräusch über die meisten Bühnen Deutschlands ging." [17] Zu
einer Zeit, in der der Räuberroman als modischer Typus der
Trivialliteratur galt, sollte Zschokkes Jugendwerk eine noch
weit grössere Verbreitung erzielen als dem Autor selbst bekannt
geworden ist. Die Geschichte des edelmütigen venezianischen
Banditen hat nichts geringeres als eine "veritable Abellino
saga" verursacht,[18] die ganz Europa in ihren Bann zog und
sogar den Weg über den Atlantik gefunden hat.[19] Die englisch-
sprachige Fassung, die M. G. Lewis 1804 unter dem Titel *The
Bravo of Venice, A Romance, Translated from the German*
vorlegte, gehört zu den populärsten englischen Unterhaltungs-
romanen in der ersten Hälfte des 19. Jahrhunderts. M. G.
Lewis hat dabei nicht, wie man zunächst meinte,[20] eine freie
Bearbeitung von Zschokkes Drama *Abällino* vorgenommen,
sondern der Verfasser des *Monk* hat sich damit begnügt, eine
recht treue Übersetzung von Zschokkes Roman zu bieten.[21]
Zusammen mit Beckfords *Vathek* und Walpoles *Castle of Ot-
ranto* ist Zschokkes Räuberroman im Dezember 1849 auch in
die Hand Herman Melvilles gelangt, der seinen Londoner Aufenthalt dazu benutzte, sich im literarischen Bereich der Gothic
Novel umzusehen.[22] Wahrscheinlich las Melville seine Londoner Neuerwerbungen während der fünfwöchigen Heimreise
auf der "Independence." Wenn man bedenkt, dass bald nach
seiner Rückkehr *Moby Dick* entstehen sollte, so tritt das von
Zschokke selbst so abfällig beurteilte Jugendwerk des *Abällino*
wenigstens von fernher in den Gesichtskreis der Weltliteratur.

Als Zschokke seine *Prinzessin von Wolfenbüttel* abfasste,
hatte er bereits von der Räuberromantik seiner Frühzeit einen
erheblichen Abstand gewonnen. Im Rahmen der umfassenden
Entwicklungsgeschichte des deutschen Romans gehört die *Prinzessin* zu denjenigen Erzählungen, die nach Erzählhaltung und
Stil die Periode von der späteren Klassik zum Biedermeier
überbrücken.[23] Die Geschichte von der Prinzessin aus dem
Hause Braunschweig-Wolfenbüttel, die in einer zerrütteten
Ehe am Zarenhof schwere Demütigungen und Misshandlungen
erfahren muss, von der sie eine abenteuerliche Flucht befreit,
die schliesslich zum Beginn eines neuen Lebens in den glücklichen Gefilden am unteren Mississippi führt, bringt alle Vor-
aussetzungen mit, um nach dem Geschmack des Zeitalters den
Kult der Sentimentalität in ein exotisches Gewand zu hüllen.
Im Erscheinungsjahr von Zschokkes Roman mochte man überdies für das Problem einer ehelichen Verbindung von deutschen und russischen Fürstenhäusern um so empfänglicher sein,
als soeben Karl Friedrich, Erbprinz des Grossherzogtums von
Sachsen-Weimar-Eisenach, die russische Grossfürstin Maria
Paulowna heimführte. Aus Anlass der Ankunft des hohen
Paares in Weimar hat der bereits vom Tode gezeichnete Schiller sein kleines Festspiel *Die Huldigung der Künste* geschrieben, das am 12. November 1804 zur Aufführung kam.

Doch in unserem Zusammenhang ist nicht der erste Teil von
Zschokkes Roman mit der Schilderung der leidvollen Jahre in
Petersburg von Belang, sondern der zweite Teil, der von dem
Schicksal der Siedler in Louisiana berichtet. Zschokke begnügt
sich dabei nicht mit der Häufung von abenteuerlichen Zügen
und der freien Entfaltung emotionaler Regungen, wie sie so
oft im deutschen Amerika-Roman um die Wende vom 18. zum
19. Jahrhundert die Frage nach der Wahrhaftigkeit und Zuverlässigkeit der Berichterstattung überhaupt nicht aufkommen
lassen. Zschokke weiss einen erstaunlichen Vorrat an realisti-
schem Detail auszubreiten. Er schildert den Vorgang einer
deutschen Siedlung in Louisiana mit einer Eindringlichkeit,
welche die entsprechenden Kapitel der *Prinzessin von Wolfenbüttel* zum besten literarischen Kommentar macht, den wir

überhaupt zur Geschichte der kleinen und kurzlebigen Siedlung am unteren Mississippi besitzen. Man wird deshalb versuchen müssen, den Quellen nachzuspüren, die den Autor zu einer so sachkundigen Berichterstattung befähigt haben.

Eine unmittelbare persönliche Verbindung Zschokkes mit Gewährsmännern aus Louisiana, die ihm mündlich oder schriftlich Auskunft erteilten, dürfte kaum zu erweisen sein. Amerikanische Graduierte, die ihr Studium in Deutschland fortsetzten und dabei zugleich willkommene Informationen über ihr Land vermittelten, sind erst nach dem Erscheinen von Madame de Staëls *De l'Allemagne* (1813) zu erwarten. Es ist hinlänglich bekannt, welchen Nutzen Goethe daraus zu ziehen wusste.[24] Aber auch in Weimar war man fast ausschliesslich auf amerikanische Besucher angewiesen, die aus den Neuengland-Staaten stammten.[25] Jesse Burton Harrison aus Virginia, der im März 1830 in Weimar weilte, hat als "the only direct link that ever existed between Goethe and the South-Central region of the United States" zu gelten.[26]

Zur Zeit der Abfassung seiner *Prinzessin von Wolfenbüttel* hatte Zschokke kaum auf irgend eine mündliche Auskunft zu hoffen. Er war noch nicht einmal in der Lage, sich wie Goethe der Erfahrungen zu bedienen, die Alexander von Humboldt in Mittel-und Südamerika gemacht hatte. Humboldt kehrte erst im Herbst 1804 von seiner ausgedehnten Forschungsreise zurück, die nicht nur die Grundlage seines weiteren Lehrens und Wirkens bilden sollte, sondern geradezu als "ein deutsches und ein europäisches Ereignis" angesprochen werden darf.[27] Aber die Veröffentlichung seines monumentalen dreissigbändigen Reisewerks *Voyage aux régions équinoxiales du Nouveau Continent* sollte erst 1807 einsetzen und sich bis zum Jahre 1834 erstrecken. Der Verfasser der *Prinzessin von Wolfenbüttel* hat dadurch freilich nichts verloren, denn Humboldt hat niemals den Boden Louisianas betreten. Immerhin trug der Naturforscher sich vorübergehend mit dem Gedanken, es dem englischen Botaniker John Fraser gleichzutun, den er Anfang 1801 auf der Insel Cuba kennen lernte. Fraser, der im Auftrage des Zaren Paul Pflanzen sammelte, hatte 1799 die Stromfahrt auf dem

Ohio und Mississippi nach New Orleans zurückgelegt. Humboldt war nicht abgeneigt, dem Beispiel Frasers zu folgen,[28] um dann jedoch der weiteren Erforschung Südamerikas den Vorzug zu geben.

Die Reiseberichte Humboldts sind für die *Prinzessin von Wolfenbüttel* noch ohne Bedeutung. Als jedoch Zschokke fast drei Jahrzehnte später mit seiner Erzählung *Der Pflanzer von Cuba* (im *Rheinischen Jahrbuch* für 1832 erschienen) erneut den Blick nach dem Golf von Mexiko lenkte, nahm er ausdrücklich Bezug auf Humboldt als einen Gewährsmann, der bisher mehr als irgend ein anderer getan hatte, um Europa eine Anschauung jener Regionen zu vermitteln. Zschokke versichert zu Eingang seiner Erzählung, er möchte den Lesern Briefe mitteilen, "welche schon dadurch ein gewisses Interesse erhalten, dass sie uns mit der einfachen Lebensweise eines westindischen Pflanzers, mit Eigenthümlichkeiten einer Insel näher bekannt machen, welche, meines Wissens, seit Alexander von Humboldt Niemand näher geschildert hat." [29] Der Umstand, durch den Zschokke in den Besitz von Briefen eines Pflanzers kam, wird in der Erzählung selbst angedeutet, aber doch fiktiv verschleiert. Zuverlässiger berichtet darüber die Autobiographie: "Ein auf seinen Pflanzungen in Cuba wohnender Schweizer hatte seinen Sohn, Kind einer schönen Negerin, in eine Erziehungsanstalt nach Unterseen am Thuner-See geschickt, mir aber die Geldzahlungen für ihn anvertraut." [30] Die persönliche Verbindung regte offensichtlich Zschokke dazu an, ein Bild des Lebens auf Cuba zu entwerfen, wobei er durch authentisches Material wirksam unterstützt wurde.

Bei der Abfassung der *Prinzessin von Wolfenbüttel* sah sich Zschokke in einer weit ungünstigeren Lage. Doch es entspricht der Rechtlichkeit seines Denkens, die zuweilen einen leichten Schein von Pedanterie erhält, wenn er auch in diesem Falle willfährig dem Leser Auskunft gibt, woher er sein Wissen um das abenteuerliche Schicksal der Prinzessin bezogen hat. Im Vorwort wird als Quelle für die "ausserordentliche Begebenheit," welche die Fabel des Romans bestimmt, unter anderen der "Chevalier le Bossu" mit seinen "Nouveaux voyages d'Amérique septentrionale" genannt.³¹ Die Angabe des Verfassernamens und des Titels ist ungenau.³² Ob Zschokke tatsächlich Bossu gelesen hat oder sich mit Informationen aus zweiter Hand begnügte, die ihrerseits auf den Franzosen zurückgehen, ist ungewiss. Überdies kam es dem deutschen Erzähler allein darauf an, für das Unglaubliche und schlechthin Fabelhafte, das dem Bericht vom Leben der Christine von Wolfenbüttel anhaftet, sich durch einen Hinweis auf seine Quellen gewissermassen zu entlasten. Auf welche Weise er jedoch über das Ziel der Auswanderer, nämlich Louisiana, in historischer, geographischer und wirtschaftlicher Hinsicht Aufschluss erlangte, wird an keiner Stelle des Romans vermerkt.

Bossu gehört als Reiseschriftsteller einer Zeit an, in der das Amerika-Bild der Franzosen eine entscheidende Wandlung durchmachte: "It was . . . in the 1760's that citizens of the French and American cultures first came into direct contact and communication." ³³ Eine Folge solcher persönlicher Beziehungen, die mit dem Eintreffen Benjamin Franklins in Paris wirksamen Antrieb erhielten, ist es zweifellos gewesen, wenn der seit Montesquieu im Denken der Franzosen tief eingenistete Verdacht, dass neue Staatengründungen allein schon durch ihre Traditionslosigkeit einem Primitivismus der Gesinnung ausgeliefert sind, allmählich entkräftet wurde. Man war nun bereit, die Lebens-und Entwicklungsmöglichkeiten, welche die neue Welt bot, mit anderen Augen zu sehen. Das mag in erster Linie für die amerikanischen Nordstaaten gelten, deren Freiheitskampf von Frankreich mit grösster Aufmerksamkeit verfolgt worden ist. Die Kundschafter, die der französische Premierminister Choiseul seit 1764 in Englands nordamerikanischen Besitzungen unterhielt, brachten zuverlässige Nachrichten über deren erstaunliche Entwicklung zu wirtschaftlichem und kulturellem Wohlstand mit.³⁴ Doch dieses neue Interesse musste auch dem Süden zugute kommen, wo soeben Louisiana zu einer spanischen Kolonie geworden war (1763), in der jedoch die neuen Herren es keineswegs leicht fanden, französische Sprache und Gesittung mit spanischer zu vertauschen.³⁵ Bossu konnte zuverlässig damit rechnen, dass Nachrichten über das ehemalige

französische Besitztum im Mutterland willkommen waren. Er
hat es auch nicht unterlassen, die deutsche Siedlung zu erwäh-
nen, deren wirtschaftliche Bedeutung er hoch veranschlagt.
Den Deutschen wird nachgesagt: "Ces Peuples sont très la-
bourieux, on les regarde comme les Pourvoyeurs de la Capi-
tale." [36]

Als Zschokke seine *Prinzessin von Wolfenbüttel* schrieb, hatte
sich freilich an den von Bossu geschilderten Zuständen bereits
wieder manches geändert. Inzwischen war Louisiana für wenige
Jahre an Frankreich zurückgefallen, um kurzfristig an die
Amerikaner abgetreten zu werden. Die alten französischen
Familien haben diesen erneuten politischen Wechsel nicht ohne
Bitternis über sich ergehen lassen.[37] Die Politiker in Paris
mögen dadurch in geringem Masse beunruhigt worden sein, da
ihre Entscheidung von "strategic necessities" bestimmt wurde.[38]
Aber man konnte es der französischen Öffentlichkeit nicht ver-
denken, wenn sie neuen Anteil am Ergehen der Bevölkerung
am unteren Mississippi nahm. Reiseschriftsteller wie Claude C.
Robin,[39] François Marie Perrin Du Lac[40] und Berquin-Duval-
lon[41] hielten reiche Informationen bereit. Die Veröffentlichung
von Berquin-Duvallon kam gerade noch zeitig genug, um als
Quelle für Zschokke dienen zu können. Dies umso eher, als der
Buchausgabe (1803) ein Abdruck von Auszügen im *Mercure de
France* vorhergegangen war. Für die Beliebtheit Duvallons
spricht, dass bereits 1804 in Weimar eine gekürzte deutsche
Übersetzung erschien, die unter dem Titel *Schilderung von
Louisiana* von Ehrmann verfasst worden war. Zschokke konnte
es mithin gar nicht so schwer fallen, sich mit Material zu ver-
sorgen, das ihm erlaubte, von der Kolonie ein leidlich zuverläs-
siges Bild zu entwerfen.

Für seine *Prinzessin von Wolfenbüttel* wählte Zschokke die
Form eines Brief-Romans, wobei freilich die Briefe mit Tage-
buchblättern durchsetzt sind und das Ganze am Schluss durch
ein Kapitel "Mündliche Überlieferungen" und eine "Nach-
schrift" abgerundet wird. Diese Art der Darbietung mag auf das
Vorbild von Bossus Reisewerken zurückgehen. Damit hängt
wohl auch zusammen, dass Zschokke, der doch den Lebenslauf

einer deutschen Prinzessin erzählt, einen Franzosen zur zweiten
Hauptfigur macht. Wesentliche Teile des brieflichen Berichtes
fallen der fiktiven Gestalt des Chevalier d'Aubant zu, der einem
Freunde in Frankreich von seinem Ergehen in Petersburg Mit-
teilung macht. Er wird dort Zeuge der Demütigungen, welche
die von ihm selbst tief verehrte und geliebte Grossfürstin Christine an der Seite des haltlosen Zarewitsch Alexis erdulden muss.
Am Hofe in Ungnade gefallen, entschliesst sich der Chevalier
zur schleunigen Rückkehr nach Frankreich, wo er zu seiner
äussersten Bestürzung die Nachricht von dem Tode Christines
erhält. Als Ausweg aus der heftigen Krise, in der er sich be-
findet, bietet sich ihm die Abkehr von Europa und die Erneue-
rung seines Lebens in einem anderen Erdteil. Das Stichwort
"Louisiana" wird mit grossem erzählerischen Geschick ange-
bracht, so dass es seine Wirkung nicht verfehlt. In der Art des
pikaresken Romans fällt es dem Diener d'Aubants zu, seinem
ratlos und tatenlos in Paris weilenden Herrn die Kunde vom
gelobten Land zu bringen und ihm ein "Fürstenthum" zu
versprechen. Die ungläubige und ironisch gehaltene Frage des
Chevalier, wo denn sein Fürstentum liegen solle, wird mit der
Antwort quittiert: "In der neuen Welt, Herr Hauptmann; da
—warten Sie —ja, —am Mississippi, in dem grossen Königreich
Louisiana, nicht weit von Amerika. Alles läuft jetzt dahin. Ich
habe mit sechszehn Familien gesprochen heut' an der Wirthsta-
fel; sie kommen weit her; es sind sogar Deutsche und Schweizer
darunter. Alles geht nach der Louisiana." [42] Der Plan, der
zunächst als absurd erscheint, nimmt rasch einen konkreten
Umriss an. Wenig später kann der Chevalier d'Aubant seinem
Freunde Laurent Bellisle brieflich melden: "Mein Handel mit
dem Schiffskapitän de Blaizot ist im Reinen. Ich verlasse
Europa und gehe in die Louisiana. An den schönen Ufern des
Mississippi will ich meine Wohnung bauen, und Oberhaupt
einer kleinen Kolonie werden, die mich zu ihrem Führer gewählt hat. Es sind sechs Handwerksleute, welche auf eigene
Kosten nach Nordamerika gehen wollen; diese treten in meine
Dienste. Schon habe ich ansehnliche Bestellungen in Bordeaux
zum Ankauf von allerlei Samen, Vieh, Acker-und Hausgeräth

gemacht." [43] Der Auswanderer lässt keinen Zweifel darüber aufkommen, dass es nicht Abenteuerlust oder Gewinnsucht ist, was ihn zu diesem Entschluss bestimmt. Vielmehr versteht er sich selbst als einen "Europa-Müden," der den Entartungen des privaten und des öffentlichen Lebens im alten Erdteil zu entrinnen hofft: "Ich sehne mich nach einem schönern Leben. Ich will der Stifter einer glücklichen Gesellschaft werden, welche durch Arbeitsamkeit blühend, durch Unterricht weise, durch bürgerliche und religiöse Freiheit kraftvoll und beneidenswürdig sein soll." [44]

In paralleler Führung der Hauptfiguren lenkt der Erzähler nun zunächst wieder unseren Blick auf Christine. Wir erfahren, dass die Nachricht vom Tode der Grossfürstin ein Irrtum war. Die misshandelte Gemahlin des Zarewitsch gilt zwar in Petersburg als tot und hat sogar ein Scheinbegräbnis erhalten. In Wirklichkeit handelt es sich jedoch dabei um ein Trugspiel, das es ihr ermöglicht, mit Hilfe eines treuen Dieners und ihrer Hofdamen die Flucht aus unerträglichen Verhältnissen zu vollziehen. Eine beschwerliche und gefahrvolle Reise führt sie durch Russland, Polen und Deutschland nach Frankreich, wo sie nun ebenfalls das Heil in der Auswanderung sucht. In Paris wird die Vereinbarung mit einem Kapitän getroffen, sie selbst und ihre wenigen Begleiter "nebst mehrern hundert Deutschen nach Amerika überzufahren. Diese Deutschen waren mehrentheils verarmte Leute, welche ihr Vaterland zu verlassen gedachten, um ihr Glück unter fremden Himmelsstrichen bei der Gründung neuer Kolonien in Louisiana zu finden." [45]

Die hochgespannte Erwartung auf das gelobte Land, wo man "im Schatten tausendjähriger Haine verborgen und vergessen leben" möchte, [46] wird zunächst gründlich enttäuscht. Traum und Wirklichkeit stimmen nicht überein. Was sich dem Auge der Auswanderer bei der Ankunft darbietet, wird nun wiederum in einem Brief des Chevalier d'Aubant an seinen Freund festgehalten. An dieser Stelle gelangt Zschokke zu einer klaren und eindringlichen Darstellung, wie sie nur aus der Kenntnis historischer und geographischer Quellen erwachsen konnte. Vorübergehend wird das fabulöse Element ganz zurückge-

drängt, um der sachkundigen Beschreibung Platz zu machen.
D'Aubant berichtet mit spürbarer Ernüchterung: "Als wir von
Pensacola absegelten, längs den Küsten von Westflorida, erwar-
teten wir Ausgewanderten alle mit ungestümem Verlangen den
prachtvollen Anblick des hochgelobten Louisiana. Wir träum-
ten uns schon die malerischen Ufergegenden, mit ihren grünen
Hügeln, reichen Fluren und ungeheuern Waldungen aufs
Schönste vor, und beschlossen so im Vorbeifahren die behag-
lichsten Landungsplätze, und was sonst sich zur Errichtung
einer Pflanzstadt eignen würde, sorgfältig zu bemerken. Aber,
ach! wir fanden uns abscheulich getäuscht. Von Pensacola hin-
weg dehnt sich eine lange, kahle, niedrige Küste von fünfzig bis
sechszig Stunden hin; überall nur todter Sand, auf welchem hin
und wieder eine verkrüppelte Meerkiefer und magere Ge-
sträuche grünten." Im gleichen Zusammenhang heisst es dann
weiter: "Der Kapitän landete endlich in der allertraurigsten
und unfruchtbarsten Gegend dieser Küste. Da lagen einige er-
bärmliche Hütten umher, worin etliche halbverhungerte Menschen wohnten, Überbleibsel einer frühern, hier angelegten
Kolonie. Bei diesem Anblick entfiel uns Allen der Muth; wir
sahen einer traurigen Zukunft entgegen; unsere stolzen Erwar-
tungen schlichen demüthig neben der Wirklichkeit hin. Es
fehlte wenig, dass nicht viele Ausgewanderte wieder mit einem
Schiffe nach Europa zurückgekehrt wären, welches eben von
Biloxi absegeln wollte zum vaterländischen Welttheil." [47]
Der Missmut der Auswanderer wird noch einmal durch den
Kapitän beschwichtigt, der sie dazu ermahnt, New Orleans
nicht mit "dem grässlichen Biloxi" zu verwechseln. So setzt man
die Reise fort, um dabei nur neue und höchst unangenehme
Überraschungen zu erleben. Mit den Worten d'Aubants: "End-
lich erreichten wir die Mündung des ungeheuern Mississip-
pistroms, von welchem jetzt alle Zungen Europens sprechen. Er
bietet viele Einfahrten dar; aber die meisten haben nur wenig
Wasser, vielen fehlt es zu gewissen Jahreszeiten ganz daran. Das
Ufer ist überall flach und niedrig, und scheint weit umher, so
wie der grösste Theil der Küste, erst durch das Meer und den
Strom gebildet worden zu sein. Man findet dort beinahe keinen

Stein, sondern Alles ist Schlamm, Sand, Schilf und verfaultes
Holz, wie es der Mississippi von seinen entfernten, noch nie
gesehenen Quellen, bis hieher, in einer unermesslichen Strecke
aufnahm und gegen den Ozean ausspülte." [48] Nach zweitägiger
Fahrt auf dem "Schilf-und Schlammeer" ist New Orleans er-
reicht: "Als man uns sagte, wir seien nun an Ort und Stelle,
rieben wir uns verwundert die Augen; denn aller Mühe un-
geachtet, konnte keiner von uns Neu-Orleans entdecken, oder
was sonst einem so berühmten Orte ähnlich sah. Am östlichen
Ufer des Flusses, wo er eine weite Krümmung bildet, in welcher
alle Schiffe landen können, standen überall zerstreute Hütten,
von Holz und Rohr aufgeführt. Hin und wieder zeigte sich
auch wohl ein Gebäude, von Holz und gebranntem Thon er-
richtet, was etwas europäischere Physiognomie hatte. Man er-
klärte mir den Mangel aller grossen und massiven Häuser damit,
dass der Boden nicht Festigkeit genug habe, schwere Gebäude
zu tragen. Das war nun die Hauptstadt von Louisiana." [49]
Bei der Schilderung von New Orleans wird den wirtschaft-
lichen Gegebenheiten ausführlich Rechnung getragen. Zschokke
bemüht sich, alles mit den Augen der Siedler zu sehen: "Neu-
Orleans liegt auf einer grossen Insel, die ungefähr fünfzig bis
sechszig Stunden lang sein mag. Sie wird vom Mississippi, vom
Meer, vom Landsee Pont Chartam [*sic*] und vom Manchac,
einem Abfluss des Mississippi, gebildet. Der grösste Theil dieser
Insel aber ist durchaus unanpflanzbar, ist den Überschwemmungen des Mississippi ausgesetzt, und eines schlammigten feuchten
Grundes. Man hatte den Bau des Zuckerrohrs versucht; allein
die zuweilen eintretenden, wenn gleich geringen Fröste zur
Regenzeit, besonders beim Nord-dund Nordwestwind, verderben die Ärnten. Auch mit Baumwollenstauden werden ziemlich
glückliche Versuche gemacht; am besten gelingen die Pflanzungen des Indigo, und dieser kann allerdings einst ein ansehn-
licher Artikel der Ausfuhr werden, so wie der Tabak. Für Alles,
was einen feuchten Boden fordert, ist das Land sehr ergie-
big." [50]
Die ersten Schritte zur planmässigen Ansiedlung werden damit
getan, dass die Ankömmlinge dem Gouverneur vorgestellt wer-

den und d'Aubant seine Empfehlungsbriefe überreicht. Er
erhält die Erlaubnis, "auf neue Entdeckungen auszugehen, und
für mich und alle diejenigen, welche mit mir gekommen waren,
eine neue Pflanzstadt anzulegen, wo es mir belieben würde." [51]
An der Spitze seiner Expedition setzte der Chevalier "nach dem
rechten Ufer des Mississippi über, und ging den grossen Fluss
hinauf. Das Land wurde immer schöner und trockener, je
weiter wir zogen; die Ufer hörten auf niedrig zu sein; sie be-
standen meistens aus Kalkfelsen." [52] Man entschliesst sich dazu,
sich vom Mississippi zu entfernen und "die Richtung gegen
Nordost" zu nehmen, "um die Ufer des rothen Stromes zu
finden, der in den neumexikanischen Gebirgen entspringt, und
seine Gewässer in den Mississippi stürzt." [53] Hier findet man
"das prachtvolle Land," das man ersehnt hat. Der Chevalier
gründet seine Siedlung "Christinenthal" und kann dem Freund
in der Heimat mitteilen: "Die Ankömmlinge hatten mich von
jeher zu ihrem Haupt erkoren; der Gouverneur hatte mich als
solches bestätigt, mir obrigkeitliche Rechte ertheilt, und für
den König von Frankreich, unsern Souverän, der anderthalb-
tausend Meilen von uns entfernt lebt, in Eid und Pflicht genom-
men." [54] Der Chevalier wird zwar in Feindseligkeiten zwischen
Indianerstämmen verwickelt, aber es gelingt ihm, seiner Siedlung die nötige Sicherheit zu verschaffen und durch harte Arbeit die Pflanzungen ertragreich zu machen. Sein Glück ist voll-
kommen, als er zu seiner grössten Überraschung in einer be-
nachbarten Siedlung die geliebte Christine wiederfindet. Nach
langen Wirrnissen und schweren Schicksalsschlägen werden die
Liebenden in ihrem "selbstgeschaffenen Paradiese" [55] vereint.
Wie der Autor am Schluss seines Briefromans zusammenfassend
berichtet: "Die glücklichen Kolonisten lebten lange in benei-
denswürdiger Abgeschiedenheit von der übrigen Welt und vergessen von Europa. Ihre Pflanzungen, meist Indigo und Tabak,
erreichten bald den höchsten Flor." [56]

Zschokke ist es im allgemeinen gelungen, in seiner Spielart
des "exotischen Amerika-Romans" fabulös-romanzenhafte und
realistischdeskriptive Elemente verhältnismässig bruchlos miteinander zu verbinden. Wenn man die historischen Gegeben-

heiten zum Vergleich heranzieht, wird man zunächst bemerken, dass Zschokke in der Datierung und Lokalisierung sich leichte Abänderungen gestattet hat. Nach der Zeitangabe der Briefe landen die deutschen Siedler unter Führung des Chevalier d'Aubant im Frühjahr 1718 in Louisiana, während in Wirklichkeit die Werbung der Compagnie des Indes in Deutschland erst 1720 einsetzte. Zschokke sah sich zu einer geringfügigen Vordatierung gezwungen, weil er die Übereinstimmung mit dem chronologischen Ablauf der Ereignisse am Zarenhof wahren musste. Da Aleksej Petrowitsch, der Sohn Peters des Grossen, im Juli 1718 von seinem Vater zum Tode verurteilt wurde, musste Christine von Wolfenbüttel derzeit bereits einer ihr unerträglichen Ehe entrückt sein und die Flucht angetreten haben. Aber auch in der Lokalisierung der deutschen Siedlung war für den Autor des Romans eine leichte Korrektur erwünscht. Die deutschen Niederlassungen an der Côte des Allemands sind für Jahrzehnte nicht über kärgliche wirtschaftliche Verhältnisse hinausgekommen, während Zschokke ein in jeder Hinsicht blühendes Gemeinwesen brauchte, wenn er schliesslich dennoch das vollendete Glück seiner leidgeprüften Hauptfiguren demonstrieren wollte. Als Ausweg bot sich ihm an, seine Romangestalten ins Innere von Louisiana vordringen zu lassen, "um die Ufer des rothen Stromes zu finden." [57] Dabei wahrt er noch immer eine leidliche Übereinstimmung mit dem geschichtlichen Ablauf: eine kleine Gruppe deutscher Siedler ("three or four families") ist in der Tat von New Orleans aufgebrochen und hat sich am Red River niedergelassen.[58]

Von solchen Freiheiten abgesehen, auf die ein Erzähler selten verzichten kann, bleibt es erstaunlich, mit welcher Zuverlässigkeit Zschokke den historischen und geographischen Gegebenheiten zu entsprechen weiss. Wenn er den niederschmetternden Eindruck von Biloxi auf die Ankömmlinge schildert, so steht das in Einklang mit den Erfahrungen, welche die Louisiana-Auswanderer bei der Landung an einem Orte machten, an dem keinerlei Vorkehrungen für ihren Aufenthalt getroffen waren.[59] Diese erste Enttäuschung löst bei Zschokkes Reisegesellschaft den Wunsch aus, möglichst umgehend in den alten Erdteil

zurückgebracht zu werden. In der Tat hatte Gouverneur Bienville sich mit solchen Anträgen der deutschen Siedler zu befas-
sen.[60]

Die Funktionen des Gouverneurs, von denen Zschokke be-
richtet, stehen gleichfalls in Einklang mit den landesüblichen
Gepflogenheiten. Der Romanheld d'Aubant teilt mit, dass der
Governeur, da es in New Orleans an Wirtshäusern fehlte, ihn in
seiner Wohnung beherbergt habe, bis er sich eine Gegend zur
Ansiedlung gewählt haben würde.[61] In einer Flugschrift aus
dem Jahre 1720, die im Dienste der Anwerbung von Louisiana-
Auswanderern auf deutschem Boden steht, heisst es: "Von dem
Zustande des Landes Louisiana hat auch ein Mann an seine
Frau folgenden Brieff nach Frankreich voriges Jahr geschrie-
ben: Ich halte mich bey einem guten Freunde auf, biss mir der
Herr Gouverneur mein Stück Landes wird anweisen lassen." [62]
Als der Chevalier d'Aubant dann die Wahl getroffen hat, wo
er seine kleine Gemeinschaft ansässig machen will, gibt er der
Siedlung zu Ehren der ihm unvergesslichen Prinzessin den
Namen "Christinenthal." Das deutsche Dorf "Marienthal," das
schon 1722 genannt wird, bietet sich daher als historische Ent-
sprechung an.

Auf die klimatischen Bedingungen, von denen die Pflanzungen bestimmt werden, hat Zschokke mit Sorgfalt geachtet. Der
Roman unterrichtet uns darüber, dass "die zuweilen eintretenden, wenn gleich geringen Fröste zur Regenzeit" den Anbau
des Zuckerrohrs beeinträchtigten, während Indigo- und Tabak-
Kulturen sich empfehlen.[63] Damit sind getreulich die klimatischen Eigenheiten eines Landes wiedergegeben, in dem winter-
liche Kaltlufteinbrüche den Anbau tropischer Gewächse er-
schweren.[64] Bis zur Mitte des 18. Jahrhunderts war man sich
nicht ganz im klaren darüber, welche Handelspflanzen am
zweckmässigsten im Mississippi-Delta angebaut würden.[65]

Es gehört zu den Erfordernissen des Romans der Goethezeit,
dass der Hauptgestalt eine exponierte Stellung eingeräumt
wird, die im geistigen wie sozialen Rang zum Ausdruck kommt.
Zschokke konnte deshalb den Anführer seiner Auswanderer
schlechterdings nicht auf dem Niveau halten, das einem deut-

schen Kleinsiedler zukommt, der in der Heimat nichts zu ver-
lieren hat und deswegen sein Glück in fernen Zonen sucht. Von
den namenlosen Reisegefährten wird allerdings gesagt, dass es
sich dabei um "mehrentheils verarmte Leute" handelt.[66] Gewiss
hat auch der Chevalier d'Aubant in Frankreich empfindliche
Vermögensverluste erlitten, aber er bleibt doch der grosse, wil-
lensstarke, unternehmungslustige Aristokrat, der in einer aus-
gesprochenen Persönlichkeitskultur wurzelt. Zunächst scheint es
ganz abwegig, in der historischen Überlieferung nach einer
Parallele Umschau halten zu wollen. Und doch gibt es eine
Entsprechung zum Romanhelden Zschokkes, nämlich die historische Gestalt von Karl Friedrich (d'Arensbourg), der 1721 das
Kommando über 330 Auswanderer führte. Karl Friedrich
stammte aus Arensburg auf Ösel, war Hauptmann im schwedi-
schen Heere und hatte bei Poltawa gekämpft.[67] Bei Zschokke
wird gleich auf den ersten Seiten seines Briefromans "das
Schlachtfeld von Pultawa" erwähnt.[68] Dieser Anknüpfungspunkt
zwischen der historischen und der fiktiven Gestalt sollte sich
für Zschokke als fruchtbar erweisen. Der historische Karl Friedrich emigrierte, als seine Heimat an Russland kam, legte sich
den Titel eines "Chevalier d'Arensbourg" bei und bot seine
Dienste der Compagnie des Indes an. Vierzig Jahre lang ist er
bis zu seinem Tode im Jahre 1777 Kommandant der deutschen
Siedlung gewesen, als "Père des Allemands" verehrt und vom
französischen König ausgezeichnet.[69] Seinen Wohnsitz hat man
ihm zu Ehren "Karlstein" genannt. Er befehligte die Miliz an
der Côte des Allemands und mag an Feldzügen gegen die
Indianer teilgenommen haben.[70] Er hat sich in so hohem Masse
Geltung und Wohlstand erworben, dass "the family of d'Arensbourg" zu den angesehensten Geschlechtern des Territoriums
von New Orleans zählte.[71]

Der fiktive Chevalier d'Aubant wahrt weitgehend den von
der Geschichte vorgezeichneten Umriss. Zschokke lässt seinen
Helden ebenfalls dem Herrschaftsbereich des Zaren entfliehen,
macht ihn in Frankreich zum Haupt der Louisiana-Auswanderer, lässt ihn in der neuen Heimat eine blühende Provinz
gründen, wobei er über eine achtbare Miliz gebietet und in

kämpferische Auseinandersetzungen mit Indianerstämmen verwickelt wird. Nur die Verbindung seiner Lebenslinie mit der der ebenfalls landesflüchtigen Prinzessin Christine ist freie Zutat des Erzählers. Damit kommt das Fabulöse zu seinem ungeschmälerten Recht, ohne jedoch die verhältnismässig sachkundige Darstellung der historischen und geographischen Situation zu beeinträchtigen.

Mit der *Prinzessin von Wolfenbüttel* ist der deutsche Amerika-Roman in eine neue Phase seiner Entwicklung eingetreten. Das Thema der Auswanderung und Siedlung ist vielseitig und beziehungsreich mit der Romanhandlung und der Charakteristik der Hauptfiguren verbunden. Zschokkes Briefroman enthält nichts mehr von der Sturm- und Drang-Gesinnung, die in der deutschen Literatur der 70er und 80er Jahre des 18. Jahrhunderts Amerika als Eldorado der Freiheit erscheinen lässt, in dem sich ungezügelte Temperamente auszuleben vermögen. Nach der Überzeugung Zschokkes sind harte Arbeit und der Wille zu selbstloser Unterordnung die unabkömmlichen Vorbedingungen, unter denen allein eine echte Gemeinschaftsgründung zustande kommen kann. Von reiner Abenteuerlust ist hier nichts mehr zu spüren. Ebenso weit bleibt Zschokke davon entfernt, in der Art Jung-Stillings (*Geschichte Florentins von Fahlendorn,* 1781–83) Amerika als eine "Besserungsanstalt" auszugeben, der es gelingt, auch denjenigen, der in der Heimat zu den Unbelehrbaren gehört, in Zucht zu nehmen.[72] Zwar lässt Zschokke uns wissen, dass eine harte Prüfung die Kolonisatoren erwartet, aber die von Menschenhand noch unberührten Gebiete sind ihm "heilige Wildnisse," in denen der Mensch in seinem "harmlosen Selbst" zu leben vermag.[73]

Da er sich selbst als Lehrer und Erzieher verstand, war es Zschokke daran gelegen, im Schlusskapitel seines Romans sinnfällig die moralische Folgerung aus den mitgeteilten Lebensläufen zu ziehen. Er wollte mit seinem Erzählwerk dartun, wie "das harte Schicksal unter eigenen Willen gebeugt" werden kann, sofern der Mensch fähig ist, sich "siegend über die Vorurtheile der Welt" zu erheben und sich "selbstschöpferisch" zu betätigen.[74] Zschokkes Hauptfiguren, der Chevalier d'Aubant und

Prinzessin Christine, verfügen über solche Eigenschaften, mit denen die Ungunst der Verhältnisse dann doch noch zu Heil und Segen verwandelt werden kann. Ähnlich hatte bereits Sophie Mereau Brentano gedacht, die in ihrem Roman *Das Blüthenalter der Empfindung* (1794) Held und Heldin eine Zuflucht in den Vereinigten Staaten finden lässt, denn dort "freut sich der Genius der Menschheit wieder seiner Rechte." [75] Das ist eine Ansicht, die im deutschen Amerika-Roman um 1800 allenthalben begegnet. Dorothea Schlegels *Florentin* (1801) zeigt beispielhaft, wie in der Hauptgestalt der Entschluss reift, die Sache der Amerikaner zur eigenen zu machen, um die Geburt eines mustergültigen republikanischen Staates mitzuerleben. Diesen Grundgedanken sprach Friedrich Schlegel ein Jahrzehnt später (*Über die neuere Geschichte*, 1810) mit dem Leitsatz aus, Nordamerika habe als eine "Pflanzschule europäischer Menschheit und europäischer Freiheit" zu gelten.[76]

Nach der Meinung Friedrich Schlegels hatte Goethe in *Wilhelm Meisters Lehrjahren* in dieser Hinsicht nicht genug getan. Goethe hätte, wie Schlegel kritisch anmerkt, an der Figur des Lothario die amerikanischen Erfahrungen zu einem Beispiel für die "Lehrjahre des Menschen" machen sollen, wodurch Wilhelm Meisters "Lehrjahre des Künstlers" in sinnvoller Weise ergänzt und kontrastiert worden wären.[77]

Friedrich Schlegel konnte derzeit nicht wissen, wie eingehend das Thema "Amerika" den Verfasser des *Wilhelm Meister* noch beschäftigen sollte. Mit den *Wanderjahren* ist dann das Problem der Auswanderung und Siedlung zu zentraler Bedeutung gelangt. Freilich ist damit die Entwicklungsphase des deutschen Amerika-Romans, an der sich Zschokke beteiligte, bereits abgeschlossen und durch neue Perspektiven von Grund auf verändert. Zschokke denkt ausschliesslich an das Schicksal des grossen Einzelnen, Goethe jedoch an das Geschick der Gruppe, der Gemeinschaft, des Bundes. In der Anlage der Fabel kam es Zschokke allein auf eine Bewährung der Herzen an, nicht aber auf eine Bewährung des Bundes im gemeinsamen Planen und Handeln, wie sie ein Vierteljahrhundert später in *Wilhelm Meisters Wanderjahren* von Goethe zum Kern seines Romans

gemacht wurde. Allerdings ist bei Zschokke nicht anders als bei
Goethe der Gedanke der transatlantischen Kolonisation in den
Ablauf des Romans eingefügt, um—mit den Worten der *Wanderjahre*—"zu zeigen, wie man eigentlich von vorn beginnen
und einen Naturweg einschlagen könne." [78] Goethe hatte als his-
torisches Vorbild für einen solchen "Auswandererstaat" die Harmony Society Georg Rapps im Sinn, über deren dritte Nieder-
lassung in der Nähe von Pittsburgh ihn Prinz Bernhard aus
eigener Anschauung unterrichten konnte.[79] Diese Gesellschaft,
die nach dem Bericht Prinz Bernhards "durch das Band der Religion" zusammengehalten wurde, ist nach dem Stand der Gesittung und Bildung kaum noch mit der kleinbäuerlichen Siedlung an der Côte des Allemands zu vergleichen. Und doch ist
für den deutschen Amerika-Roman der Goethezeit nach Ausweis von Zschokkes *Prinzessin von Wolfenbüttel* der Blick nach
dem unteren Mississippi und dem Red River nicht weniger
reizvoll gewesen als der Blick nach dem Ohio und dem Susque-
hanna.

Occasional German Verse at Westphalia, Missouri, in the 1880's*

by
W. A. Willibrand

THE TERM, "occasional verse," as used in this paper, is the equivalent of the German word, *Gelegenheitsdichtung*. It designates pieces of popular poetry written as a contribution to the commemoration of certain events. At Westphalia, Missouri, as elsewhere, such verse usually made its appearance in connection with anniversary celebrations. This kind of popular verse was often the product of local versifiers. Normally it did not survive by many days the events it celebrated, unless it got into print, which sometimes happened at Westphalia, or unless it found its way into song—the fate of the first piece mentioned here which was associated with a parish event in the 1880's. In 1935, the year of the Westphalia centennial celebration, I found the five pieces concerning that Central Missouri village in the St. Louis *Amerika,* a German-language newspaper which appeared for some decades in a daily and a semiweekly edition.

A feeling for popular German poetry remained alive in the Low German community of Westphalia for a century or more after its founding in 1835.[1] The leaders of Westphalia's German

---

* This is the substance of a paper read at the Sixteenth Annual Meeting of the South-Central Modern Language Association, Houston, Texas, November 6, 1959.

pioneers were educated men who had some kind of contact with
German Romanticism and its far-reaching influence on the development of German poetry. For more than a century all of
Westphalia's pastors were conversant with German. To a large
extent this was also true of the teaching nuns and of lay teachers
in the outlying communities. Some of the early lay teachers had
been students at German universities. They came over from the
fatherland as political exiles after the abortive revolutionary
movement of 1848. In one way or another the rather constant
stream of newcomers from the old country added to the endur-
ing appreciation of popular German poetry.

Popular verse accompanied one from the cradle to the grave.
When you were just beginning to speak you were taught little
rhymed-prayers. Years later you heard your children recite them
and even your grandchildren. You heard German verse in the
form of jingles and games. You heard it spoken by the man who
rode through the neighborhood to invite people to a wedding.
Verse was the medium used by a little girl, dressed in white, as
she greeted newlyweds at the home where the postnuptial fes-
tivities were held, usually the home of the bride.[2] And verse
sometimes appeared at the end of obituary notices in the weekly
Volksblatt. Even after the turn of the century one schoolmaster
of a neighboring community could always be depended upon
to produce a poem for almost any important event.[3] To be sure,
most popular poetry was sung. But there were people who could
not sing and these got much enjoyment out of reading aloud
or memorizing whatever popular texts came their way. And the
nonsingers, especially children who could not do anything musical by ear, were known to "sing" and "chant" their verses if
there was no one around to stop them.

Two events of the 1880's, the dedication of church bells and
the celebration of Westphalia's first fifty years as a parish, called
forth some interesting and readable pieces of occasional verse.

On May 14, 1883, the new bells of Westphalia's stone Church
of St. Joseph were consecrated. This event was the occasion of a
poem which appeared in the St. Louis *Amerika.*[4] The author

makes a city out of the village and steep mountains out of the
gently sloping Ozark hills of Osage County, Missouri. But these
hills come affectionately to life in their relationships with Westphalia—Goethe's "Mignon" lies in the author's romantic background. The first stanza, among others, is worth quoting:

> Kennt ihr die Stadt auf steiler Höhe liegend,
> Umringt von Bergen, die noch steiler sind:
> Von grünen Bergen, die im Kreis sich biegend,
> Die Stadt umarmen, wie ihr liebstes Kind?
> Das ist Westphalien, die frohgelaunte—
> Die liebste Stadt, die Perl' von Osage County!

Not only the hills surround Westphalia affectionately, but also
the blue waters of the Maries, the creek above which Westphalia stands. Our poet continues to romanticize the landscape:

> Kennt ihr die Stadt, um deren Brust sich windet
> Der Blauen Maries waldumrauschte Flut;
> Die Stadt, die auf dem grauen Fels gegründet
> Doch inselartig in den Wassern ruht?

A public relations element comes into the third stanza in which
the church steeple and the new bells in it are duly praised.
Some of the neighboring villages, Reichbronn,[5] Loose Creek,
Linn, and St. Thomas, are asked if they have anything compara-
ble to such beauty of form enclosing such lovely chimes:

> Kennt ihr die Stadt: ein Turm strebt auf nach oben,
> So stark von Bau, so künstlich von Gestalt;
> Und Glocken tönen drinn, die muss man loben,
> Ihr klarer Klang hinauf nach Koeltztown schallt.
> Von Reichbronn ihr, von Loose Creek, Linn, St. Thomas,
> Ihr Lieben sagt, habt ihr bei euch auch so was?

The opening question of the fourth stanza is the last one to
follow the *Kennst du das Land* pattern of Goethe's song. In this
stanza attention is drawn to the attractive church property at
Westphalia, which includes the convent, the parochial school,

and the rectory. Stanzas five and six inquire about the sturdy
Low German builders of this prosperous community. Most of
them are no longer living, and a reply is imagined as coming
from the graves of the cemetery. The pioneers are resting after
hard labors, for which religious faith and courage gave them the
required strength. The people of the 1880's are asked in the
seventh stanza to remember the struggles of the pioneers and to
hold in reverence the surviving early settlers. To all, the living
and the dead, there are final salutes in the closing stanza which
correspond to four lines of rhetorical questioning in most of the
other stanzas. There the questions are answered by two lines of
reply. Here at the end the stylized salutes are followed by a
prayer, conventional in tone, for the temporal and eternal hap-
piness of all Westphalians:

> Heil denen, die da ruh'n in kühler Erde!
> Den Siedlern Heil, die noch am Leben sind!
> Ein dreifach Heil den guten Bürgern werde!
> Ein dreifach Heil für Mann und Weib und Kind!
> O möge Gott Westphalien stets beglücken,
> Und alle einst mit Himmelslohn entzücken.

According to the Westphalia centennial booklet,[6] the author
of these carefully executed rhymed pentameters was Father
Schlechter, S.J., a pastor at Westphalia and at nearby Loose
Creek during the 1880's.[7] *Amerika* had published them anony-
mously on May 23, 1883.

A little more than a month later, on June 27, it gave its readers a reply to the query, "Do you know the city . . . ?"[8] Also in
iambic verse, it consists of seven stanzas, each containing three
four-foot lines plus a two-foot line, the rhyme-scheme being
abba. It came from Milwaukee and was initialed H. E. Was
H. E. perhaps a Jesuit then in residence at the newly established
Marquette College? In any case these initials do not correspond
to the name of anyone mentioned in the index to the three volumes of Father Garraghan's *The Jesuits of the Middle United
States.*

H. E. had obviously lived in the Westphalia community. The pattern, with its feminine rhymes, takes good care of the nostalgic note with which the lyric begins:

> Ich kenn' die Stadt, o dass mich länger
> Beglücket hätt' ihr süsser Friede!
> Ihr Frohsinn tönt aus deinem Liede,
>   O werter Sänger.

The Milwaukee writer finds only sorrow and pain in his northern abode. He would like to share in the joys of the Westphalia singer and derive from him the experience of pure and genuine delight:

> Allhier find' ich nur Leid und Schmerzen;
> An deinem Glücke möcht' ich weiden
> Und schöpfen echte, reine Freuden
>   Aus deinem Herzen.

His syntax is sound and so is his versification, but his sentiments seem a bit trite. He recalls the church whose spire points heavenward, the school and the children, the nuns who do the teaching, and the homes where noble thoughts and good old German customs flourish. He asks the new church bells to proclaim both joy and sorrow and to send their sounds abroad in the forest for the pleasure of Christian people. Flowers become the image of young people, who could hardly have been as satisfied with their lives as the writer seems to be when he portrays them as ever striving for a purity that is pleasing to God.

There is a bit of local history in the last stanza. Four of the Jesuits whose names had become associated with the growth of the parish are mentioned: Krier, Vallazza, Gonser, Schlechter. One surmises that a Jesuit writer was paying a tribute of respect to colleagues who were still doing missionary work in the area. But their Osage County days were numbered. In September of 1883, a matter of three or four months after the dedication of the church bells, the Jesuits turned Westphalia over to the

Reverend Anton Diepenbrock, a German-born priest, the first secular pastor of Westphalia.

Five years later, 1888, the parish could celebrate its fiftieth anniversary. (It was actually the fifty-third year after the arrival of the first German settlers.) That year a cycle of three little poems appeared in *Amerika* under the title, "Westphaliens Lied im Jubeljahr." [9] The poems consist respectively of six, six, and eight four-line stanzas. Again each stanza has three tetrameters, but this time the rhymes are masculine and there is a trimeter refrain. Actually all three of the poems have two alternating rhyming refrains. Thus the first piece, "Auf der Reise, 1838–40," has the alternating refrains, *Lieb Heimatland, ade,* and *Du Stern auf dunkler See.* The "Star on darksome Sea" is the Blessed Virgin, protectress of the immigrants who came to West-phalia at different times between 1838 and 1840. The entire poem is concerned with the immigrants' getting safely across the stormy waters of the Atlantic. I quote two stanzas to illustrate the connection of the refrains with the tetrameters and with each other:

> Die Väter fuhren übers Meer
> Mit nassem Aug' und sorgenschwer;
> Es kam ein starker Sturm daher,
> Lieb Heimatland, ade!

> Die Blitze züngeln blutigrot;
> Es geht einher der nasse Tod;
> Erlöse uns aus dieser Not,
> Du Stern auf dunkler See.

The double refrain gives the three pieces a certain sturdiness and holds them together rather effectively.

The second poem of our cycle symbolizes twenty-five years in the primeval forest: "Im Urwalde, 1838–1863." Here the terrors of the long ocean voyage are left far behind. Instead there is the lively activity of reducing a virgin forest to a tamed state for agricultural purposes; prosperity comes without fail to the new farms. Unlike other folk poetry that has to do with the hardships of pioneering, there is nothing more painful here than earning your bread by the sweat of your brow. With plenty of livestock and abundant harvests there is much to do. People are busy at clearing, harvesting, spinning, weaving, and knitting. On Sundays a thousand voices are heard in the village church, where Father Helias, the first Jesuit pastor, urges his flock to think of something more than material prosperity.

Listen for a moment to the activities of the woodsmen, to the passing of the swamp, and to the forest coming painfully to life as it is being destroyed:

> Die Säge klirrt, der Hammer schallt,
> Es fällt der Baum, es keucht der Wald,
> Der Sumpf versiecht, der Felsen knallt,
> Im Urwald wurde Licht.

And then the result of all this labor:

> Fest steht das Haus, der Hof sich dehnt,
> Das laute Vieh zum Stall sich sehnt,
> Die Rebe an den Berg sich lehnt:
> Doch ohne Schweisz gings nicht.

There is more poetry in the terrors of the sea and in the destruction of the forest than in the sentiments that end with, *Doch ohne Schweisz gings nicht.*

"Im Jubeljahr 1888" is the title of the third poem of the cycle. It looks upon fifty years of spiritual and economic community building as a sort of triumph. Attention is called to the church, the convent school, the boys' school, and the rectory. There is praise of some neighboring village communities which are daughter parishes of Westphalia. We hear again of prosperity, of loyalty to things of old as embodied in the things that are new. The verses lend themselves well to song. I quote the first and the last stanzas:

> Die Kinder blieben gut und treu,
> Das alte bauten sie aufs Neu',
> Dass heut' sich jedes Herz erfreu':
> Bringt Gott ein Loblied dar!
>
> . . . .
>
> Behüt uns Gottes Engelschaar
> Vor aller Sünde und Gefahr,
> Dass wir einst feiern wunderbar—
> Das ewige Jubeljahr.

An effort has been made here to rescue from oblivion some pieces of occasional poetry which are intimately connected with the history and the life-sustaining beliefs of a German community. The traditional quality of this verse cannot be denied. Like most folk art it follows established patterns in both form and content. During the post-pioneer era of intense community consciousness and community effort, it fulfilled its function of emphasizing values which might have been lost through more independent and more one-sided pioneering. It is of course true that some of the emphasis seems repetitious and trite. Viewed, however, in the context of their era these values were—and are —extremely important. Religion was the center of community life and often the prime mover in folk festivals and their attendant popular verse. Other cultural values brought over from Germany, most of all the language, were likewise cherished, for they were destined to become vital elements in the Americanism of the immigrants and their more immediate descendants.

To the folklore of the German immigrants belonged an awareness of the German contribution to the development of America. At Westphalia the German settlers could see at first hand that their farming was superior to that of the earlier Americans from whom they bought their land. Hence the emphasis upon work and their pioneering history. The comparatively few pieces of verse which I was able to find in newspaper files reveal nothing of the drabness, loneliness, poverty, and even the angry sarcasm sometimes found in verses about sod-house dwellers living on their claims.[10] Our Missouri home-steaders must have had similar trials but their religious faith and their cultural myth tended toward a more optimistic out-look. The verse, which reflects beauty in their lives and stability in their achievements, cannot be compared with creative poetry. But it bears comparison very well with English popular poetry in the United States.

Joseph de Laporte's Evaluation
of German Literature

by
Erich A. Albrecht

LETTER 299 OF Volume XXIII of Laporte's[1] *Voyageur Fran-çois*,[2] which appeared in 1777 in Paris and in a German transla-tion in 1782,[3] contains a discussion of German literature which is noteworthy for the following reasons: first, it is a hitherto un-recorded plagiarism from Friedrich Melchior Grimm; second, it extends the significance of Grimm as a critic of German lit-erature; third, it is most likely the last instance of a late Gott-schedian influence; fourth, it illustrates the existence of a sig-nificant time lag between the appearance of contemporary works of literature and their recording in popular critical writ-ings; fifth and finally, it gave to the eighteenth-century Ger-man readers—in its translated form—additional reason to be-lieve in their own literature.

Although Laporte's contributions to the field of literature were somewhat pedestrian, they were so widely read that even the best French and German journals had to review them.[4] However, from the appearance of the earliest volumes of his *Voyageur François* in 1765 to the appearance of Volume XXI, the attention that was paid to them became progressively more reluctant.[5]

As far as the *Voyageur François* is concerned, no review of its twenty-third volume can be found in the *Journal Encyclo-pédique,* the *Journal Historique et Littéraire,* the *Année Lit-*

48

téraire, the *Mercure de France,* or the *Goettingische Anzeigen* after 1780, when Laporte's death occasioned a flurry of positive and negative notes, including a favorable one by Jean de Laharpe, and one by Friedrich Melchior Grimm, who seems to have been unaware of the fact that Laporte had lifted the bulk of his evaluation of German literature from Grimm's *Lettres à l'auteur du Mercure sur la littérature Allemande.*[6]

When one considers the astonishing quantity of Laporte's publications, of which, according to Wilhelm Heinsius, sixteen were translated into German,[7] it becomes obvious that this *compilateur infatigable* was unlikely to have read himself many of the German writers he discusses in Volume XXIII of his *Voyageur François.* The following statement in the *Goettingische Anzeigen von Gelehrten Sachen:* "Vom *Voyageur François* hat Henri de la Porte den 17. und 18. Band A. 1773 bey Collet abdrucken lassen, worinn er von England handelt. Ueberhaupt hat Hr.B. hier bessere Urkunden abzuschreiben gehabt . . . ," [8] challenges one to search for the original of the source which Laporte was bound to have used for the compilation of his data on German literature.

Since Laporte pretended to have edited letters written by a French traveler in 1757, it seemed likely that he would have copied or used material concerning German literature which had appeared in a French publication somewhat before that time. After checking a number of French accounts of German literature which were published between 1750 and 1766, it became obvious that Laporte had used primarily Grimm's *Lettres à l'auteur du Mercure,*[9] and secondarily a book by a Michael Huber entitled *Choix de Poésies Allemandes.*[10]

In support of the claim made regarding the dependence of Laporte upon Grimm the following two passages are furnished:

(1) Grimm writes in the *Mercure de France* (1750): "Plusieurs d'entre eux ignorent qu'il y ait une littérature allemande, et peut-être ne sont-ce pas ceux-là qui en pensent le moins avantageusement. Des beaux esprits allemands! Quels termes pour des oreilles francaises! Cependant l'esprit, ainsi que la sottise, est de toutes les nations. Horace et Moevius, Boileau et Cotin, ont été compatriotes;

et si la Thrace a eu ses Orphées, pourquoi l'Allemagne n'aurait-elle pas ses poètes?" [11]

(2) Laporte, in the *Voyageur François* (1777), writes: "Bien des gens ignorent qu'il y ait une littérature Allemande. Des beaux-esprits dans la Germanie! Quels mots pour la plupart des oreilles Européennes! comme si l'esprit et la sottise n'estoient pas de tous les pays. La Thrace a bien eu ses Orphées, pourquoi l'Allemagne n'aurait-elle pas ses littérateurs et ses poètes?" [12]

In regard to Laporte's dependence upon Huber's *Choix de Poésies Allemandes,* it can be shown that the register of Huber's anthology agrees to a very large extent with the selection of names of German poets discussed by Laporte.[13] Both compilers, moreover, tellingly list the *Juedischen Schaefergedichte* of the German poet Breitenbauch (!).

Because of the discovery of this hitherto unrecorded paraphrase of Grimm's evaluation of German literature in Laporte's *Voyageur François,* which was widely read both in France and Germany, Professor J. R. Smiley's comment that "Grimm's position as a significant factor in the dissemination of French culture throughout Europe needs to be given greater emphasis," [14] should be extended to read: "Grimm's position as a significant factor in the dissemination of French *and German* culture . . . needs to be given greater emphasis"—especially since it seems likely that other studies of German literature by Grimm may yet be located in French and German periodicals.[15]

The evaluation of German literature originally written by Grimm and paraphrased and enlarged by Laporte in his *Voyageur François* is of even greater interest, when one considers that the essence of Grimm's critical survey of the literature of his native country stems from Johann Christoph Gottsched, Grimm's admired teacher, who was said to have sent Grimm to Paris as a propagandist of German literature.[16] Whether Grimm wrote his letters concerning German literature to the editor of the *Mercure de France* in obedience to Gottsched's wishes or not, the interesting fact remains that, thanks to Grimm and Laporte, Gottschedian ideas make, in 1782, what is presumably their last appearance in a German publication.

Laporte's discussion of German literature in the German translation of the *Voyageur François* (*Reisen eines Franzosen*) is of still greater interest by virtue of the fact that the translator, Christian August Wichmann (1735–1805),[17] added a considerable number of remarks in the form of footnotes and corrections to the translated text. While these contribute little or nothing to the understanding of the poets referred to in the text, they unintentionally reveal the fact that the translator, Wichmann, an academically trained minor poet, had not caught up with the literary events of his time. It is significant that he does not use the privilege extended to him by Johann Gottlob Immanuel Breitkopf, namely of adding copious footnotes, for the purpose of really bringing Laporte's obviously dated account of German literature up to date.

Instead of referring to the later Lessing, to Bürger, Herder, Wieland, and Goethe, he added in 1782 (!) in connection with Laporte's opening sentences, "Schöne Geister, witzige Köpfe in Deutschland? Welche Worte für die mehresten Ohren in Europa," the following footnote: "Das kann wohl mitten in Deutschland von einem oder dem anderen Hofe gelten: (denn leider haben die Deutschen immer das Schicksal, in ihrem Vaterland am meisten verkannt zu werden); aber gewiss ist keine einzige Nation mehr in Europa, die eine solche Exklamation ausstossen kann—ja, schon 1757 (von welchem Jahr dieser Brief unseres Autors datiret ist), fing sich das Vorurtheil an zu verliehren." [18]

In spite of the somewhat obsolete character of this third-hand discussion of German literature in the twenty-seventh volume of the *Reisen eines Franzosen,* it can be said that it undoubtedly deserves attention for one more reason, namely, for recommending German literature to the average eighteenth-century German reader. An endorsement of this kind by any French writer was looked upon as a welcome and reassuring thing, as can be seen by the remarks of F. W. Zachariä:

Die Franzosen, die sonst am bittersten auf unseren Mangel schmaehten, lassen uns seit einiger Zeit am meisten Gerechtigkeit widerfahren; und ein Haller, ein Gellert, ein Klopstock, ein Gessner sind itzo in Paris mehr gekannt, als an den meisten deutschen Höfen, wo man einige unserer Dichter aufs höchste nur noch in einer französischen Uebersetzung liest, und von den übrigen, wenig oder gar nichts weiss.[19]

The German version of the *Voyageur François* especially, for the various reasons given above, should be considered important source material for studies of the literary scene in late eighteenth-century Germany. There is much in Laporte's evaluation and the asides of Wichmann, his translator, which can be used to extend such studies as Viktor Hehn's *Goethe und das Publikum*[20] concerning the level of the general reading public of that period.

Ein Franzose als Beschützer deutscher Universitäten

by
G. Waldo Dunnington

EINE DER ERSTEN Regierungsmassnahmen Jérômes, des Sommer-
königs von Westphalen, war die Schliessung der altehrwürdigen
Universitäten Helmstedt, Paderborn und Rinteln, da wegen
der vielen anderen Abgaben die Unterhaltskosten von 600 000
Frs. für die sechs Landeshochschulen (ausser den genannten
noch Marburg, Göttingen und Halle) von den zwei Millionen
Einwohnern nicht mehr aufgebracht werden konnten. Wenn
diese drei Universitäten damals in Jahre 1808 von einem ähn-
lichen Schicksal verschont blieben, so verdankten sie das dem
unermüdlichen Eintreten des französisch-deutschen Gelehrten
und Schriftstellers Charles François Dominique de Villers.

Villers wurde am 4. November 1765 zu Boulay (Lothringen)
geboren, und trat 1782 als Offizier in die französische Armee
ein. Er diente einige Monate als Freischärler im Korps Condé.
Wegen seiner vier Flugschriften *De la Liberté* wurde er gezwungen, 1792 sein Vaterland zu verlassen. Er wandte sich nach
Deutschland und kam nach mancherlei Irrfahrten im November
1796 nach Göttingen, wo er sich an der *Georgia Augusta* imma-
trikulierte.

Villers hatte es sich zur Lebensaufgabe gemacht, bei seinen
Landsleuten Verständnis für den deutschen Geist zu erwecken,
sie insbesondere mit der deutschen Literatur bekannt zu machen. Als Franzose steht er im deutschen Geistesleben des be-

ginnenden 19. Jahrhunderts als Dritter im Bunde neben Adalbert von Chamisso und de la Motte-Fouqué. Von urteilsfähigen Zeitgenossen wie Jean Paul oder den Gebrüdern Grimm wurde er höher geschätzt als die politische Literatin Mme de Staël.

Im Juli 1798 hatte Charles de Villers erstmals sein Kulturprogramm verkündet, als er im Hamburger *Spectateur du Nord,* der bedeutendsten von und für Emigranten geschriebenen Zeitschrift Deutschlands, den ersten seiner 67 Beiträge veröffentlichte, nämlich seine *Idées sur la destination des hommes de lettres sortis de France et qui séjournent en Allemagne.* Er forderte darin die vom Schicksal nach Deutschland verschlagenen federgewandten Landsleute auf, unter Verzicht auf alle politischen Absichten aus wohlmeinender Liebe zu ihrem eigenen Volke die geistigen Schätze des Gastvolkes zu heben und sie dem eigenen Heimatvolk zu vermitteln.

So erschloss Villers z.B. als erster den Franzosen die Kantische Philosophie mit seinem Werk: *La philosophie de Kant ou principes fondamentaux de la philosophie transcendentale* (1801, 1802). Schon im Jahre 1797 hatte Villers in seinen *Lettres Westphaliennes* einen ersten Versuch unternommen, namentlich seinen Lieblingsdenker Kant für Franzosen begreiflich zu machen, ein Unternehmen, dem er noch manche Jahre des Studiums und des Schrifttums widmete.

Wie sehr er aber auch einem Denker wie Fichte nahe stand, beweist ein anderer Aufsatz derselben Zeitschrift: *Considérations sur la prééminence des deux langues allemande et française,* worin er sieben Jahre vor den Berliner *Reden an die Deutsche Nation* feststellt, die deutsche Sprache sei ursprünglicher und schöpferischer als die französische, weil letztere eine zusammengesetzte Mischsprache und in ihrem Grundbestand nur ein deutscher Stammesdialekt sei. Bezeichnend, dass er nach einer scharfen Pariser Erwiderung aus der Feder Fontanes gerade deswegen seine Mitarbeit am *Spectateur* aufgeben musste.

Für das französische Nationalinstitut verfasste er eine grosse Arbeit: *Essai sur l'esprit et l'influence de la Réformation de Luther* (1804; 5te Ausgabe, 1851; deutsche Übersetzung, 1805;

verkürzte Ausgabe, 1836). Darin versuchte Villers den grossen
Reformator seinen früheren Landsleuten näher zu bringen,
obgleich er selbst katholischer Konfession war. Bald darauf
erhielt er eine hohe Ehrung von der Stadt Bremen in Anerken-
nung seines nächsten Buches: *Les Doléances des Peuples du
Continent de l'Europe au Sujet de l'Interruption de leur Com-
merce.*

In Göttingen hörte Villers Vorlesungen bei August Ludwig
von Schlözer (1735–1809), ordentlichem Professor für Geschichte
1769–1809. Er genoss jahrelang gastfreundliche Aufnahme
bei der Tochter seines Lehrers, Dorothea von Schlözer, die als
erste deutsche Doktorin rühmlich bekannt ist.[1] Sie heiratete
später den reichen Lübecker Kaufmann Rodde und blieb Villers volle 18 Jahre in ungetrübter Freundschaft verbunden. In
dieser Zeit erschlossen sich ihm Klopstock, Schiller, Goethe und
besonders Jean Paul als die typischen Vertreter deutscher Denk-
und Dichtungsart, obgleich ihm anfangs das rechte sprach-
liche Verständnis viel Mühe kostete. Villers verkehrte auch mit
dem Eutiner Kreis um Graf Stolberg, besonders auch mit Friedrich Heinrich Jacobi und Heinrich Wilhelm von Gerstenberg.
Bekanntlich blieb Goethe damals durch einen zufällig am
Schreibtisch liegenden Brief Villers' vor französischer Einquar-
tierung verschont. 1797 ging Villers nach Lübeck; im selben
Jahre erschien seine anonyme Arbeit: *Lettre à Mademoiselle
D(orothea) S(chlözer) sur l'abus des grammaires dans l'étude du
français* (Gottingue). Später wirkte er an der Schriftleitung der
Archives littéraires und der *Mélanges de Littérature etrangère*
mit.

Angeregt durch eine Preisfrage der Akademie von Lyon:
"Verdient die französische Nation den Vorwurf der Leichtig-
keit, den ihr die fremden Nationen machen?" arbeitete Villers
mit gewissenhafter Kritik eine wirklich unvoreingenommene
Studie aus, die 1806 erschien unter dem Titel: *Sur la manière
essentiellement différente dont les poètes français et allemands
traitent l'amour.*[2] Durch zahlreiche Belege aus den Literaturen
beider Völker wies er nach, wie sehr den Deutschen die Liebe
ein heiliges Lebensideal, den Franzosen dagegen nur allzusehr

eine sinnlich-materielle Leidenschaft sei, auf Genuss und Ge-
winn berechnet. Hier behauptete Villers, dass die französischen
Dichter "ont confié la plupart à leur creuset poétique des élé-
ments pris dans le règne sensuel et matériel de l'amour, dans
l'attrait passionné des plaisirs et de la jouissance," während
Deutsche "ont choisi presque constamment les leurs dans ce que
l'amour a de plus saint, de plus idéal, de plus mystique." Diese
Ansicht stammt aus Jean Pauls *Vorschule der Ästhetik,* wo er
erklärt, "die grössten Dichter waren die keuschesten," und die
französischen Dichter kritisiert, weil ihre Dichtung "schamlos"
sei.[3]

An diese Studie fand Goethe so grosses Gefallen, dass er sich
von Villers eine französische Übersetzung seiner Farbenlehre
erbat, freilich vergeblich, da dieser sich nicht auf naturwissen-
schaftliche Abwege drängen liess. Jedenfalls war in jener Studie,
welche die vergleichende Forschungsmethode in die Literatur-
wissenschaft einführte, Villers' Grundthese vom Gegensatz zwischen deutschem Idealismus und französischem Materialismus,
vom höheren Wert der deutschen Klassik im Vergleich zum
französischen Klassizismus erstmals klar formuliert und belegt.
War er doch überzeugt, dass Deutschlands geistige Waffen einst
Frankreich schlagen würden, wie es eben die überlegenen ma-
teriellen Waffen Frankreichs bei Jena und Auerstedt gegen
Deutschland getan hätten.[4] Goethe hielt Villers für eine Per-
sönlichkeit von Bedeutung, da er zwischen den Franzosen und
Deutschen stehe und "wie eine Art Janus herüber und hinüber
sieht." Villers veröffentlichte im Maiheft 1808) der zu Amsterdam in französischer Sprache erscheinenden literarischen Zeitschrift *Le Conservateur* einen Aufsatz über deutsche Literatur
und deutschen Buchhandel.

Es war für die Universitäten des neuen Königreiches Westphalen ein Glück, dass zum Generalstudiendirektor ein Mann
ernannt wurde, auf den das gelehrte Bildungswesen die grössten
Hoffnungen setzte, Johannes von Müller. Dieser glaubte, dass
durch Napoleon ein neues Zeitalter heraufgeführt würde. Er
versuchte einmal, dem König Jérôme einige Grundbegriffe vom

deutschen Universitätswesen beizubringen und bekam diese
Antwort: "Alle eure Universitäten taugen nichts, ich werde sie
alle verbrennen, ich will nur Soldaten und Ignoranten." Einmal behauptete man sogar, Anatomie als Lehrfach sei überflüs-
sig. Das war nicht merkwürdig. Für den normalen Franzosen
lag Deutschland im fernen Osten.

Aber Johannes von Müller berichtete jetzt, dass auch Laplace
den westphälischen Ministern Göttingen ans Herz gelegt habe.
Der Philologe C. G. Heyne wandte sich wiederholt an seine
Freunde vom Institut de France. Eine an Napoleon entsandte
Deputation kam mit allgemeinen Versprechungen zurück; der
Kaiser soll gesagt haben: Göttingen gehöre nicht Hannover,
nicht Deutschland, sondern der Welt. Johannes von Müller
entschloss sich nun, die öffentliche Meinung um Hilfe anzuge-
hen; er fand den geeigneten Mann für diese Aufgabe, C. F. D.
de Villers, und forderte ihn auf, etwas über deutsche Universitäten zu schreiben. Bald erschien ein Bändchen: *Coup d'oeil
sur les Universités et le mode d'instruction publique de l'Allemagne protestante* (1808).

Görres rühmte diese Schrift in den *Heidelberger Jahrbü-
chern* (1808, S. 439 ff.): "Das Ganze ist durchaus so aufgefasst,
wie man Menschen, die an der Spitze der Regierungen und
grosser Geschäfte stehen, alles als Gattung nur aufzufassen
gewohnt sind . . . einen Gegenstand darstellen muss, wenn
man will, dass sie sich für ihn interessieren sollen. Die Vorurteile gegen die deutschen Universitäten konnten vor ihm nicht
mehr bestehen, und es ist schon viel gewonnen, wenn er an die
Stelle des bösen Willens Klage über Unvermögen des Dranges
der Zeiten wegen tritt."

Villers berichtete von einer Unterhaltung, die Schlözer vor
Jahren mit dem Orientalisten Deguignes in Paris gehabt hatte.
Man sprach vom Wesen der deutschen Universität, und es
kostete Schlözer unendliche Mühe, sich dem Franzosen verständ-
lich zu machen. Endlich rief Deguignes aus: "Ah, nun verstehe
ich! Sie Deutschen fangen da an, wo wir aufhören."

"Man kann hinzufügen," schrieb Villers, "dass in jedem iso-

lierten Teile sich ein engherziger *esprit de corps,* ein Sekten-
geist bilden wird, der jeden insgeheim zur Verachtung der
übrigen Wissenschaften hinleitet, die er gar nicht kennt."
Villers gehörte zu jener Zeit der Göttinger königlichen Gesellschaft der Wissenschaften als korrespondierendes Mitglied
an, und war mit Heyne, Eichhorn, Kästner, Spittler, Sieveking
und Schlözer eng befreundet. Durch gemeinsame Neigung zu
Jean Paul zählte er den Mathematiker Gauss zu seinen Freunden. Villers kam zu dem Schluss, "dass mit dem Gedanken
von irgendeinem Abbruch (der Universitäten) eine Art Schande
verbunden scheine und unersetzlicher Verlust der gesamten
Kultur drohe."
Seinen rastlosen Bemühungen blieb auch bekanntlich der
Erfolg nicht versagt. Die Göttinger Universität, die "Akropolis
der Gelehrtenrepublik," wie er die *Georgia Augusta* in seinen
Schriften nannte, blieb neben Marburg und Halle erhalten.
Seit 1811 gehörte Villers der Universität Göttingen als ordent-
licher Professor der Philosophie und französischen Literatur an.
Er war 1810 mit der Familie Rodde nach Göttingen gezogen,
wo er grosses Ansehen genoss und seine Lehrtätigkeit besonders
erfolgreich war, wenn er natürlich auch manchen Neider unter
den Professoren hatte, die es ihm nicht verzeihen konnten, dass
er, "der keine einzige Fachwissenschaft zunftmässig erlernt
hatte," zu solchen Ehren gelangt war. Er war ja von Haus aus
Artillerie-Offizier, hatte sich aber schon als junger Offizier
wissenschaftlichen und schöngeistigen Bestrebungen gewidmet.
Villers benutzte damals bald die deutsche, bald die französische Sprache, aber nicht wahllos: "Deutsch schreibe ich gern,
wenn das Gefühl sich meiner bemeistert, wenn ich dithyram-
bisch werde—Französisch brauche ich lieber zum ruhigen Er-
zählen." Er hielt Frankreichs Vorurteile gegen deutsche Art
und Dichtung für eisig und kalt. Das französische Publikum
seiner Tage wird als geistige Kastraten charakterisiert: hoch-
gebildet, aber ohne edle Kräfte der Seele. Im Jahre 1809 veröffentlichte Villers ein inhaltsreiches Werk *Introduction des am-
bassadeurs philologiques quoique allemands;* bedauernswert ist

nur dass zwei hochverdiente Meister übersehen wurden: Herder und Lessing.

1806 erschien sein Werkchen: *Lettre à Madame la comtesse Fanny de Beauharnais sur Lubeck*. Diese Schrift behandelte die französischen Ausschreitungen bei der Eroberung Lübecks, von wo ihn ein Haftbefehl General Davouts vertrieb, worauf Villers nach einer gescheiterten Vermittlung des Königs Jérôme sich gelegentlich einer Pariser Reise den unmittelbaren Schutz Napoleons erwirkte. Infolgedessen musste Villers beim Anschluss an Frankreich Lübeck verlassen. Unstet zog er in Deutschland umher, nicht selten von den eigenen Landsleuten verfolgt. Davout war sein besonderer Feind von Lübeck her; in Westfalen gewährte man ihm Schutz. In Göttingen studierte er Farbenlehre bei Benjamin Constant. Als man in Bremen eine neue Universität errichten wollte, trug sich Villers mit dem Plane, als Professor dorthin zu gehen. Abe dieser Versuch schlug fehl, wie auch seine späteren Bemühungen, in den neu gegründeten Hochschulen in Genf oder Koblenz unterzukommen. Bei seiner Berufung nach Göttingen befürchtete man, dass diese Ernennung einen Präzedenzfall schaffe, und dass man hier stets fühlen würde, dass er kein Fachgelehrter sei.

Nach Schlözers Tod geschah der wirtschaftliche Zusammenbruch des Kaufhauses Rodde, also seines Gastgebers, bedingt durch die vernichtenden Auswirkungen der napoleonischen Kontinentalsperre auf die hanseatischen Handelsstädte. Villers machte sich damals erbötig, aus dem Rest der Konkursmasse wenigstens das väterliche Erbe Dorotheens sicherstellen zu lassen, und vertiefte sich in juristische Sonderfragen. Darüber hinaus suchte er auch anderwärts neue Hilfsquellen zu erschliessen. Es spricht für seinen edlen Charakter, dass er aus selbstloser Dankbarkeit eine Eingabe an Herzog August von Gotha dichtete, so wie er auch seine Göttinger Beziehungen zu Minister Reinhard, Johannes von Müller und Jakob Grimm stets selbstlos für alle Hilfesuchenden verwertete. Diesmal wirkte Villers für die Schwester seiner Gönnerin, also für des toten Schlözers jüngste Tochter Lisette, die nunmehr kein elterliches

Heim mehr hatte und nur zu gerne ihren in Gotha weilenden Verlobten geheiratet hätte. Dessen wirtschaftliche Grundlage wollte Villers heben, und zwar durch warme Fürsprache für beide bei dem Herzog. Zu seiner grossen Enttäuschung verhielt der Herzog von Gotha sich durchaus ablehnend. Er schrieb an Jean Paul (als Vermittler in dieser Angelegenheit): "so gern ich auch oft das übernehme, was die Pflicht näherer reicher Verwandter wäre," so rate er doch dem Dichter, der mehr als er mit Gefühlen verdiene, "dem schönen J. und der eleganten L. den Weg in die Kirche und den in das Bett mit Dukaten zu pflastern"; er halte sich für viel ärmer als das zu bedenkende Liebespaar, wenigstens nach dessen äusserem Auftreten bei Hofbällen zu schliessen.[5] Trotz dieser Absage konnte Jean Paul seinem Freunde Villers mitteilen: "Sie liebt er (der Herzog) als einen 'Antikrites' wegen Ihres Patriotismus für Deutsche, welchen ich Krites ihm zu entbehren scheine."

Villers beschreibt die damals auf der Göttinger Universitätsbibliothek herrschende Liberalität: "Chaque jour, aux heures où ce superbe dépôt est ouvert, on peut voir à l'entrée deux files non interrompues de ceux qui y entrent et qui en sortent, pour y rapporter, pour en élever de nouvelles richesses, ou pour y aller faire des recherches; ce tableau mouvant ne ressemble pas mal aux abeilles, qui se pressent à la porte d'une ruche." [6] Er fährt dann fort: "Im Inneren herrscht die Ordnung, Höflichkeit und Geschäftigkeit der Gelehrten, die in diesem heiligen Bezirk die Funktionen der Bibliothekare und Sekretäre erfüllen. Man verpflichtet sie jedesmal sozusagen, wenn man ihren Dienst in Anspruch nimmt. Die wissenschaftlichen Interessen anderer scheinen ihre persönlichen zu sein."

Als es sich freilich darum handelte, die Stadt Göttingen von Kriegslasten zu befreien, zur Zeit als die Armee des Kronprinzen von Schweden vor den Toren lag (1813), bediente man sich gern seiner guten Beziehungen. Trotz seiner anerkannt grossen Verdienste um die drei deutschen Universitäten, die ohne ihn sicher den Wirren des napoleonischen Zeitalters zum Opfer gefallen wären, hatte die hannoversche Regierung, die 1814 wieder eingesetzt wurde, nichts eiligeres zu tun, als Villers seines Amtes zu entsetzen und ihn unter Zubilligung einer Pension des Landes zu verweisen; "er könne der Universität durch literarische Verbindung anderer Orte nützlicher sein." Sein Sturz empörte allgemein. Der Freiherr vom Stein und sogar der König von Preussen und der Zar von Russland setzten sich für Villers ein. Constant erreichte wenigstens eine Milderung: das Gehalt wurde ihm belassen und die Verbannung rückgängig gemacht. Diese planmässig angezettelte Intrige, ein Werk schnöden Undanks, bleibt eine Schmach für die hannoversche Regierung einem Manne echt deutscher Gesinnung gegenüber. Man sprach damals sogar von Beschimpfung der deutschen Nation durch die hannoversche Regierung. Auch der Einspruch des mächtigen Grafen Münster fruchtete nichts. Erst auf dem Sterbebett widerfuhr Villers die Ehrenrettung einer Berufung an die Universität Heidelberg.

Der Kabinettssekretär A. W. Rehberg hatte diesen Schlag gegen Villers geführt. Er hat sich später zu rechtfertigen versucht. Villers' Verdienst ist gewiss gross. "Aber," so sagt Rehberg, "er hatte unter der westphälischen Herrschaft einen Einfluss erlangt, der unter solchen Verhältnissen, aber auch nur unter ihnen wohltätig sein konnte. Er modelte alles nach seinen eigenen Ansichten. Als ständiger Sekretär der Gesellschaft der Wissenschaften waren die wohlgegründeten Ansprüche anderer sehr verdienter und berühmter Männer gekränkt."

Zum Schluss sei noch bemerkt, dass der amerikanische Gelehrte George Ticknor (1791–1871) durch Villers' *coup d'oeil* auf Göttingen aufmerksam geworden war und veranlasste, dass spätere Harvard-Schüler dort studierten. Bekanntlich war Villers mit Mme de Staël sehr gut befreundet; er hat ihre Schriften über das damalige Deutschland beeinflusst. Sie hat sich anerkennend über ihn geäussert: "Man findet Herrn Villers immer an der Spitze edler und grossherziger Ideen und er scheint durch die Anmut seines Geistes und die Tiefe seiner Studien berufen, Frankreich in Deutschland und Deutschland in Frankreich zu repräsentieren." [7]

Trotz glänzender Rufe nach auswärts blieb Villers bis an sein
Lebensende in Göttingen. Kaum fünfzigjährig, starb er am 26.
Februar 1815, vielleicht an gebrochenem Herzen. Sein Schüler,
Gottfried Christian Friedrich Lücke (1791–1855), später ordent-
licher Professor der Theologie, hielt ihm die Grabrede. Auf
dem Albanifriedhof[8] liegt er neben vielen anderen grossen Män-
nern begraben.

The Changing Concept of the *Singspiel* in the Eighteenth Century

by
Alfred R. Neumann

IN THE HISTORY of the arts there have been numerous instances of changes in meaning of the terminology of criticism. As forms and critical concepts are re-examined by each generation, the nomenclature applied varies. The terms "Baroque," "Renaissance," and "Romantic," for instance, do not necessarily describe the same artistic phenomenon in each art. They certainly do not describe the same era, country by country and medium by medium, nor do we today necessarily understand these terms in the same way in which they were interpreted a generation ago.

In the present paper I should like to trace the changing use of the term *Singspiel* from its inception until it achieved its present meaning and to analyze what it meant to various eighteenth-century thinkers who wrote about musico-dramatic art forms which they called *Singspiel*.

We must begin with a purely philological determination of the actual earliest use of the word Singspiel. Jacob Ayrer probably deserves historical credit as the innovator of the word in applying it to fifteen playlets in his *Opus Theatricum*, published in Nürnberg in 1618. The first of these plays is entitled "Ein schöns neus singets Spil, ist genannt der Münch im Kess-

63

korb, mit fünff Personen. Im Thon: Wie man den Engelendi-
schen Roland singt." We must thus assume that Ayrer took a
well-known melody and, in the mode of the contrafacta, supplied new ballad-like verses which were acted out.

According to Jacob Grimm, the first lexicographical entry of
the term occurred in 1691 in Caspar von Stieler's *Der deutschen
Sprache Stammbaum,* where the word Singspiel is glossed as
"melodrama." One must bear in mind that until Goethe's time
the word melodrama indicated a drama with *melos,* melody.
Rousseau's *Pygmalion* and its German successors by Heinz
Brandes and Georg Benda, and especially Goethe's *Proserpina,*
must be mentioned as outstanding examples of that form.

In Stieler's day, then, Singspiel indicated a theatrical production with music, without necessarily delineating the precise way
in which music was used. For a long time the term was used as
a synonym of the Italian *dramma per musica,* a term which we,
as well as the Germans of the eighteenth century, usually trans-
late simply as "opera." Significantly, the twelfth chapter of
Johann Christoph Gottsched's *Versuch einer Critischen Dicht-
kunst* (1st ed.; Leipzig, 1730) is entitled "Von Opern oder
Singspielen." Gottsched thus uses the terms "opera" and
"Singspiel" absolutely interchangeably.

For practical purposes, systematic operatic criticism started
in Germany with Gottsched. We know of only two treatises on
opera prior to his, but these made no impression. However, the
imprint of Gottsched's personality and thought upon at least
two generations was such that the fate and form of opera in
Germany were partially decreed by the would-be dictator of
Leipzig.

Gottsched objected to opera as "ein ungereimter Mischmasch
von Poesie und Musik, wo der Dichter und Komponist einander Gewalt tun, und sich überaus viel Mühe geben, ein sehr
elendes Werk zu Stande zu bringen." [1] Many of his contemporaries agreed with him on that point, and it is not too difficult
to find people today who still share his view on that score.

Musicodramatic presentation, however, underwent considerable development during Gottsched's lifetime, while his opinion

of that art form underwent relatively little modification. I do not believe that Gottsched ever distinguished any more between opera and Singspiel than the creators of the new popular German Singspiel: the composers Standfuss, Hiller, Benda, Schweitzer, and Mozart, and the authors Weisse, Wieland, Herder, and Goethe. Thus Gottsched's objections against the alien Italian grand opera and his rage against Christian Felix Weisse's low-comedy Singspiel became fused and confused into a great critical veto of opera in general. This misunderstanding and rigidity cost German opera much in its struggle for acceptance and has damaged Gottsched's posthumous reputation. For whenever Gottsched speaks of opera or Singspiel, he means Italianate opera. Although he altered his opposition to that form in later life, to most of his contemporary followers opera remained an art form to be avoided and scorned.

What, then, is this distinction which I claim Gottsched failed to make? The operas of Händel, Telemann, and Keiser, at the turn of the eighteenth century, just as those of Schütz in the previous century, were examples of an essentially Italian art form, regardless of the language in which they were performed. Whether our modern opera theaters perform Verdi or Puccini in English or Italian, these works are still prime examples of an Italian art form. Instead of producing grand tragedy like Shakespeare in England, Lope de Vega in Spain, Corneille and Racine in France, or Lessing and Schiller in Germany, Italy gave to the world the flowering of its tragic muse in the form of opera. Laboriously recuperating from the ravages of the Thirty Years' War, Germany was not in a position to participate in the expensive luxury of developing its own operatic theater. In Italy opera was a business enterprise, supported by the general population through admission fees. In France and England opera was the province of a single, centralized court. In Germany, however, the political subdivision into more than three hundred principalities prevented opera from finding a lasting home in more than a few of the wealthiest, or most exploitative courts. Let us not forget that the flowering of the Italian opera in Stuttgart under Niccolo Jomelli and Jean-Georges Noverre coincides with the events described in Schiller's *Kabale und Liebe,* the selling of troops to provide funds for princely entertainment. The other courts and princely homes had to search for artistic forms more suitable to their economy. It is no accident, I believe, that eighteenth-century chamber music is definitely a German form. Even a small court could afford four or five musicians to perform at court functions.

The artists had to fit themselves into this economic picture if interested in creating works for a "visible stage." In imitation of the *Beggars' Opera* by John Gay and Johann Christoph Pepusch (1728) and Charles Coffey's *The Devil to Pay,* Christian Felix Weisse produced his *Der Teufel ist los* in 1752, with music by J. J. Standfuss, adapting an earlier translation by Caspar Wilhelm Borcke, the first German Shakespeare translator. Analogous with the almost contemporary French *Opéra comique,* the Italian *Opera Buffa* and its immediate English ancestor, *Der Teufel ist los,* dealt with comic everyday situations, had few characters, and thus needed few actors, was presented in the vernacular and included spoken dialogue. This form not only was economically feasible, but also won immediate acclaim. Aesthetically, however, the essence of its form and purpose was radically different from the Italian grand opera, whose name it carried still in many minds and mouths. The 1778 edition of what we refer to as Weisse's *Singspiele* is still captioned "C. F. Weissens Opern."

The synonymous use of "opera" and "Singspiel" was thus the general rule among mid-eighteenth-century writers. One of the worst anti-opera diatribes ever written, inserted by its author, Christian Gottlob Ludwig, in Gottsched's *Beyträge zur critischen Historie der deutschen Sprache* in 1732, under the title "Versuch eines Beweises, dass ein Singgedicht oder eine Opera nicht gut seyn könne," could be cited as an additional example. However, among Gottsched's disciples we find already one who begins to make a distinction between the two terms. In 1749 Johann Adolf Scheibe, who is sometimes referred to as the composer of the Gottsched school, wrote a work which we would call an "opera," entitled *Thusnelda,* with the avowed purpose of showing that an opera could be written that followed Gottsched's rules of tragedy and still avoided his objections. He prefaced his work with an essay "Von der Möglichkeit und Beschaffenheit guter Singspiele." To Scheibe, Singspiel simply meant an opera that was sung in German.

The line of development then leads us to the startlingly similar viewpoint of Christoph Martin Wieland, whom we must discuss here briefly as the author of a full-length grand opera in German, *Alceste,* set to music by Anton Schweitzer, as well as the author of concomitant critical essays on what he meant by Singspiel.

The collaboration between Wieland and Schweitzer began with a conventional little Singspiel *Aurora,* written for the birthday of the Duchess of Weimar in the fall of 1772. (Schweitzer's success with a setting of Rousseau's *Pygmalion* had led Wieland's attention to this conductor of the Seyler troupe of actors, residing then at Weimar.) The climax of this collaboration was the opera *Alceste,* first performed in Weimar with great success on May 28, 1773, and repeated many times there. Some have hailed this work as the first German opera, which it hardly is. We only have to think of Opitz-Schütz's *Dafne,* and the work of Keiser, Mattheson, and Händel in Hamburg. It was, however, a new start, a completely new tradition that in no way represented a continuation of those previous operas in the German language. German singers were expected finally to sing in their native tongue rather than in Italian or French, and the audience was presented with an opera accessible to more than those capable of understanding a foreign language. Secondly, for the first time since the Baroque operas of Opitz, Harsdörffer, and their contemporaries a recognized literary figure was here actively taking part in the forward development of music. Whereas Gottsched ostensibly blasted opera and Lessing largely left music to the musicians, Wieland, not satisfied with criticism and aesthetic speculation, lent a hand in the movement toward a more balanced relationship between literature and music in opera.

Considering that Wieland's *Alceste* was produced only five

years after Gluck's masterpiece of the same name, the choice of
subject might be called presumption. Quite the contrary is true:
it is an act of veneration for the acknowledged master of opera,
and a deed of patriotism. Alfred Einstein observes that Wieland's patriotism gave the first impetus to his desire to write an
opera in German: "He had been annoyed by Burney, who had
seemed to him to deal too contemptuously with German vocal
music, and wished to prove that German could be at least as
sonorous an operatic language as French." [2] There was also a
personal reason for his choice: in 1772 Wieland's wife almost
died in childbed, and was saved miraculously, a little biographical detail which makes the selection of the subject more com-
prehensible. But that was not reason enough. He had to choose
a theme that would be familiar, could be understood at the first
hearing, and could attract an audience immediately. Eight other
Alceste operas prior to 1773 are known. The plot was therefore
familiar to the listeners. Furthermore, Gluck's operas were
geared to the great stages of Vienna and Paris. Wieland, like
Kurt Weill and Gian-Carlo Menotti today, wanted to provide
the small provincial stages with an opera that they could readily
perform with modest means. Rather than to try to storm the
strongest bastions of Italian opera—the large stages of Vienna,
Dresden, and Berlin—Wieland wanted to introduce German
opera through the back door. Once a demand had been aroused
and an audience educated, the metropolitan stages would have
to follow. Unfortunately, Wieland's efforts were about a generation too early.

Wieland's *Alceste* never became as famous as Goethe's parody
of the opera, deriding Wieland's eighteenth-century Greeks.
Goethe later admitted that his *Götter, Helden und Wieland* was
by no means a cool polemic, but an impulsive act; he even
called it *verfluchter Dreck*. As with Heinrich von Kleist, Goethe's rejection of the moment undeservedly became the opinion
of generations. In Konrad Burdach's opinion, *Alceste* is a dramatic poem which deserves an honored position in the annals
of German dramatic style. For the first time since the Winckel-
mann Renaissance, Hellenic tragedy was heard on the German

stage, leading the way to Goethe's *Iphigenie* and Schiller's
Braut von Messina. But Wieland's opera remained no more
than a milestone. Only too soon it disappeared from the stage,
as Schweitzer's music could not fully play the role allowed to
music in Wieland's libretto.

The opera did give rise, however, to a series of aesthetic writings in which Wieland clarifies his views on musicodramatic
arts. These are his *Versuch über das deutsche Singspiel* (1775)
and a series of *Briefe an einen Freund über das deutsche Singspiel Alceste,* all published in Wieland's periodical *Der Teutsche
Merkur*. The friend to whom the letters were supposedly addressed was Johann Georg Jacobi. They mark the first organized
positive interest in opera on the part of a major German man of
letters.

Wieland's occasional divertissements with music, like *Aurora,*
pass under the same name as his *Alceste*, which is "durchkom-
poniert." The naming means much to Wieland, since he realizes
that the word "opera" denotes something French or Italian to
his contemporaries. He writes in the *Versuch über das deutsche
Singspiel:*

> Lassen wir immer, wenns darauf ankommt, die Italienische und
> Französische *Oper* im Besitz dieses wunderbaren Namens, und aller
> Vorzüglichkeiten die man damit verbinden will; und fragen wir uns
> dagegen lieber: ob wir nicht mehr Ehre davon hätten, wenn wir die
> Schöpfer einer neuen und interessantern Art von Schauspielen
> wären; nämlich eines Singspiels, welches ohne viel mehr Aufwand
> zu erfordern als unsre gewöhnlichen Tragödien, durch die blosse
> Vereinigung der Poesie, Musik und Aktion, uns einen so hohen
> Grad des anziehendsten Vergnügens geben könnte, dass kein
> Zuschauer, der ein Herz und ein paar nicht allzu dicke Ohren mit-
> brächte, sollte wünschen können, seinen Abend angenehmer zuge-
> bracht zu haben.[3]

Just like Gluck and Wagner, Wieland is conscious of the need
for a new terminology in order to differentiate his efforts from
those of others, who may hide traditional form under the accepted name. For the same reason he borrows from the French
the expression *lyrisches Drama* and uses for the first time the
term *musikalisches Drama*. However, he failed in giving an old

term a new meaning. Still, behind the brave patriotism of these essays, Wieland remains an apologist for his own work when he talks about the Singspiel in contrast to the Italian and French operas. There is a constant undertone of self-justification. At the same time, his observations are sincere and professional, born of his own experience.

Wieland's *Versuch* is an application of the teachings of the Italian opera reformer, Count Algarotti, to German circumstances. Algarotti preached reform and return to the principles of the Renaissance opera of Florence. Since there existed no German opera to be reformed, Wieland wanted to apply the products of that reform directly to the German stage, to transplant the best results of the Italian and French opera, and to make it an organic part of the German stage tradition. He refused, however, to be induced by the Grecomania inherent in Algarotti's viewpoint to transplant the ancient Greeks as such onto the eighteenth-century stage, but accepted them only as ideal figures. He also cites Algarotti to remind the composer that music and poetry are sister-arts and are only all-powerful in concert. But he warns that in this union music must be subordinate, otherwise the balance will be endangered.

In the wake of Wieland's effort on behalf of a German Singspiel, Joachim Schubauer, a Benedictine monk from southern Bavaria, published a treatise "Ueber die Singspiele" in 1781. A polemic against Italian style opera, this essay pits the simplicity of the bourgeois Singspiel of Benda, Hasse, Neefe, and Hiller against the flowery grand opera and the Italian *Opera Buffa*. In a summary statement Schubauer states: "Mit dem Singspiel . . . könnte Deutschland vielleicht in wenigen Jahren eine ganz eigentümliche, dem Character ihrer Sprache, und dem Geiste ihrer Biedernation rein angemessene Theatermusik haben."

Schubauer thus combines the patriotic-aesthetic intent of Wieland with the definition of Singspiel as a light, entertaining, middle-class drama. His essay, however, appears to have received very little attention and as a result must be viewed as a symptom rather than as a shaper of critical opinion.

With Schubauer, however, we have reached the end of the

semantic development of the term Singspiel, since he essentially uses that term in the sense in which it is usually applied today: a light opera with intermingled spoken dialogue, akin to an operetta. No less a person than Goethe contributed six librettos in this form, and Mozart's *Entführung aus dem Serail* and *Zauberflöte* must be reckoned as its most outstanding examples. Out of an attempted translation of an Italian word came a distinct national musicodramatic form which was a direct forerunner of the German romantic opera of E. T. A. Hoffmann, Carl Maria von Weber, and finally Richard Wagner.

Schillers *Wilhelm Tell* und der "Edle Wilde"

by
Hellmut A. Hartwig

Seit Schillers berühmtestes Theaterstück zum ersten Male auf der Bühne erschien, wird gegen sein Schauspiel Sturm gelaufen aber gleichzeitig auch manch eine Lanze zu seiner Verteidigung gebrochen. Die streitenden Parteien scheinen sich ziemlich einig zu sein, was die reichlich lockere Struktur des Werkes anbetrifft; auch scheint man sich damit abgefunden zu haben, dass die Berta-Rudenz-Affäre wie ein Anhängsel wirkt und dass die Parricida-Einlage des fünften Aufzugs auch bei den treuesten Schiller-Jüngern ein gewisses Unbehagen erzeugt. Was ist also der wirkliche Zankapfel? *Was* an dem Stück erregt immer noch die Gemüter? Doch wohl die Gestalt des Tell.

Wie bei der Gestalt des Don Carlos in dem Stück gleichen Namens, scheint die Figur des Titelhelden auch im *Tell* im Verlauf des Dramas abzublassen. Zuerst sieht man einen starken und mutigen Einzelgänger, der überall eingreift, wo Not am Mann ist: ". . . dem Mann muss Hilfe werden," sagt er zu Ruodi, dem Fährmann, der sich weigert, den flüchtigen Baumgarten über den stürmischen See zu setzen. "Der brave Mann denkt an sich selbst zuletzt," meint Tell, wenn es sich darum handelt, einen Bedrängten zu retten. Durch diese Worte und durch die gleich darauf folgende mutige Tat erweckt Schiller in uns Bewunderung für Tells uneigennützige Hilfsbereitschaft und für seine starke Männlichkeit. Der nachdenkliche Be-

72

Wilhelm Tell *und der "Edle Wilde"* 73

schauer wird sich aber auch darüber klar, dass er es hier mit einem Primitiven zu tun hat. Der Ausspruch: "Mit eitler Rede wird hier nichts geschafft" drückt Tells Primitivität aus. Lange Reden und das Denken, das solchen Reden vorausgeht, sind nicht Tells Sache. Dies wird besonders augenscheinlich, wenn er auf Stauffachers Frage: "So kann das Vaterland auf Euch nicht zählen, wenn es verzweiflungsvoll zur Notwehr greift?" mit den Worten antwortet: "Der Tell holt ein verlornes Lamm vom Abgrund und sollte seinen Freunden sich entziehen? Doch, *was* ihr tut, lasst mich aus eurem *Rat!* Ich kann nicht lange prüfen oder wählen; bedürft ihr meiner zu bestimmter *Tat*, dann ruft den Tell, es soll an mir nicht fehlen." Noch klarer wird dieser Anti-Intellektualismus Tells kurz nach seiner Miss-achtung des Gesslerschen Gebots, den Hut auf der Stange zu grüssen. Sagt doch da unser "Held" zum Tyrannen Gessler: "Verzeiht mir, lieber Herr! Aus Unbedacht, nicht aus Verach-tung Eurer ist's geschehen." Und nun kommt die für die Ab-sicht dieses Versuchs wichtigste Stelle im ganzen Stück: "Wär' ich besonnen, hiess'ich nicht der Tell.[1] Ich bitt' um Gnad,' es soll nicht mehr begegnen."

Die eben zitierte Rede stellt den Tiefpunkt im Verblassungs-prozess des Titelhelden dar. Vorher schon hat man die Augen-brauen peinlich berührt hochziehen müssen, als Tell den um Mithilfe am geplanten Volksaufstand bittenden Stauffacher mit einer Phrase nach der anderen abspeiste. Am Anfang helden-haft, solange der Not an *einem* Manne abzuhelfen war, scheint aus Tell geradezu ein Biedermeiertyp zu werden, dem Ruhe die erste Bürgerpflicht ist ("Dem Friedlichen gewährt man gern den Frieden"), der durchblicken lässt, dass die Vögte von der Bevölkerung provoziert wurden ("Die Schlange sticht nicht un-gereizt") und der dem Stauffacher-Bund der Schwächeren ("Ver-bunden werden auch die Schwachen mächtig") hochmütig sein: "Der Starke ist am mächtigsten allein," hinschleudert. Über-rascht ist man dann, wenn Tell am Ende dieses Zwiegesprächs dem Stauffacher doch noch seine Hilfe zusagt, falls es zu "be-stimmter Tat" kommen sollte. Doch ganz unverständlich wird diese Zusage, wenn man kurz vorher Tell hat sagen hören:

"Beim Schiffbruch hilft der einzelne sich leichter," und: "Ein jeder zählt nur sicher auf sich selbst."

Ist der Mann bei Sinnen? fragt man sich. Er hat doch Baumgarten und anderen geholfen. Wie kann man diese krass egoistisch anmutenden Aussprüche mit Tells voriger Opferfreudigkeit vereinbaren? Aber im nächsten Augenblick ist er wieder bereit, sein Leben für andere, diesmal für die Aufständigen, aufs Spiel zu setzen. Ist da Tells spätere Bemerkung dem Gessler gegenüber, "Wär' ich besonnen, hiess' ich nicht der Tell," der Schlüssel zu diesem anscheinenden Widersinn?

Bemerkenswert in diesem Zusammenhang ist nun Gesslers Rede, die auf Tells anfängliche Weigerung folgt, vom Kopfe seines Kindes den berüchtigten Apfel zu schiessen:

> Ei, Tell, du bist ja plötzlich so besonnen!
> Man sagte mir, dass du ein Träumer seiest
> Und dich entfernst von andrer Menschen Weise.
> Du liebst das Seltsame—drum hab' ich jetzt
> Ein eigen Wagstück für dich ausgesucht.
> Ein andrer wohl bedächte sich—du drückst
> Die Augen zu und greifst es herzhaft an. (1903–1909)

Durch diese Worte (die er seinem Gessler in den Mund legt) lässt uns der Verfasser wissen, dass Tells Primitivität kein Spiel des Zufalls ist, etwa bedingt durch die grosse Eile, mit der das Schauspiel geschrieben wurde, sondern bewusst von ihm gewollt ist. In dieser einen Rede Gesslers ist Tells Menschentyp fast völlig umrissen. Er ist nicht besonnen. Er ist ein impulsiver Mensch, der nicht lange nachdenkt, wenn—beispielsweise—Not am Mann ist. Er ist demnach auch kein richtiger Held, der in völliger Erkenntnis der Lage und trotz der Gefahr aus Prinzipien oder um der "grossen Sache" willen etwas wagt. Held-Sein ist zu neunzig Prozent eine intellektuelle Angelegenheit. Jetzt fällt es einem wie Schuppen von den Augen: Solange man Schillers Tell als den konventionellen Helden sieht, starren seine Reden, Taten und Unterlassungssünden von Widersprüchen. Sieht man ihn aber, wie ihn Schillers Gessler zu sehen scheint, dann ist alles klar. Tells Benehmen durch das ganze

Stück hindurch wirkt nun völlig logisch. Tells Sprache ist allerdings nicht immer die eines simplen Bergbewohners; der Menschenerzieher Schiller kann nicht umhin, von Zeit zu Zeit mit Tells Stimme zu dozieren, sowie überhaupt mit den Zungen vieler anderer im Drama zu tönen. Jedoch soll hier diese Tendenz unseres Verfassers, sich im *Tell* (wie die Romantiker es so gern in ihren Werken taten) unter die eigenen Gestalten zu mengen und aus ihrem Mund zu sprechen, nicht gerügt werden. Im Gegenteil, ein objektiverer *Tell*, wie Goethe ihn geschrieben hätte, wäre nie im Stande gewesen (um mit Karl Schmid zu sprechen), die Welt im gleichen Masse zu begeistern.[2] Doch dieses Sprachlich-aus-der-Rolle-Fallen erschwert es dem Betrachter, in Schillers Titel-Helden den redlichen aber nicht sehr "besonnenen" *Edlen Wilden der Schweizer Berge* zu erkennen.

Ganz gleich ob Schiller bewusst den "Edlen Wilden" in Tellscher Gestalt heraufbeschwören wollte oder nicht, hier möchte ich nur versuchen, durch eine Gleichstellung des Menschen Tell mit dem Idealtyp des Edlen Wilden die bei Tell immer wieder konstatierte Inkonsequenz des Handelns als einen Irrtum zu erweisen. Dieser Irrtum musste schon dadurch entstehen, dass man bei der Bewertung einen europäischen oder sogenannten zivilisierten Maszstab anlegte.

Steckt man Tell zu Bewertungszwecken in die recht naive Zwangsjacke des gängigen Helden—vom Typ, den Karl Mays Old Shatterhand glänzend darstellt—dann wird man bald zu einem Meister Anton,[3] der die Welt (Tells) nicht mehr versteht. Erst ist Tell heldenhaft, dann weigert er sich plötzlich, mit "Rat" an der Verschwörung gegen die österreichischen Tyrannen teilzunehmen, aber zur etwaigen späteren "Tat" sei er bereit. Er spricht mit Schillerschem Schwung davon, dass der Starke am mächtigsten allein sei. Doch viel später, in der "Hohlen Gasse, durch die ER kommen muss," sagt Tell zum redseligen Stüssi: "Dem Schwachen ist sein Stachel auch gegeben." Redet er jetzt von sich, dem früher so Starken? Wieso ist er jetzt schwächer als vorher? Kurz nachdem er von diesem "Stachel" (oder Pfeil?) spricht, fällt sein erstaunlicher Spruch: "Es kann der Frömmste nicht im Frieden bleiben, wenn es dem

bösen Nachbar nicht gefällt." Sofort denkt man natürlich an
Tells frühere Entgegnung auf Stauffachers verzweifelte Frage,
ob man denn ertragen solle, was unleidlich sei:

> Die schnellen Herrscher sind's, die kurz regieren.
> —Wenn sich der Föhn erhebt aus seinen Schlünden,
> Löscht man die Feuer aus, die Schiffe suchen
> Eilends den Hafen, und der mächt'ge Geist
> Geht ohne Schaden spurlos über die Erde.
> Ein jeder lebe still bei sich daheim;
> Dem Friedlichen gewährt man gern den Frieden. (422–28)

Und auf Stauffachers ironisches "Meint Ihr?" sagt derselbe
Mann, der später Stüssi vom Frömmsten erzählt, der nicht in
Frieden leben kann: "Die Schlange sticht nicht ungereizt . . ."
Der heldenhafte Erretter Baumgartens sieht sich also jetzt als
Schlange, die sticht, weil Gessler sie direkt, persönlich, am eige-
nen Leibe, am eigenen Blute gereizt hat. Und diese Schlange
Tell sticht aus dem Hinterhalt, nicht sofort und tapfer auf die
Apfelschussprovozierung hin mit dem ersten Pfeil.[4] Allerdings
wäre dies "unbesonnen" gewesen, denn sofort hätten Gesslers
bewaffnete Knechte ihn und seinen Knaben erschlagen.[5] Ja,
besonnen war die Schlange Tell, aber nicht einmal so mutig
wie die wirkliche Schlange und viel tückischer.

"Jetzt schlägt's aber dreizehn," sagt der Meister-Anton-Typ
unter uns. "Ein seltsamer Heiliger, dieser Tell! Der redet und
tut ja wie ein prinzipienloser Schuft! Das soll der Held des
Schauspiels sein?" Ist der nächste Schritt nun ein Angriff auf
Schiller? Gott behüte! Der Meister-Anton-Typ hat doch *seine*
Prinzipien, und diese schliessen als unumstösslichen Grundstein
absolute, blinde Verehrung für alle Grossen der Nation ein. Da
versucht man lieber eine "Ehrenrettung." Man ignoriert den
Wechselbalg Tell und sucht sich einen neuen Helden für das
Stück aus. Da wird das Schweizer Volk zum Helden gemacht.[6]
Oder es ist die Schweizer Gegend, die Kulisse, die als Heldener-
satz dient. Dann wird das Opernhafte des Schauspiels vermerkt.
Die musikalische Sprache wird herausgestrichen. "Die *Sprache*
Schillers macht das Tell-Schauspiel zu dem, was es ist," schreibt

Melitta Gerhard.[7] Wird nun das Musikalische des Werkes über-
betont, dann braucht man wohl nicht zu sehr auf das Logische
darin zu achten. Bei so einer "Oper" ist ja das Libretto nicht zu
genau zu nehmen, ausser man ist (wie Wagner) auf ein "Ge-
samtkunstwerk" aus.

Hin und wieder befasste sich ein Kritiker ohne Beschönigungs-
oder Ablenkungsversuche mit der Titelgestalt. Was Hans Rudolf Hilty[8] in den Gestalten der eidgenössischen Bundesgrün-
der sieht, jene " 'edle Einfalt und stille Grösse,' welche die
Klassiker sonst in den Werken der Antike bewunderten," sucht
wohl Böhtlingk im Tell selbst und findet nur ein grosses Schil-
lersches Dilemma. Er findet nur Einfalt und alles andere als
stille Grösse. Der mythische Tell besitzt Winckelmanns Eigenschaften nicht. Schiller will sie dem Mythos abringen. Im dritten Band von Böhtlingks *Shakespeare und unsere Klassiker*
heisst es:

Noch fataler war die Klippe, welche der Mythus Schillern dadurch
in den Weg legte, dass er aus der legendarischen Gestalt des Tell
einen lebenswahren, wirklichen Menschen, eine glaubhafte Persön-
lichkeit machen musste. Der Apfelschuss, der Sprung aus dem
Nachen auf den Felsen am Ufer, inmitten des tosenden Sturmes—
diese beiden entscheidenden Momente mussten aus dem Reiche der
Phantasie ins Reich der greifbaren Wirklichkeit, das Epos ins Drama
umgesetzt werden. Vor allem aber musste der meuchelmörderische
Schuss aus dem Hinterhalt heraus ethisch zureichend gerechtfertigt
werden, ohne die Sympathie mit dem Helden, der als der Tapferste
der Tapfern dastehen soll, zu ertöten. Die Letztere hat Schiller selbst
offenbar am meisten Kopfzerbrechen gemacht. Was hat er hierzu
nicht alles für Untaten auf das Haupt des ebenfalls mythischen
Gessler geladen! nicht alles aufeinander getürmt, um den Schuss
aus dem Hinterhalt heraus uns erträglich, annehmbar zu machen!
Durch die hohle Gasse muss erst ein fröhlicher Hochzeitszug kommen, der das friedliche, unschuldige, glückliche Menschentum vor
Augen stellt, auf dem sich das finstere Bild des blutigen Tyrannen
abhebt. Muss die verzweifelte Gattin und Mutter, der Gessler den
Gatten und Vater geraubt hat, kommen, sich mit ihren Kindern vor
die Füsse von Gesslers Pferd niederwerfen und vergeblich an dessen
versteintes Herz appellieren. Erst angesichts dieses Notstandes,
dieser Ungeheuerlichkeit, die unser Mitleid und unsere Entrüstung
aufs Höchste steigert, gibt Tell den Schuss ab.[9]

Wie viele vor und nach ihm, meint Böhtlingk, dass die Johann-Parricida-Szene Tells Mord an Gessler "beschönigen" musste. Böhtlingk findet keinen zu grossen Unterschied zwischen den beiden Mordtaten. Beide Mörder rächten sich *für erlittene Schmach:*

> War es nicht die Rache dafür, dass er (Gessler) ihn (Tell) genötigt hatte, den Apfel vom Haupte seines Kindes zu schiessen? Schon der Umstand, dass Tell sich hierzu hergegeben hatte, war wahrlich wenig dazu angetan, dessen HELDENMUT ins Licht zu setzen—dass er, statt gleich den ersten Pfeil gegen den "Tyrannen" auf dessen ungeheuerliche Zumutung hin abzuschnellen, diesem erst den zweiten zudachte, war eher—feig. Man sieht, wie die überlieferte Sage, der Mythus, wie ihn die Volksphantasie naiv ausgestaltet hatte, durch den nur die Treffsicherheit des Schützen verherrlicht werden sollte, Schiller auch hier bedenklich in die Quere gekommen ist.[10]

Vor Böhtlingk deutet schon Ludwig Bellermann an, dass Schiller durch die Sage arg behindert wurde. Tschudis Überlieferung der Tellsage zwang Schiller, den Schuss geschehen zu lassen, meint Bellermann.[11] Auch er kritisiert die Parricidaszene als unerwünscht.[12] In diesem Zusammenhang ist Reinhard Buchwalds Hinweis auf Schillers Haltung zum Monolog Tells vor der Ermordung Gesslers wichtig. Buchwald zitiert aus einem Brief des Dichters an Iffland, der den Monolog bei einer *Tell*-Aufführung streichen wollte: "Der Casus gehört vor das poetische Forum, und darüber kann ich keinen höheren Richter als mein Gefühl erkennen." [13] Das gilt wohl auch für die Parricidakontroverse. Sicherlich drückt Lily Hohenstein Schillers eigenes Empfinden aus, wenn sie schreibt:

> Wie er dann wirklich die göttliche Hilfe zum zweitenmal erlebt und der Vogt gerichtet vom Ross stürzt, da ist Tell wieder der Alte, der unschuldige Naturmensch mit der freien, ungespaltenen Seele, der beim Anblick des Parricida schaudernd erschrickt, weil Mord, und gar Mord am verwandten Blut, die unfasslichste Schandtat ist, die ein Mensch begehen kann.[14]

Die Parricida-Einschaltung wäre demnach notwendig gewesen, um den Kontrast zwischen der Tat des Naturmenschen

Tell und der des "unnatürlichen" Herzogs offensichtlich zu machen. Wenn wir nun weiter Lily Hohensteins Auslegung folgen, dann hat Schiller seinen Tell als Naturmenschen gesehen—oder gar als edlen Wilden, oder den "sanften Wilden" der Romantiker und vor allem Herders. In einer Rezension von Hoxie Neale Fairchilds *The Noble Savage. An Inquiry into a Phase of Romantic Naturalism*[15] weist Camillo von Klenze darauf hin, dass der "Edle Wilde" in der europäischen Literatur gebraucht wurde, um den Gedanken der universellen Toleranz zu fördern. Der Rezensent rügt an Fairchild, dass er bei der Aufzählung der Völker, unter denen die "Edlen Wilden" zu finden sind, nur die Neger und Indianer erwähnt. Skythen und Zigeuner müssten auch dazugezählt werden, meint von Klenze. Man denke an Voltaires *Les Scythes* und Goethes *Iphigenie,* wo gerade der klassische Wilde, gerade der Skythe, die edelste Gattung des primitiven Menschen darstellt, während, zum Beispiel, bei Cervantes die "Gitanella" in den *Novelas Ejemplares* besagte Gattung enthält. Interessant und für meine These sehr wichtig ist es, dass von Klenze auch Goethes Götz unter die "Edlen Wilden" stellt.[16] Also warum nicht Schillers Tell?

Herders Propagierung des guten Naturmenschen[17] hat viel dazu beigetragen, dass seine Zeitgenossen, die Romantiker und andere (darunter Schiller), jenen Begriff nicht vergassen. Die Romantiker besonders vergassen ihn so wenig, dass Fairchild in seinem oben erwähnten Werk, fast am Ende seiner Ausführungen, schreiben konnte: "I have created a hero, Right Reason; a villain, Romanticism; and a villain's tool, the Noble Savage!"[18] Dies deutet an, dass (wie z.B. in Goethes *Faust II* im Zusammenhang mit der Anwendung klassisch-griechischer Begriffsträger,[19] auch der "Edle Wilde" als Träger des Toleranzgedankens schliesslich zu oft, nicht zu wenig gebraucht wurde. Auf jeden Fall ist es demnach kaum notwendig, beweisen zu müssen, dass Schiller vom "Edlen Wilden" wusste. Es ist auch unwichtig hier festzustellen, ob gerade Herders Schriften den Hauptanteil an diesem Vermittlungsprozess trugen. Was mir wichtig ist, ist zu betonen, dass Herders Beschreibung des "Edlen Wilden" nicht wesentlich von denen seiner Vorgänger (Las Casas, Montaigne, Marmontel, Dobrizhoffer, Sir Walter Raleigh usw.) abwich, Mehr sogar als in seinen berühmten *Ideen* hat Herder in seinen *Briefen* den "Edlen Wilden" als ein Toleranzwerkzeug verwendet, wie Professor Robert T. Clark, Jr. schon darauf hinwies. In seinem Artikel, "The Noble Savage and the Idea of Tolerance in Herder's *Briefe zu Beförderung der Humanität,*" bespricht Clark den Typ des "Edlen Wilden," den Herder in seinen *Briefen* zitiert und der dem Letzteren vorschwebte.[20]

Wenn wir uns Herders "Wilden" ansehen, dann leuchtet es gleich ein, warum das Eigenschaftswort "edler" oft mit "sanfter" ersetzt wurde. Diese "Edlen Wilden" Herders sind alle gut und anhänglich, treu bis in den Tod und melancholisch. Sie stehen alle schon in dem Schatten ihres kommenden traurigen Schicksals durch die bösen Europäer. Sie erwecken Sympathie, sind aber unheroisch, wie Schillers Tell es im Grunde ist, obwohl ihm das traurige Schicksal der "Edlen Wilden" Herders, Las Casas' usw. erspart bleibt. Dieses Unheroische (ganz im Gegensatz zu den Dramenhelden aus Schillers früherer und mittlerer Periode) hat man natürlich während der verschiedenen nationalistischen Perioden nach Schiller nicht wahrhaben wollen. Er soll der "Tapferste der Tapfern" sein, haben wir eben von Böhtlingk gehört, jedoch ist er—schreibt Böhtlingk— eher feig, doch wohl "feig" im Sinne von "All good soldiers run away, so's to fight another day." Diese vernünftige Regel ist die des einfachen Soldaten, des unkomplizierten Mannes vom Volke, wie Tell ihn darstellt. Bellermann sagt: "Tell ist durchaus keine heroische Natur, auch nicht, wie sonst alle Haupthelden Schillerscher Dramen, ein erlesener, hochbegabter Geist."[21] Dann weiter unten: [Er ist ein] "schlichter, einfacher Landmann von ruhigem, friedliebendem, auf sein Tagewerk beschränktem Sinne. Allmählich erst streift Tell (in der Schuszszene) die Unterthänigkeit [*sic*] ab."[22] Buchwald beschreibt in seinem 1959 erschienenen Werk über Schiller den Tell als geduldig, unterwürfig, selbst zu Ausreden bereit (also wie ein Kind oder kindhafter "Wilder Mann" Herderschen Gepräges), "aber dabei ein naturhafter Mensch, der den fürchterlichen Kampf in seiner Seele mit den Händen zuckend, mit rollenden Augen ausficht und nach seiner Tat [dem Apfelschuss] kraftlos zusammenbricht." [23]

Bei fast allen Beurteilern des Schillerschen Tell ist trotz aller klugen und gewiss meistens richtigen Einsicht immer wieder zu verspüren, dass die Tellgestalt Unbehagen verursacht. Wie schon erwähnt, lenkt man oft die Aufmerksamkeit ab von dem Hauptakteur. Man tut dies entweder durch Hinweise auf das Opernhafte des Stückes (von Schiller selbst bestätigt),[24] oder—wie Melitta Gerhard—durch Hinweis auf die "Sprache Schillers" (was wohl alle sogenannten Unebenheiten des Schauspiels völlig belanglos machen soll?), oder durch das Auffinden des Heroischen beim Schweizer Volke, da man nicht zu genau auf den "Helden" Tell hinsehen möchte.

Nun scheinen mir aber alle diese geistreichen Purzelbäume nicht in jedem Falle gerechtfertigt oder nötig. Wo es sich um Beschönigungen oder Ablenkungsversuche handelt, werden sie durch die Annahme bedingt, dass Tell nicht konsequent handelt, sich also nicht wie der konventionelle Held (im heutigen wie auch in Schillers eigenem, sonstigem Sinne) benimmt. Bei Tell ist keine Spur von edler Selbstaufopferung, wie zum Beispiel bei dem Marquis Posa. Was ich nun behaupten möchte, ist, dass alles Unbehagen über Tells Tun und Sprechen verschwindet, wenn man in ihm den "Edlen oder sanften Wilden" à la Herder sieht. Von Interesse dürfte es an dieser Stelle sein, dass Schiller seinen edlen Schweizer Bergmenschen einige Male wie einen typischen Indianerhäuptling Coopers oder des noch späteren Karl May sprechen lässt. Wie bekannt, radebrechen deren edle Rothäute von sich nur in der dritten Person, wie etwa: "Ugh, Winnetou hat gesprochen!" oder: " 'Chingachgook hilft jetzt Bleichgesicht!' sprach der edle Mohikaner, mit dem roten Finger seine eigne stolze Brust berührend." Ähnlich gibt doch Tell dem Stauffacher die Hand und spricht: "Der *Tell* holt ein verlornes Lamm von Abgrund und sollte seinen

Freunden sich entziehen? . . . Zu dem Fischer (Vierter Aufzug, erste Szene, Zeile 2294 ff.):

> Ihr werdet meinen Schwäher bei ihr finden
> Und andre, die im Rütli mitgeschworen.
> Sie sollen wacker sein und gutes Muts:
> Der *Tell* sei frei und seines Armes mächtig;
> Bald werden sie ein Weiteres von mir hören.

Nicht "Ich sei frei," sondern "Der Tell sei frei," sagt er von sich selbst. Man könnte einwenden, hier wolle er sich nur dem Fischer zu erkennen geben, doch der wusste ja schon längst, wen er vor sich hatte, und hatte ihn sogar schon in Zeile 2271 mit "Tell, Tell" angeredet. Und nun nochmals tut Tell, als ob er von einer dritten Person spreche, wenn er dem Parricida die von diesem geforderte Hand reicht und fragt: "Kann ich Euch helfen? Kann's ein Mensch der Sünde?" und dann, wie ein Humanitätsapostel Herders, fortfährt:

> Doch stehet auf! Was Ihr auch Grässliches
> Verübt—Ihr seid ein Mensch—ich bin es auch;
> Vom *Tell* soll keiner ungetröstet scheiden—
> Was ich vermag, das will ich tun. (3222–26)

Was Tell dann für Parricida tut, ist weniger ein Tun als ein Nichts-Tun. Er wahrt das Geheimnis der Identität seines unglücklichen Gastes, sogar vor der eigenen Familie. Wie öfters der "Edle Wilde" Herders, ist Tell hier edel durch *Nichts-Antun*. Es ist die Anwendung der Goldenen Regel der Urchristen, dem Nächsten nicht das anzutun, was man von ihm nicht gerne erleiden würde. Wenn Tell dabei wie ein edler Wilder von sich in der dritten Person spricht, ist das dann sehr apropos.

Man vergleiche nun, da ich Herder schon öfters erwähnt habe, und da seine *Ideen zur Philosophie der Geschichte der Menschheit* (1784) und die schon zitierten *Briefe zu Beförderung der Humanität* (1793) dem Weimarer Mitbürger Schiller bekannt gewesen sein dürften, die Herdersche Anschauung über die edlen Wilden Amerikas mit Tells Natur, wie sie in Schillers *Tell* zutage tritt:

... Soll man nach dieser Gestalt [des "rothäutigen" Amerikaners] einen gewissen Haupt-und mittlern Charakter der Amerikaner angeben: so scheints Gutherzigkeit und kindliche Unschuld zu seyn, die auch ihre alte Einrichtungen, ihre Geschicklichkeiten und wenigen Künste, am meisten ihr erstes Betragen gegen die Europäer beweisen. Aus einem barbarischen Lande entsprossen und *un*unter-stützt von irgend einer Beihülfe der cultivirten Welt gingen sie selbst, so weit sie kamen, und liefern auch hier in ihren schwachen Anfängen der Cultur ein sehr lehrreiches Gemählde der Mensch-heit.[25]

Sieht man jetzt Tell als ähnliche Gestalt, wo sind dann die Widersprüche in seinem Handeln? Wie Bellermann schon schrieb,[26] Tell lindert direkte Not, aber die Verletzung ver-briefter Freiheitsrechte der Schweizer Kantone lässt ihn kalt. Sobald aber seine Freunde in Bedrängnis geraten, ganz gleich was der Grund (Verschwörung gegen die Tyrannen oder sonst eine Handlung) sein mag, wer zuerst angegriffen worden ist— und von wem—da ist er wieder bereit zu helfen. Wie der primi-tive Mensch begreift er nur das, was er sehen kann und was direkt an ihn herantritt. Die erhabene Rede, die "weisen Sprüche" wechseln mit realistischer Bauernsprache ab, weil der Edle Wilde Tell eben nicht ein *echter* Wilder ist, sondern die Idealgestalt des *"Edlen* Wilden" darstellt.

Wo Tell *"un*besonnen" ist, oder treuherzig, wie sofort in seiner Erzählung von der Begegnung mit Gessler an der Ge-birgswand augenscheinlich wird, oder als er Gessler den Grund für den zweiten in Bereitschaft gehaltenen Pfeil angibt, da ist Tell der naive Naturmensch. Wo er *besonnen* handelt, wie während des Apfelschusses, wo er durch Ausführung des bru-talen Befehls die überrasche und *heroische* Tat und den si-cheren darauffolgenden Tod vermeidet, ist Tell immer noch der primitive Mensch, der instinktmässig handelt und nicht auf Grund von Erwägungen. Wenn aber aus seinem bäuerlichen Munde hohe Weisheiten quellen, oder wenn er Parricida ge-genüber einerseits den entrüsteten Unschuldsengel spielt, anderseits bereit ist, dem bösen Verwandtenmörder christlich zu begegnen, dann ist er das Sprachrohr der Humanitätsapostel Herder und Schiller. Diese zwei Typen, realistischer Bewohner einer rauhen Welt und Idealist auf höchster Ebene,[27] ergeben in einer Person verschmolzen den "Edlen Wilden der Schweizer Bergwelt," Schillers Wilhelm Tell, welcher, in diesem Lichte gesehen, keine Apologie mehr benötigt, sondern im Gegenteil unter den grössten Bühnengestalten der europäischen Literatur seinen Platz nimmt.

Hölderlin, *Der gefesselte Strom / Ganymed**

by
Walter Silz

A

Der gefesselte Strom

Was schläfst und träumst du, Jüngling, gehüllt in dich,
Und säumst am kalten Ufer, Geduldiger,
   Und achtest nicht des Ursprungs, du, des
      Oceans Sohn, des Titanenfreundes!

5   Die Liebesboten, welche der Vater schikt,
   Kennst du die lebenathmenden Lüfte nicht?
     Und trift das Wort dich nicht, das hell von
      Oben der wachende Gott dir sendet?

    Schon tönt, schon tönt es ihm in der Brust, es quillt,
10   Wie, da er noch im Schoose der Felsen spielt',
     Ihm auf, und nun gedenkt er seiner
      Kraft, der Gewaltige, nun, nun eilt er,

    Der Zauderer, er spottet der Fesseln nun,
   Und nimmt und bricht und wirft die Zerbrochenen
15   Im Zorne, spielend, da und dort zum
      Schallenden Ufer und an der Stimme

---

* This article was written in April, 1961.

85

Des Göttersohns erwachen die Berge rings,
  Es regen sich die Wälder, es hört die Kluft
    Den Herold fern und schaudernd regt im
20   Busen der Erde sich Freude wieder.

Der Frühling kommt; es dämmert das neue Grün;
  Er aber wandelt hin zu Unsterblichen;
    Denn nirgend darf er bleiben, als wo
      Ihn in die Arme der Vater aufnimmt.

B

Ganymed

Was schläfst du, Bergsohn, liegest in Unmuth, schief,
  Und frierst am kahlen Ufer, Gedultiger!
    Denkst nicht der Gnade du, wenn's an den
      Tischen die Himmlischen sonst gedürstet?

5   Kennst drunten du vom Vater die Boten nicht,
      Nicht in der Kluft der Lüfte geschärfter Spiel?
        Trift nicht das Wort dich, das voll alten
          Geists ein gewanderter Mann dir sendet?

Schon tönet's aber ihm in der Brust. Tief quillt's,
10   Wie damals, als hoch oben im Fels er schlief,
        Ihm auf. Im Zorne reinigt aber
          Sich der Gefesselte nun, nun eilt er

Der Linkische; der spottet der Schlaken nun,
  Und nimmt und bricht und wirft die Zerbrochenen
15   Zorntrunken, spielend, dort und da zum
          Schauenden Ufer und bei des Fremdlings

Besondrer Stimme stehen die Heerden auf,
  Es regen sich die Wälder, es hört tief Land
    Den Stromgeist fern, und schaudernd regt im
20   Nabel der Erde der Geist sich wieder.

Der Frühling kömmt. Und jedes, in seiner Art,
  Blüht. Der ist aber ferne; nicht mehr dabei.
    Irr gieng er nun; denn allzugut sind
      Genien; himmlisch Gespräch ist sein nun.

The two texts here confronted and designated for convenience as *A* and *B* are two versions of the same poem as printed on pages 67 and 68 of the second volume of Friedrich Beissner's monumental *Grosse Stuttgarter Ausgabe*. A, written probably in the spring of 1801, was first published in Hölderlin's *Gedichte*, edited by Ludwig Uhland and Gustav Schwab in 1826. B, developed from A probably as early as 1802, was revised by its author for publication as one of the so-called "Nachtgesänge" in December, 1803 and printed in a *Taschenbuch* for the year 1805.[1] Both versions are in the Alcaic strophe. Between them falls the onset of Hölderlin's madness.

On the following pages I shall attempt to substantiate, by means of a critical comparison of the two texts in detail, my opinion that *Ganymed* is a deranged reworking of *Der gefesselte Strom*, with confusions of thought and expression, repetitions, patchwords, and prosy lapses that make it indubitably inferior to the original.

In this opinion I stand, as far as I can see, alone. Writers on Hölderlin, when they have dealt with the poem in particular, have invariably rated *Ganymed* as superior.[2] Wilhelm Michel, in his essay "Hölderlins Ode *Ganymed*" (1924, last reprinted in his *Hölderlins Wiederkunft* [Wien, 1943], 123–38), considers it an improvement over the first version in both language and thought. For him it is an example of a new poetic language, Hölderlin's "Spätsprache," "schärfer im Profil, karger im Umriss, härter im Stoff, reicher und verdichteter in der Substanz," discarding "das Blühende und Gerührte" in favor of an ultimate "Eigentlichkeit des Ausdrucks." The comparative study by Leopold Liegler, *"Der gefesselte Strom* und *Ganymed,"* in the *Hölderlin-Jahrbuch 1947* (Tübingen, 1948, pp. 62–77), is an elaborate and at times rationalizing endeavor to prove the later version in every respect preferable to the earlier one. He too finds a new and superlative diction in B, "eine beinah unirdische Sprache, die durch ihre gläserne Klarheit erschüttert." What I find *erschütternd* about B is the spectacle of a great deranged genius deranging his own work.

Five years after Liegler, Alfred Romain contributed to the

Hölderlin-Jahrbuch a long and laborious discussion designed to demonstrate that *Ganymed* is "ein in sich zusammenstimmendes, gerundetes Kunstgebilde, dessen veränderte Wortgestalt bis ins letzte Ausdruck des neuen Sinngehaltes ist." Romain dismisses any criticism of the shift to the Ganymede-theme: "Vielmehr ist die Eingestaltung der Ganymedidee folgerecht durchgeführt und mit so hoher Kunst, dass von Nachlassen des dichterischen Vermögens keine Rede sein kann." [3] Richard M. Müller, the author of a monograph on the river-motif in German Classicism, also finds in *Ganymed* an essential *Korrektur*, realized above all in its final strophe.[4]

Let us consider the evidence of the text afresh. What of the change in title? The natural phenomenon underlying the poem is the breaking-up of the ice on a swollen river in the early spring, presumably the Swiss Rhine (Hölderlin was at Hauptwyl during the early months of 1801). The original title, *Der Eisgang*, designated this subject matter directly, naïvely; the title of A gives it a personal, dramatic aspect, raises it to the symbolic: we are reminded of Goethe's *Mahomets Gesang*. Is B's title an improvement on A's? Wilhelm Michel, in his *Das Leben Hölderlins* (Bremen, 1940, p. 405), attributes the title *Ganymed* to Hölderlin's wish to represent the *Hinauswandern* of the river as a *Heimgang zum Ozean,* the limited individual life returning to the divine *Lebensfülle*. But is the addition of a name from the mythology book of any help in expressing this? Is it not said clearly at the end of A, and badly obscured at the end of B? What confusion the Ganymede-motif can invite is shown by Ernst Müller's interpretation of B's closing stanza: "Diese letzte Strophe . . . fasst die Deutung zusammen. Der Fluss hat seine Aufgabe erfüllt und ist mit der Wolke [of which Hölderlin says nothing], in die sich sein dem Ozean zueilendes Wasser verwandelte, zum Himmel aufgefahren, weil er als Götterbote Ganymed dorthin gehört, um als himmlischer Mundschenk lebenspendenden Nektar zu kredenzen. So ist er jetzt ferne und 'nicht mehr dabei.' " [5]

Paul Böckmann, in his *Hölderlin und seine Götter* (München, 1935, p. 314), sees Ganymede symbolizing the "Heros, der in die Arme des Vaters aufgenommen wird." But Ganymede was no *Heros;* he was only a beautiful boy who became the object of Zeus's homosexual love. It is impossible to reconcile the Ganymede of Greek myth with the *zorntrunken* self-liberator of B, to say nothing of the *Gewaltige* of A. The violence in the poem is wholly on the part of the river; in the myth it is on the part of Zeus. Yet Robert Ulshöfer thinks to justify Hölderlin's *mythische Betrachtungsweise* in B by saying "er sieht in dem Strom den Liebling des Göttervaters, der ihn mit Gewalt den irdischen Banden entreisst." [6]

Böckmann believes that the use of Ganymede's name gives the poem "ein noch freieres, mythisches Gepräge"; I should say on the contrary that it reduces the original Nature-myth of A to mere mythology and introduces an unfortunate confusion of reference and imagery into the poem. "The [ice-]fettered Stream" as a title is both picturesque and precise; *Ganymed* is both artificial and misleading, for the poem has nothing to do with Ganymede. Only B lines 3–4 may be taken as a (none too intelligible) allusion to the cupbearer of the gods; to see a hint of the Ganymede-motif in A line 22, as Liegler does, seems to me utterly far-fetched. The level *wandelt hin* for the movement of the river flowing away into the distance is completely contradicted by the sharp upward movement of Ganymede in the eagle's talons.[7]

Liegler considers the opening stanza of B "wesentlich energischer im Ton, zupackender und schärfer" than A's; verbal changes, he argues, alter the lines *ins entschieden Schroffe.* But what is gained, poetically, by such *Schroffheit* at this point? *Bergsohn* may be harsher and more specific than *Jüngling* (although no better in suggesting a river), but it is, for Hölderlin, far less evocative and characteristic: youthfulness is a high quality of his rivers, especially the Rhine and the Neckar.[8] Michel, in his essay, praises the designation *schief* (B line 1) as *scharf und sinnlich* in contrast to the *gehüllt in dich* of A. To me, *liegest in Unmut, schief* suggests a petulant child, rather than a river, in its bed;[9] in any case, it yields no poetic image. The *gehüllt in dich,* however, is both in the real and the figurative

sense more "sharp and sensuous," for the ice-clad river is indeed
wrapped up in itself, in its own frozen element! The stretched
liegest covers a metrical difficulty, as does *tönet* (B line 9); there
are no such forms in A. B line 2 is more physical and less poetic
in expression than A line 2. The meaning and application of
Gnade are obscure, and one can hardly make sense of B lines
3–4, whereas A is entirely clear.

The bold inversion of A line 5, which gives such emphasis
to the object and impetus to the sentence, is lost in B's heavier
order. The *drunten* squints between *du* and *Boten,* but is true
of neither, and the whole stanza again does not equal A in
clarity. The "sharpened play" of the winds caught in the chasm
(B line 6) is to be sure an original and vivid perception in itself; but by using *Kluft* here, the poet sacrifices the personification of A lines 18–19: the canyon hearkening to the yet distant
voice of the oncoming torrent. In A there are clearly two sum-
monses that bid the sleeping stream awake: the *Liebesboten*
(A line 5) are the mild "life-breathing airs" from the sea, from
Father Ocean; the *Wort* coming down "bright from above" (A
line 7 f.) is the touch of Light, the "ever-wakeful god" the
Sun.[10] B confuses this situation by injecting *drunten* and the
keener winds (which do not suggest a thaw) and the figure of a
mysterious wanderer. Who is this *gewanderter Mann* who appears so suddenly in B line 8? Is it Hölderlin? Norbert von Hellingrath, in his Hölderlin edition (IV, 309) concludes that it is
"der Dichter"; but why should it seem *sinnlicher und zutreffen-
der* to have the poet enter his poem at this one place? Beissner's
classical parallels (II, 547) are distant and inconclusive. We are
left puzzled.

B line 9 sacrifices the eager repetition of *schon tönt* of A line
9 and substitutes a choppy line with a patchword *aber*—to be
followed by a second *aber* in the same stanza. *Hoch oben im
Fels* (B line 10) is less vivid than *im Schosse der Felsen* (A line
10). Liegler finds a special subtlety in the juxtaposition of *tief*
and *hoch* (B lines 9, 10); but these two words stand in different
connections and are not contrastable; their juxtaposition is
probably an inadvertence. In the replacement of *spielt'* by

schlief (B line 10) Liegler would have us see a "Verfestigung des Ausdrucks, . . . eine umso glücklichere Korrektur" as *spielen* now occurs at the only possible place, in B line 15. But the play-motif was already used in B line 6, and the sleep-motif in B (and A) line 1; these repetitions do not strengthen but weaken the expression.

The introduction of the idea of *Reinigung* in B line 11 Liegler regards as a *Hauptleistung* that renders the image of the frozen river-god *wesentlich anschaulicher*. Rather, one must object, it muddles the image: a prisoner strives for liberation, not purification; he casts off fetters, not dross. The picture of the awaking river throwing off its bonds of ice floes was beautifully clear in A; the intrusion of *Schlacken* and *reinigen* in B has blurred it. The *Zerbrochenen* made complete sense with *Fesseln* (A lines 13–14) ; it makes much less sense with *Schlacken:* whether *they* are broken or not is unimportant, so long as they are eliminated (*ausgeschieden*). In this detail, again, B detracts from the congruity of the poem. Yet Romain, whose most original contribution is to interpret B as not dealing with an *Eisgang* at all but with the river's breaking through an obstructing *Erdmasse,* reasons (p. 71): "Das Wort 'Fesseln' für das Hemmende, hier ohnehin nicht mehr brauchbar wegen des schon vorangegangenen Wortes 'der Gefesselte,' und weil mit der 'Reinigung' die Fesselung innerlich bereits überwunden ist, wurde bedeutsam ersetzt durch 'Schlacken'!"

In the shifting of *im Zorne* forward from A line 15 to B line 11, Liegler manages to see a "manic" improvement, and even Beissner commends it as "eine Verdopplung, eine Verstärkung des Zorn-Motivs" (II, 547). One could say to the contrary that the wrath-motif is thus brought in too early, before it has been fully motivated, and that the *zorntrunken* of B line 15, despite its heightening suffix, becomes thereby weak and anticlimactic. The replacement of *der Zauderer* by *der Linkische* (B line 13), noted by Liegler with approval, again seems to me out of keeping with the logic of the poem, for the river is represented as slow, not as awkward, in liberating itself. *Zaudern* and *eilen* make a clear antithesis; *linkisch* and *eilen* do not.[11] I can see no

gain, but only a slight jar, in the substitution of *dort und da*
(B line 15) for the idiomatic *da und dort* of A line 15, as well as
in the needlessly demonstrative and colloquial *der* (the second
of three) in B line 13; yet the German interpreters are at pains
to discover subtle significance even in these petty differences.[12]

Of greater moment is the change from *schallenden* to *schauenden* in line 16. It has given rise to some amazing interpreta-
tional gymnastics. Hellingrath (IV, 309) comments: "es ist
nötiger[!] das Staunen [which is not what *schauen* says] der
schauenden Ufer zu betonen als ihr selbstverständliches[!] Wi-
derhallen," and he praises the ensuing passage as "eine wunder-
bare Steigerung der vorher schon so schönen Stelle." Liegler
opines: "Erst das 'schauende Ufer' sichert die Gedankenrich-
tung, in die der Dichter den Hörer getrieben[!] haben will: zum
Eindruck einer aufwachenden, aufhorchenden Welt"—neither
of which *schauen* says! Beissner supports Hellingrath in the
opinion "dass das aufmerkende Schauen [the 'aufmerken' is
again added] gegenüber dem blossen Widerhall des Schallens
in der 1. Fassung eine Steigerung bedeutet" (II, 547). Romain
(p. 72) likewise reads into *schauenden* an "erstauntes Aufmerken der nahen Umwelt," and, since he conceives of the river as
a sort of colossal ditcher, he finds *schallen* no longer appropriate to the dull thud of the excavated earth-masses as they fall!

One wonders whether, had Hölderlin written *schaukelnden*
or *schaffenden* or some other word, the interpreters would not
strain equally hard to rationalize it. For me, *schauenden* makes
nonsense of "der vorher schon so schönen Stelle": the "resound-
ing shores," as the rising river flings its broken ice on them, is
a poetic perception of natural truth and classical quality. Of the
six words that Hölderlin considered for this place, *schauenden*
is the only one that does not make sense.[13] I should guess that
schauenden, if it is not simply a miswriting for *schallenden*, is
a deranged echo of the original word. We know from other evidence that in his *Umnachtung* Hölderlin's acoustic and rhyth-
mical sense remained relatively unimpaired while his logical
faculty gave way. Perhaps his mind played with the sound-
relation between the two words in disregard of their meanings,

as it may have done with *schlief* and *spielt'* in line 10. We cannot say. But we can at least refrain from reading into his words meanings that are not there.

The dramatic—for Hölderlin, almost violent—character of the fourth strophe and the acoustic quality of the fifth have not been seriously diminished in B (it is interesting to note that line 14, with its three energetic monosyllabic verbs, is the only line of the poem left unchanged), but the language and the concepts in these strophes show considerable deterioration. "Des Fremd- lings/Besondrer Stimme" (B lines 16–17) is bare prose in comparison with "der Stimme/Des Göttersohns" (Liegler explains: "die Ufer schauen, *weil* ein Fremdling . . . gekommen ist"). The picture of herds getting to their feet (B line 17) is far inferior to that of the encircling hills "awaking" with sound (A line 17).[14] "Es hört die Kluft/Den Herold fern" (A lines 18–19) suggests a fine acoustic effect: the empty gorge already echoing with the sound of the rushing waters that will soon fill it. *Tief Land* (B line 18) is mysteriously suggestive but vague by contrast with *Kluft,* and *Herold* (the river as herald of the spring) is stirring and proud as against *Stromgeist,* which adds nothing new and causes an awkward collision with a different *Geist* in the next line (there is a third *Geist* in B line 8). *Nabel* is more arresting, but more limited and physiological and less poetic than *Busen* (line 20).

The delicate *dämmert* for the tender young green of early spring (A line 21) has no equivalent in B. This line, "Der Frühling kommt; es dämmert das neue Grün," is a spring poem in itself, a gem of Volkslied-like simplicity and evocative power and fluid movement; B can only garble it sadly. B line 22 is metrically bad: *blüht* and *nicht* require an accent and do not get it; *der* and *mehr* receive the accent and do not want it; a patchy, choppy line results which cannot bear comparison with the grace and dignity of A line 22. Even the minor word *aber,* by virtue of its placing in this line, has a lesser poetic value than in A.

In fact, the whole last strophe of B is jerky and prosaic. It consists of seven pieces, disconnected in syntax and thought, with patches of flat literalness like *jedes in seiner Art* and *nicht mehr dabei*. It is bare of all metaphor. It has lost, save in a syllable-counting sense, its Alcaic form. It has lost the father-son reference and hence the "arch" which that motif, coming at the beginning and end of A, stretches over the whole poem. Yet Michel, in his essay, holds this strophe to be superior to the final one of A and admires its *ruhiges, grosses Sagen*. Romain commends its *wortkarge, sinndichte Sätze*. Liegler finds it *unerhört eindrucksvoll*, and in general maintains "aus der Frühlingsmetapher vom 'gefesselten Strom' ist nun ein Lied vom Erdenwandel eines Genius . . . geworden." I doubt that anyone could derive this meaning from B if he did not have A to guide him.

The ending of A, for its part, is beautifully clear and coherent, with no intrusive notions of *Irrgang* and *allzugute Genien* to cloud the issue. The river, having released itself, releases the spring and renews the life of the earth. But it cannot stay to enjoy the beauty it has called forth; it must complete its course, like the great spirits such as Hölderlin who pass through the everyday on their way to immortality. Rivers in Hölderlin's poetry (*Heidelberg* is an example) often symbolize his sense of the flux and urgency of life, especially the self-spending of genius fulfilling its destiny. The final picture of the river in the far distance ending in the embrace of its father, Ocean, is graphic and satisfying; there is nothing like it in B. After the agitated crescendo of the fourth and fifth stanzas comes (in A) a quiet receding, a majestic withdrawal. This movement of rise and fall, of conflict and resolution, marks the structure of many of Hölderlin's poems. *Der gefesselte Strom* is not one of his greatest and profoundest odes, but it is one of his clearest, most characteristic, and loveliest, one that the tragically disabled poet, so soon after, could not improve but only impair.[15]

Das Motiv der Einsamkeit in der modernen deutschen Lyrik

by
Gilbert J. Jordan

"LIEBE UND EINSAMKEIT, Liebe und unerfüllbare Sehnsucht sind die Mütter der Kunst," sagt Hermann Hesse in seinem Gedicht "Blick nach Italien" und will damit natürlich sagen, dass die Kunst und die Dichtung ihre Hauptquellen in der Liebe, in der Sehnsucht und in der Einsamkeit finden, und dass die Künstler und die Dichter sich immer wieder mit diesen elementaren Gefühlen beschäftigt haben. Warum Hesse an dieser Stelle nichts von den anderen Urquellen der Kunst, wie zum Beispiel Gott, Tod, Natur usw., zu sagen hat, wollen wir dahingestellt sein lassen, denn es handelt sich ja hier nur um ein Nebenmotiv des Gedichtes. Aber wie steht es nun mit den drei benannten "Müttern der Kunst?" Dass die Liebe und die Sehnsucht nicht nur die Mütter, sondern auch zwei der wichtigsten Themen der Literatur—vor allem der Lyrik—sind, braucht gar nicht mehr betont zu werden, aber das gilt nicht immer in demselben Masse von der Einsamkeit. Man wird gerne zugeben, dass die Einsamkeit oft eine Triebfeder für die Dichtung ist, aber als eigentlicher Gegenstand erscheint sie auffallend selten vor dem Ende des neunzehnten Jahrhunderts in der deutschen Dichtung. In der vorliegenden Arbeit soll nur ziemlich oberflächlich einmal darauf hingewiesen werden, wie stark aber dieses Problem der Einsamkeit in der modernen deutschen Lyrik zu Worte kommt.

Wenn man die deutsche Lyrik des neunzehnten Jahrhunderts, besonders die der Romantik, auch nur vorübergehend daraufhin durchsieht, so fällt bald auf, dass es sich an den verhältnismässig wenigen Stellen, wo man überhaupt auf die Einsamkeit zu reden kommt, um ein frohes Erlebnis handelt. Nehmen wir je ein Gedicht von Goethe, Tieck, Heine und Brentano als bekannte Beispiele dafür! In Goethes Gedicht "An den Mond," das zwar noch aus dem achtzehnten Jahrhundert stammt, lesen wir:

> Jeden Nachklang fühlt mein Herz
> Froh- und trüber Zeit,
> Wandele zwischen Freud und Schmerz
> In der Einsamkeit.

In diesem Gedicht ist die Einsamkeit also eine Zuflucht, wo man zwischen Freude und Schmerz wandeln kann, bei Tieck aber wandelt man nur noch in Freude, und die "Waldeinsamkeit" wird symbolisch für, und fast gleichbedeutend mit, Glückseligkeit:

> Waldeinsamkeit,
> Die mich erfreut,
> So morgen wie heut
> In ew'ger Zeit,
> O wie mich freut
> Waldeinsamkeit.

Zu dieser Waldeinsamkeit flieht auch Heinrich Heine in seinem gleichnamigen Gedicht:

> Ich floh den gelben Menschenneid,
> Ich floh in die grüne Waldeinsamkeit.

Und schliesslich in Clemens Brentanos "Nachklänge Beethovenscher Musik" wird die Einsamkeit die Quelle, die Mutter und der Zauberspiegel innerer Sonnen:

> Einsamkeit, du stummer Bronnen,
> Heil'ge Mutter tiefer Quellen,
> Zauberspiegel innerer Sonnen,

Die in Tönen überschwellen,
Seit ich durft' in deine Wonnen
Das betörte Leben stellen,

. . . .

Hab' zu funkeln ich begonnen.

Die Stimmung in diesen Gedichten könnte man wohl als typisch für die Lyrik des früheren neunzehnten Jahrhunderts betrachten. Die Dichter sehnen sich nach der Natur und nehmen ihre Zuflucht zur Einsamkeit, wo sie Ruhe, Frieden und Wonne finden. Nur ganz allmählich erst im Laufe des neunzehnten Jahrhunderts fängt man an, die Einsamkeit auch als etwas Unerwünschtes, etwas Liebloses, etwas Trauriges zu empfinden. In Nikolaus Lenaus Sonnett "Einsamkeit" lesen wir zum Beispiel:

Hast du schon je dich ganz allein gefunden,
Lieblos und ohne Gott auf einer Heide,

. . . .

Warst du auf einer Heide so allein,
So weisst du auch, wie's einen dann bezwingt,
Dass er umarmend stürzt an einen Stein;
Dass er, von seiner Einsamkeit erschreckt,
Entsetzt empor vom starren Felsen springt,
Und bang dem Winde nach die Arme streckt.

Hier haben wir es nicht mehr mit der Wonne der Einsamkeit zu tun. Das Alleinsein ist auch nicht nur die Wehmut der Verlassenheit; es ist eher eine Daseinsangst, fast eine Verzweiflung, dass man nicht nur allein, sondern auch lieblos und ohne Gott in der Welt steht. Damit ist auch schon das Motiv der Einsamkeit, wie es in der neueren Lyrik so oft erscheint, nicht nur berührt, sondern auch tief empfunden worden.

Eigentlich aber fängt es erst recht mit Nietzsche an. In seinem *Also sprach Zarathustra* wird viel von der Einsamkeit geredet und zwar hauptsächlich von der ersehnten Einsamkeit des Propheten, des Wanderers und des Einsiedlers. "Hungernd, gewalttätig, einsam, gottlos: so will sich selber der Löwen-Wille," schreibt er ("Von den berühmten Weisen," 2. Teil). Zarathustra fühlt sich reich in der Einsamkeit: "Immer noch bin ich der Reichste und Bestzubeneidende—ich der Einsamste!" ("Das Grablied," 2. Teil) und er trachtet nach der Einsamkeit und findet sie: "Allein bin ich wieder und will es sein." ("Vor Sonnenaufgang," 3. Teil) Diese Einsamkeit in den Bergen ist für ihn die Heimat: "O Einsamkeit! Du meine Heimat Einsamkeit! Wie selig und zärtlich redet deine Stimme zu mir!" ("Die Heimkehr," 3. Teil) ruft er und geniesst diese Einsamkeit in der Wüste. Aber er weiss auch von der Gefahr der Einsamkeit und er warnt vor der Vereinsamung ("Vom Wege des Schaffenden," 1. Teil): "Furchtbar ist das Alleinsein . . . ; einst wird dich die Einsamkeit müde machen. . . . Mit meinen Tränen gehe in deine Vereinsamung, mein Bruder."

Sehr tief empfindet er auch die Verlassenheit unter den Menschen: "Ein Anderes ist Verlassenheit, ein anderes Einsamkeit: Das lerntest du nun! Und dass du unter Menschen immer wild und fremd sein wirst:—wild und fremd auch noch, wenn sie dich lieben." ("Die Heimkehr," 3. Teil). Dieses Thema der Verlassenheit haben dann auch die Dichter immer wieder aufgenommen, bis es zu einem Leitgedanken der neueren Lyrik geworden ist. Nietzsche selber hat diesen Gedanken auch in seinen Gedichten behandelt, und hier ist es wieder meistens die Einsamkeit des Wanderers und Suchers. In dem Gedicht "Dem unbekannten Gott" heisst es zum Beispiel:

> Noch einmal, eh' ich weiterziehe
> Und meine Blicke vorwärts sende,
> Heb' ich vereinsamt meine Hände
> Zu Dir empor, zu dem ich fliehe.

Der Mensch ist ohne Ruhe in seiner Verlassenheit. Er ist wie ein Wandervogel, der "vor Winters in die Welt entflohn," und nirgends halt macht, wie es in dem Gedicht "Vereinsamt" heisst, das mit Worten der Einsamkeit schliesst:

> Die Krähen schrein
> Und ziehen schwirren Flugs zur Stadt:
> Bald wird es schnein,
> Weh dem, der keine Heimat hat!

Für Nietzsche ist "der Einsamste," wie der Titel eines anderen Gedichtes lautet, der Wanderer, dessen "dunkles Herz" müde wird aber nicht ruhen kann. Endlich aber ist es die "siebente Einsamkeit" ("Die Sonne sinkt"), seine "siebente letzte Einsamkeit" ("Das Feuerzeichen"), in der er, der Suchende (Zarathustra), "auf hohen Bergen" die "süsse Sicherheit" empfindet und in der er zur Flamme, zur Fackel, für alle Einsamen wird.

Ein ähnliches Motiv vom einsamen Wanderer, wie man es so oft bei Nietzsche findet, sieht man auch in Rainer Maria Rilkes "Herbsttag":

> Wer jetzt kein Haus hat, baut sich keines mehr.
> Wer jetzt allein ist, wird es lange bleiben,
> wird wachen, lesen, lange Briefe schreiben
> und wird in den Alleen hin und her
> unruhig wandern, wenn die Blätter treiben.

Diese kosmische Einsamkeit bringt Rilke auch in dem Gedicht "Herbst" zum Ausdruck:

> Und in den Nächten fällt die schwere Erde
> Aus allen Sternen in die Einsamkeit.

Das Motiv der inneren Einsamkeit findet man oft in der modernen Literatur—man denke bloss unter anderen an Nietzsches *Zarathustra* und an Titel wie Gerhard Hauptmanns *Einsame Menschen*, Arthur Schnitzlers *Der einsame Weg* und Hermann Hesses Gedichtsammlung *Musik des Einsamen*—aber für die Lyrik ist dieses Thema geradezu charakteristisch. Der Mensch steht ganz allein, so sehr er sich auch nach Verbindung mit anderen sehnt; immer ist der Mensch einsam, nicht nur weil er von anderen entfernt oder verlassen ist, sondern weil die Menschen einander fremd sind. So lesen wir in Ludwig Fuldas Gedicht "Allein":

> Alle sind wir so allein . . .
> Was kann einer dem andern sein?
> Kann wohl in die Augen sehn,

> Aber nicht in des Herzens Grund,
> . . . .
> Alle sind wir einander fremd.

Ähnliches hat auch Ricarda Huch in ihrem Gedicht "Einsamkeit" gesagt:

> Wohl strömt ein jedes Ding des eignen Wesens Hauch
> Den andern Dingen ein;
> Doch will ihr Sehnen überfliessen auch,
> Sie sind allein.
> . . . .
> Schlaft ihr umarmt auf einem Kissen, ihr erwacht
> Wie Sonnen fern im Raum;
> Kaum dass ihr einmal träumt vielleicht bei Nacht
> Den gleichen Traum.

Gegen diese überwältigende Macht der Einsamkeit muss der Mensch seine eigne Kraft anwenden, denn "Dir ward kein andres Gut als deine Kraft." Obwohl er allein sein muss, kann er trotzig aufrecht stehen, ermahnt Ricarda Huch. Bei Hermann Hesse aber gibt es nicht einmal diese Hoffnung der menschlichen Kraft.

> Leben ist Einsamsein.
> Kein Mensch kennt den andern,
> Jeder ist allein,

klagt er in dem Gedicht "Im Nebel." Und dieses Einsamsein ist so gross, dass alle Menschen, sogar Brüder, einander fremd sind. Also heisst es in Hesses "Der Maler malt eine Gärtnerei":

> Wir mögen Menschen und mögen Brüder sein,
> Wir stehen doch allein,
> Einer weit vom andern verirrt,
> Jeder traurig, weil er älter und einsamer wird.

Sogar Christian Morgenstern, der wohl eher als manch anderer seine Mitmenschen versteht und einen gemeinsamen Weg mit ihnen wandeln kann, spürt es auch, dass die Menschen die tie-

feren Gefühle des Leidens und der Freude nicht miteinander
teilen können.

> Ein jeder mit seiner Lust,
> ein jeder mit seiner Pein,
> jedes Herz in seiner Brust
> allein, allein, allein,

schreibt er in "Heimkehr einer einsamen Frau aus einer Gesellschaft."

Immer wieder hört man diese Töne der unerbittlichen Welteinsamkeit. In grosser Gesellschaft, mitten im Gedränge der
Massen, in der Stille der Heimat, überall empfindet man die
grosse Einsamkeit, hört man das Wehgeschrei der Dichter. So
klagt Anton Wildgans in "Tiefer Blick":

> Oh, du kannst einsam sein, dass Gott erbarm,
> und es dich mitten in dem Fliegenschwarm
> der Menschen jäh befällt wie Scham und Grauen!
> . . . .
> Und Freunde kannst du haben, Weib und Kind,
> und so allein sein wie ein Baum im Wind,
> . . . .
> nur manchmal hörst du's rauschen innerlich
> und hältst erschrocken inne: Bin das ich?!—
> So einsam kann man sein auf Gottes Erde.

Die Einsamkeit kann auch so grenzenlos, so entschieden
und so unabänderlich sein, dass nicht einmal die Liebe die
Befreiung bringen kann, wie Nietzsche es ja auch schon in
seinem *Zarathustra* gesagt hat. So schreibt Thassilo von Scheffer
wehklagend:

> Einsamer werd ich nicht im Grabe liegen,
> Als einsam ich schon hier im Leben bin.
> Ins tiefste Herz dringt nie ein andrer hin,
> Und wenn dich tausend Liebesarme wiegen.

Nur hier und da spürt man inmitten der Wehklage dieser un-
aufhaltsamen Einsamkeit einen schwachen Hoffnungsstrahl,

aber er bringt wenig Trost. Am schönsten hat Josef Weinheber
es in seinem Gedicht "Nur im Brausen des Blutes" in Worte
gefasst:

> Nur im Brausen des Blutes, das ineinander rinnt,
> wähnen wir, dass unsere Seelen eins und beisammen sind.
> Sonst sind wir immer einsam.
> So wie die Seele des Windes, der durch die Wälder singt,
> so wie die Seele der Wolke, die sich im Blauen schwingt,
> ewig einsam die Menschenseele.
> Was wir auch grübeln und fürchten und weinen und wandern,
> keiner findet Brücke und Weg zu dem andern,
> was er auch tut.

Diese schöne Metapher von der Brücke als Weg von einem
Menschen zum andern, die trotz aller Sehnsucht und Suche
schwer zu finden ist, oder nicht einmal existiert, von ihr hören
wir auch in dem Gedicht "Familie," in dem Paula von Prera-
dovic, wie auch Hesse und Wildgans, das Alleinsein unter
Freunden und in der eignen Familie äussert:

> Muss jedes fürbass wandern,
> allein in Weh und Wind;
> kann keines je zum andern,
> weil keine Brücken sind.
> In seiner dunklen Kammer
> ist jedes ganz allein.

Bei Rudolf Paulsen, "Vergessenheit," ist die Brücke wohl noch
da, aber sie "trägt nicht mehr":

> Die Hälfte bricht . . . sie sinkt im Sturm von dannen . . .
> Und einsam-grausig halb steht über Meer die Brücke.

Und so geht es immer weiter; einer nach dem andern spricht
von der grossen Einsamkeit. Überall hört man ihre Stimmen:

> Es ist so schwer allein zu gehn.
> (Eva Katharina Dechow)

> Und das Herz bricht vor Einsamkeit.
> (Jakob Haringer)

Steigt in mir die Einsamkeit zum Rand.
(Franz Werfel)

Du stehst vereinsamt auf und weinst.
(Anton Schnack)

Des Abends hör' ich . . . den Wagen der Einsamkeit.
(Camill Hoffmann)

Ich friere weit in weisser Einsamkeit.
(Paul Zech)

Uns ist viel Einsamkeit.
(Rudolf Paulsen)

Es folgte treu durch Tod und Leid,
durch ihre grosse Einsamkeit.
(Emil Hadira)

Bei den meisten Dichtern gibt es einfach gar kein Entrinnen von der Einsamkeit, und man möchte fast mit Werner Bergengruen (in "Der Gezeichnete") schreien:

Niemand, niemand ist, dich freizubitten
und dein Ort ist einsam in der Mitten.

Aber Bergengruen spricht auch von "verborgener Gnade," und wir haben schon gesehen, dass Ricarda Huch das Gefühl der Einsamkeit durch ihre eigene Kraft überwinden will, und dass Weinheber nach der grossen Vereinigung fleht und ahnt, "dass unsere Seelen eins und beisammen sind." Christian Morgenstern findet dann auch Erlösung in der Liebe in seinem Gedicht "An den andern," wenn er schreibt:

Da traf ich Dich, in ärgster Not: den andern!
Mit Dir vereint, gewann ich frischen Mut.

Franz Werfel aber findet in typisch expressionistischer Ekstase vollkommene Lösung in dem Gedicht "Ich habe eine gute Tat getan":

Herz frohlocke!
Eine gute Tat habe ich getan.
Nun bin ich nicht mehr einsam.
Ein Mensch lebt,
es lebt ein Mensch,
dem die Augen sich feuchten,
denkt er an mich.
Herz frohlocke:
Es lebt ein Mensch!
Nicht mehr, nein nicht mehr bin ich einsam,
denn ich habe eine gute Tat getan,
frohlocke Herz!

Und in "Veni Creator Spiritus" findet er vereint mit dem
Heiligen Geist den Frieden, so

Dass wir gemeinsam und nach oben
Wie Flammen in einander toben!

Wenn dann der Friede, die Freude und die innere Flamme im
Herzen aufleuchten, so findet Cäsar Flaischlen die Überwin-
dung der Einsamkeit in "Hab Sonne im Herzen":

Hab ein Lied auf den Lippen,
Dann komme was mag:
Das hilft dir verwinden
Den einsamsten Tag.

"Sonst sind wir immer einsam," könnte man fast mit Weinheber sagen, wenn man die Dichter beim Wort nehmen will.
Bei Hermann Hesse aber beziehen sich die Worte der Einsamkeit nicht immer auf die Menschheit überhaupt, sondern
manchmal gerade auf den Künstler und auf den Dichter. In
diesem Sinn nennt er ja auch seine schon oben erwähnte
Gedichtsammlung eine *Musik des Einsamen,* und er schreibt
von sich selbst und dieser Künstlereinsamkeit ("Der Dichter"):

Nur mir, dem Einsamen,
Scheinen des Nachts die unendlichen Sterne,
Rauscht der steinerne Brunnen sein Zauberlied,

Mir allein, mir dem Einsamen
Ziehen die farbigen Schatten
Wandernder Wolken Träumen gleich übers Gefild.

Für Hesse also—und darin ist er mit den früheren Romantikern und mit Nietzsche verwandt—ist die Einsamkeit auch einmal etwas Ersehntes, und das sieht man deutlich in den folgenden Zeilen aus dem Gedicht "Verführer":

Ich sehnte glühend fort mich von Genuss
Nach Traum, nach Sehnsucht und nach Einsamkeit.

Und wenn die Einsamkeit nicht gerade etwas Ersehntes ist, so erscheint sie doch als etwas Bittersüsses, wie zum Beispiel in "Bei der Toilette":

Wirst wieder wandern, schweifen, schauen dürfen,
Den Becher Einsamkeit zu Ende schlürfen
Und sterben in der Wildnis ungesehn.[1]

Schliesslich wäre noch etwas über Rilke und die Einsamkeit zu sagen. In ihm steckt ja auch die innere Einsamkeit, wie wir bereits gesehen haben. In diesem Sinn sagt er ja auch: "Doch sehr allein und lieblos ist ein jeder." ("Der Fahnenträger") Was aber noch zu betonen wäre, ist der Grundgedanke der Einsamkeit in dem *Stundenbuch*,[2] wo man nicht so sehr den Wunsch spürt, aus der Einsamkeit zu entrinnen, als das Verlangen nach Gottes Einsamkeit, ja nach Gott selbst. Der Mensch ist zwar einsam, aber Gott ist auch einsam, und man muss ihn in der Einsamkeit suchen, und man kann ihn nur in der Einsamkeit finden.

Denn nur dem Einsamen wird offenbart
und vielen Einsamen der gleichen Art
wird mehr gegeben als dem schmalen Einen.
Denn jedem wird ein anderer Gott erscheinen.
(Seite 27)

schreibt der Dichter und sagt auch:

> Ich bin auf der Welt zu allein und doch nicht allein genug,
> um jede Stunde zu weihn.   (Seite 15)

Er ist für Gott "der graue Mitwisser deiner Einsamkeit" und
Gott ist für ihn ein Teil seiner Einsamkeit: "Du bist der
Zweite meiner Einsamkeit." (Seite 40) Er sucht den Weg zu
Gott in der Stille und in der Einsamkeit der Nacht:

> Du Nachbar Gott, wenn ich dich manchesmal
> in langer Nacht mit hartem Klopfen störe,—
> so ist's, weil ich dich selten atmen höre
> und weiss: Du bist allein im Saal.
>   (Seite 11)

Und den Weg zu sich selbst, zu seinem eigenen Herzen findet
er in der Weite und in der Einsamkeit:

> Aber der Weg zu dir ist furchtbar weit
> und, weil ihn keiner ging, verweht.
> O du bist einsam. Du bist Einsamkeit,
> du Herz, das zu entfernten Taten geht.
>   (Seite 82)

Das also ist die Einsamkeit in dem *Stundenbuch.* Gottein-
samkeit könnte man dieses Gefühl nennen, und darin ist Rilke
eng mit Nietzsches Wanderereinsamkeit und Hesses Künstlereinsamkeit verwandt. Und alle drei haben etwas gemeinsam
mit der Tieck schen Waldeinsamkeit. Nur muss man sich klar
darüber sein, dass diese moderne Einsamkeit des Gottsuchers,
des Propheten und des Künstlers, wie vor allem auch die Verlassenheit und die Welteinsamkeit überhaupt, nur selten als
etwas Ersehntes und fast nie als etwas Glückseliges zu betrachten ist, wie die Einsamkeit der Romantiker. Es handelt sich
eher um etwas für den Schaffenden Notwendiges, um etwas für
die Menschheit überhaupt Unvermeidliches, ja um etwas Kos-
misches, das zum grossen Weltschmerz der modernen deutschen
Lyrik geworden ist.

The Modern German Drama*

by
F. E. Coenen

THE FEDERAL REPUBLIC of Germany had, at last count, 121 theaters[1] playing ten months a year. It has scores of talented actors and at least a handful of exceptionally brilliant stage directors. But it has no contemporary drama. The stagnation which began some twenty-five years ago has not yet been overcome.

Friedrich Luft, one of the most discerning observers of the theatrical scene in Germany (he is the theater critic of the West Berlin daily *Tagesspiegel*), for several years now has been writing surveys of what has happened. The title of his essay in 1956 was "Theaterfülle—Dramenleere," [2] in 1957 "Bühnenkonjunktur—Theaterlethargie," [3] in 1959 "Dreissig Millionen suchen einen Autor," [4] and in 1960 "Das multiplizierte Theater." [5] This is how Germans themselves judge the situation, while foreigners hardly find it worth their while to look into the German drama which, only a few decades ago, was discussed all over the world.

After World War I the German drama had reached one of the high points of its development. It almost seemed as if the military defeat had freed great creative energies. No such event took place after World War II. The hope that German playwrights would come into their own again has remained unfulfilled.

It is perhaps not too difficult to find the reasons for this

* This paper was written in May, 1961.

107

decline of the German drama. During World War I the cultural continuity had not been broken. Intellectuals were not restrained under the monarchy. But a process of increasing isolation from the outer world began in 1933 and culminated in the years of World War II. Even before 1939, all cultural life was strictly regimented. The climate was not favorable for creative work.[6]

Theatrical activity in West Germany after World War I continued without interruption. After World War II many theaters were destroyed and some were taken over by the occupation powers. Six months before the end of the war all theaters had been closed and the actors drafted into the army or the defense industries; thus the carefully built ensembles were scattered. Yet the theater soon emerged as a strong power. It became painfully obvious that stage and drama were not one and the same thing: the call for dramatists to step forward remained unheeded.[7] Only one playwright of note was discovered: Wolfgang Borchert. His drama, *Draussen vor der Tür,* was originally written for radio, depicting the tragedy of the returning war veteran. It was not yet a finished play, rather an outcry; but it held much promise. It was the first play of a young author and was fated to be his last. He died at the age of twenty-six, never knowing of the great success of *Draussen vor der Tür.*

In a special German issue of the *Atlantic* Luft wrote: "During the past ten years the German theater has lived largely on importations. The United States has contributed Miller and Williams, Kingsley and Wouk, O'Neill and Faulkner—all widely represented on the German stage. France has sent us Anouilh, Sartre, Giraudoux, Becket and Claudel—all to be found on the program of almost every important German theater—and England has given us Fry and Eliot, Whiting and Ustinov." [8]

In the late 1940's and early 1950's, the plays that impressed the Germans most were Thornton Wilder's *Our Town* (*Unsere kleine Stadt*) and *The Skin of Our Teeth* (*Wir sind noch einmal davongekommen*), and Paul Claudel's *Le soulier de satin* (*Der seidene Schuh*). In Wilder's plays the Germans were confronted with the "epic theater" which was first developed during the Romantic period in Germany. After World War I it was perfected by Bertolt Brecht as a theatrical form with strong political overtones.

In Germany silence was absolute as far as new and original plays were concerned, while the "Resistance" in France inspired a number of dramatists. Some German writers did oppose the Nazis, to be sure; but with the single exception of Borchert no one emerged as a great dramatist from this opposing climate.

The only worthwhile drama of the "Resistance" had been written far from Germany by Carl Zuckmayer in the solitude of his Vermont farm. *The Devil's General* has been the most successful play by a German author in the entire postwar period. But Zuckmayer had become an American. Many sources of his strength are American. Another drama showing the moral evil of the National Socialist regime, *The Diary of Anne Frank*, was also written in the United States. First performed five years ago, this drama has become the strongest indictment of the Nazi regime ever to be presented on the stage; its influence has been felt in many ways. In some theaters it has remained in the repertoires for five successive seasons—an almost unprecedented event in the case of a contemporary play.

Zuckmayer's *The Devil's General* was followed by a number of less successful dramas. Nevertheless, Zuckmayer may be considered the most important dramatist since Gerhart Hauptmann. Born at Nackenheim in Rheinhessen, he studied for a few years at the University of Heidelberg, but he devoted himself to the theater before graduating. Then he became a dramatist at Kiel. But before he reached the age of thirty, his play *Der fröhliche Weinberg* (1925) became a great success and made him financially independent. In this folk play he shows the people he knows best—those of the wine regions of his native Rhineland. Another play of this type, *Schinderhannes* (1927), met with equally great success. *Katharina Knie* (1929), another earthy drama, has the world of the circus as its background. In recent years it was made into the first authentic German musical but did not find favor with the audiences.

At the age of thirty-four, Zuckmayer wrote *Der Hauptmann von Köpenick,* his best play which he called a "German fairy tale." It was twice adapted to the screen and in the second version achieved a tremendous success in New York as well as in Germany. It was to remain his last play before his emigration. In the postwar period only *The Devil's General* made as deep an impression. The latter is a provocative and absorbing play dealing with an air force general who thought that his opposition to their regime should not keep him from serving the Nazi rulers. He chooses death, once he is cured of his illusion.

Subsequent plays by Zuckmayer have had no more than a moral success. *Barbara Blomberg, Der Gesang im Feuerofen* (taking place in occupied France in World War II, it derives its title from the death of a group of resistance fighters in a burning castle after they had been betrayed by a collaborator), *Herbert Engelmann* (based on a drama fragment left by Hauptmann), and *Ulla Winblad* (a play built around the Swedish poet Carl Michael Bellman [1741–1795]) have all remained without response. Dutifully performed at some first-rate theaters, they were soon forgotten. The same is true of *Das kalte Licht,* a dramatization of the Klaus Fuchs case first performed in 1955, and of *Der trunkene Hercules* (a comedy with a present day background, premiered in Zurich during the 1958/1959 season). In *Das kalte Licht* Zuckmayer endeavors to show the dilemma of the atomic spy but only manages to offer a scenic illustration of a tragic case. This is hardly enough. The full dimensions of a tragedy are missing because of the absence of dramatic action. It is a reportorial effort which does not need the stage.

No discussion of the contemporary German drama is complete without the inclusion of Bertolt Brecht whose plays are once again frequently performed in West Germany even though he was a Communist. The West German overlooks the ideological line that is so obvious in all of his plays. A contemporary of Zuckmayer (born in 1896), Brecht (born in 1898) also first rose to literary fame in the 1920's. He too left Germany in 1933, spent the war years in the United States and Scandinavia, then returned to Germany, but to the eastern part where he died in August, 1956.

In East Germany the political agitator in Brecht is stressed, whereas the West German is impressed by the poet. Quite frequently the cynicism shines through his plays, to be sure; but this is overshadowed just as often by a strong sense of dramatic plasticity, of true poetic passion.

Most of Brecht's plays were rewritten several times, often for the purpose of bringing out the political line more clearly. In his last years he was too busy managing a theater of his own to do much creative writing. While the topics of his plays constantly change, he always tries to moralize, to make converts to the Marxist cause. In the highly successful *Dreigroschenoper* (1928), Brecht had attacked the middle class for its lack of morals and made it responsible for the defects of the existing social order. His later works, written in exile, established his world reputation. *Galileo Galilei* (1938) is an indictment of the ruling class, here the Church. In *Das Verhör des Lukullus* (1939) the "capitalist" Lucullus is placed opposite the poor and the Roman slaves. In the framework of a Chinese legend Brecht tried to show the depravity of the upper class and the needs of the poor in *Der gute Mensch von Sezuan* (1940). "Bad" master and "poor" servant are pitted against each other in *Herr Puntila und sein Knecht Matti* (1940). *Mutter Courage und ihre Kinder* (1939) is another social indictment; it aims to show that war is a means of the ruling class to perpetuate the oppression of the oppressed. In it Brecht goes back to one of the darkest periods in the history of Germany, the Thirty Years' War. But in the execution of this theme Brecht the poet leaves Brecht the agitator far behind, for he has created one of the great figures in German literature. The tragedy of a mother is presented in such stark and elementary terms that it can be regarded as one of the most moving plays of our time.

Brecht is still popular with West German audiences. Since his death four of his earlier plays were premiered posthumously: *Der unaufhaltsame Aufstieg des Arturo Ui* (1941/1942) at Stuttgart in the fall of 1958, *Die heilige Johanna der Schlacht-höfe* (1929/1930) at Hamburg, and *Schweyk im zweiten Welt-krieg* (1942/1943) at Frankfurt am Main, both in the spring of 1959, and Brecht's excellent arrangement (1948) of *Der Hofmeis-ter* (1774) by Michael Reinhold Lenz (1751–1792) at Hamburg in the autumn of 1960.

In his *Atlantic* article Luft says of Brecht: "He was able to carry on his experiments with the 'epic drama' and the 'es-trangement' style of direction under nearly ideal conditions. Brecht is the only German playwright whose fame has passed beyond the German frontiers in recent years. But the style of his pedagogical theater, the preconceived didactic method of his productions, trapped irremediably behind the spiritual bars of Marxist thinking, remains an isolated phenomenon, in spite of his talent. It is not likely that he will have a successor." [9]

In *Theatre Arts,* the well-known scenic designer Mordecai Gorelik quotes Brecht as having told him: "I am the Einstein of the new stage form!" [10] This immodest utterance notwith-standing, Gorelik says about Brecht:

Schmalz, Quatsch and Kitsch all found their nemesis in Brecht. Outwardly matter-of-fact, he seethed inwardly with a passionate in-dignation. If the theater is to do more than pander to emotionalism, it must teach. It must teach in its own fashion, brilliantly, color-fully, entertainingly—but *teach* it must. Granted Brecht's views about the script, his rules of production logically follow. . . . There can no longer be any doubt that the epic form has become an important new factor in world theater.

Brecht's dramatic writings, his poems and his stage theories will remain as his memorial. As a dramatist his hard outward sobriety masked the tenderness of his love for the common man. As a stage innovator, his provocative theory and practice have laid the founda-tions for what may some day be a classic era of theater in an age of science.[11]

With such an evaluation no one who knows Brecht's work will quarrel, even where disagreement must be expressed with his political theories.[12]

Despite Luft's prediction, Brecht's style has been imitated by a number of German playwrights, ignored by some, and satirized by others. A recent drama definitely utilizes the Brecht method: *Korczak und seine Kinder* (1958) by Erwin Sylvanus was quite successful at Cologne, where it was first performed, and at Göttingen. The author, born in 1921 in Westphalia, had been known only as a journalist and a storyteller, but the critical response he received for his first play was favorable. It treats of a subject similar to that of *The Diary of Anne Frank* and is even a little more austere. It deals with an episode in the Warsaw ghetto in 1942: Dr. Korczak, the Jewish head of an orphanage with thirty-seven Jewish children, receives orders from the Gestapo to close the home. The SS officer who brings him word of this decision indicates that the children will be transported to one of the death camps. But he promises Korczak that he will save his life if he will lead his young charges into the camp without creating much of a stir. Korczak declines the deal; he will accompany the children to the camp and share their fate.

These happenings are acted on an almost empty stage, with little more than a door frame and two chairs before a black curtain used as "scenery." The actors slip in and out of certain characters and discuss the play as if they were rehearsing it. They no longer identify themselves with their roles but give sketches of human portraits. Nothing similar had been seen on a German stage before, for this outdoes even Brecht. But several critics attest to the deep impression the drama has made, so deep, in fact, that—as in *The Diary of Anne Frank*—the audiences leave the theater hushed and without applause. A comparative study of these two similar plays would be quite interesting. As it is home-grown, however, we must consider Sylvanus' drama as the most important one as far as the development of the contemporary German stage play is concerned. Perhaps it is along these lines that the stagnation of the German theater will finally be overcome. Sylvanus has written two other plays in recent years: *Unter dem Sternbild der Waage* (1959) and *Der rote Buddha* (1960).

That German playwrights have not yet produced superior plays is certainly not due to neglect on the part of the theater managers. In one season in recent years thirty plays by German authors saw their first performances. This looks more impressive than it actually is for, at the same time, exactly three and one-half times as many plays by foreign authors—105—were performed for the first time. As Otto Zoff says, the repertory of the German theater is the best in Europe.[13] And he quotes the critic and stage director Harold Clurman as saying, ". . . in quality of production, in scenic creation, in variety of repertory, in solidity of organization, the German theatre at this moment makes the English, French and other stages of the world look like little theatre activities."

The urge to perform foreign plays is so strong in Germany that frequently they are done there long before they are staged in the countries of their origin. This is particularly true of a number of American plays: William Faulkner's *Requiem for a Nun,* published in the United States nine or ten years ago, had already been a successful play on German stages when it saw its first United States performance off Broadway four years ago. Thornton Wilder's *Alkestiade (Life in the Sun)* has also had a number of productions in Germany and Switzerland [in 1957 after the English version had been premiered in Edinburgh in 1955]. *A Touch of the Poet* by Eugene O'Neill was given in several German cities (under the somewhat misleading title *Ein Hauch von Poesie*) before finally becoming a Broadway "hit." Archibald MacLeish's *J. B.* was performed at the Salzburg Festivals under the title *Das Spiel um Job* on July 28, 1958, long before it opened on Broadway. William Saroyan's *Pariser Komödie* was first performed in Vienna, then in Berlin. Jean Vauthier's *Les prodiges* was premiered at Kassel under the title *Die Wunder* before it was performed in Paris. J. B. Priestley's new play, titled *Die Folter* in German, and Jean Anouilh's play *Foire d'empoigne (Majestäten)* were performed in Germany before they had their *premières* in England or France.

To the generation of Zuckmayer and Brecht belong Erich Kästner, Günther Weisenborn, Hans Rehberg, Reinhold Schneider—all of them born around the turn of the century. Kästner, born in 1899 in Dresden, studied at the universities of Berlin, Leipzig, and Rostock and for the last thirty years has been a successful satirical poet, a writer of amusing children's stories, and a novelist. He turned to the drama at a relatively late stage of his career writing his first play only six years ago. *Die Schule der Diktatoren* is a satirical play; it was planned during the Nazi period, but not written at that time. In this work Kästner tried to show a bloody dictatorship being ousted through a virtuous rebellion. Then the rebel is murdered and the next dictatorship established. And so it goes on and on. Kästner calls this play a "tragic comedy"; laughter and seriousness alternate. Kästner, unlike Brecht, is not didactic but humorous. As the first dramatic attempt of a writer very successful in other fields, this play was generally accepted but without arousing much enthusiasm. Kästner obviously enjoyed this new medium. A second play of his, *Das Haus der Erinnerung*, was first performed in Munich.

Günther Weisenborn, born in 1902 at Velbert (Rhineland), writes in an entirely different vein. He studied medicine and philosophy at the universities of Cologne and Berlin and became a dramatist before he reached the age of thirty. In 1937 he joined the resistance movement, was arrested in 1942, and spent the next three years in prison. He wrote his first drama, *U-Boot S 4*, when he was only twenty-six. It brought him great success. None of his other plays, which appeared at great intervals, gave convincing proof that he was a capable dramatist even though their construction showed the hand of an expert.

During the last few years Weisenborn has written *Zwei Engel steigen aus, Lofter oder das verlorene Gesicht,* and *Die Familie von Nevada*. Also in recent years he revived for the German stage an old Chinese play, *15 Schnüre Gold*.

Hans Rehberg, born in Poznan in 1901, wrote nine dramas dealing with different personalities of the Brandenburg-Hohenzollern dynasty, then turned to other historical figures such as Mary Stuart, Henry VIII and Charles V. Rehberg's plays show his dramatic instinct; they are not lacking in psychological strength, but suffer from a bombastic style. His latest play, the first after a few years of silence, deals with the poet Heinrich von Kleist. It was performed for the first time in December,

1958, at the Oldenburg State Theater, but proved to be a disappointment for the audience. Rehberg has not gained the introspection which he needs to become a first-rate dramatist.

Reinhold Schneider is cut from a different cloth. Until his death in the summer of 1958, he was considered the foremost German Catholic poet. Born in 1903 in Baden-Baden, he had written more than a hundred works in different fields but, like Kästner, turned to the drama only after World War II. His play, *Der grosse Verzicht,* was first performed posthumously. It deals with the life of Pope Celestine V toward the end of the fourteenth century, presenting it in seventeen rather loosely connected scenes. Celestine, elected Pope at the age of eighty, abdicated five months later; yet his short reign brought some important decisions. Schneider has written a somewhat unusual play that, due to its austerity, seems to have little appeal to the average theatergoer. It is rather static despite its seventeen scenes, more of a "thought" play than one of action.

A few years older than the group we have just discussed were Ferdinand Bruckner [real name: Theodor Tagger], who died in 1958, and Hans J. Rehfisch, who died in 1960. Both were born in 1891, the former in Vienna, the latter in Berlin. After university studies both began writing during World War I, each composing more than twenty dramas and comedies with some large successes. Both left Germany in 1933 and came to the United States; Rehfisch permanently returned to Germany. Their later plays were mostly failures, while at least some of their earlier ones were considered thoroughly antiquated. Only Bruckner's thirty-year-old play *Die Verbrecher* had lost none of its appeal when it was restaged in Berlin about three years ago. Rehfisch also was more successful with his earlier plays than with his later ones. He even wrote a new version of one of his most popular comedies, *Duell im Lido.* His last plays are titled *Bumerang* and *Apostel der Hexen,* the latter dealing with the historical figure of the Jesuit Friedrich von Spee (1591–1635) who ardently opposed the witches' trials of his day. The lack of success of these two men in the postwar period may be explained, essentially, by the fact that they did not change their conception of the drama and that they held on to the old ideas derived from realism and expressionism—the literary periods in which they grew up.

Almost all the members of the younger generation of German playwrights write what for lack of a better definition could be called the intellectual drama. But rarely do we encounter that happy combination of ideas and passion which makes for great plays anywhere any time. Sartre, who may be considered the modern head of this school of intellectual drama, usually avoids the abstract. His use of psychology is skillful; his dialogues are beautiful. Many German playwrights have tried to imitate him; but none has equaled him.

The younger generation can be divided roughly into two groups: those who were born before World War I and whose formative years fell in the time of the Weimar Republic, and second, those born after World War I who went to school and studied during the Nazi period. The number of playwrights is rather large, but few are well known and there is no single dominating personality among them. Actually, not even one who exists today is able to live on the royalties from the performances of his plays. All of them must depend on radio (which pays well for "Hörspiele"), now also on television, on the movies, or on journalistic work. Some are complaining that it is not difficult for them to obtain a first production of their plays, but that the second or third is difficult to come by.[14] The reason for this is quite obvious: theatrical directors are eager to be the first to produce a play by a budding talent and be credited with the discovery of a dramatic genius. Sometimes there is spirited competition between theaters to obtain the rights for a play, but when it turns out to be mediocre, interest wanes.

One of the fairly successful young dramatists, Wolfgang Altendorf (born 1921), publicly announced his withdrawal from playwriting because it was not financially rewarding enough for him to devote his time to it. Altendorf has had more plays produced than perhaps any of his colleagues, four alone during 1955 and 1956: *Thomas Adamsohn, Das Dunkel, Die Wetter-*

maschine, and *Vorspiel auf dem Theater.* Then he went on his self-proclaimed strike against writing. However, playwriting is obviously in his blood, for in December, 1958, his latest play, *Die Schleuse,* was performed in the Stadttheater at Trier and enthusiastically acclaimed.

Another promising young man is Wolfgang Hildesheimer. Born in 1916 in Hamburg, he received his schooling in Germany and in England. From 1933 to 1936 he worked in Palestine as a carpenter and technical designer. He studied stage designing in London from 1936 to 1939; he then returned to Palestine where he became an art critic and painter, having several one-man shows. In 1946 he became an interpreter at the war criminal trials in Nuremberg where he remained for three years. Only then did he seriously turn to literature, immediately scoring a great success with his first volume of poetry. He was no less successful with his first novel and, in 1955, with his first play, *Der Drachenthron.*

Hildesheimer, now living in Germany again, has recently written several other plays, *Die Herren der Welt* which was performed in Berlin, two one-act plays, *Die Uhren* and *Der schiefe Turm von Pisa,* produced in the Schlosstheater at Celle, and a third one-act play, *Die Pastorale,* premiered by the Kammerspiele at Munich. His *Der Drachenthron* is a comedy showing great promise. It should stay in the repertoire. Hildesheimer was praised particularly for his playful seriousness, obviously one of the necessary ingredients of a successful play as will be seen later in the discussion of Friedrich Dürrenmatt.

Two Berlin playwrights have also been quite productive in recent years although great success has escaped them. Richard Hey, born in 1926, first turned to symbolism in *Thymian und Drachentod* and in *Lysiane.* Early in 1958 he wrote a one-act play *Margaret oder das wahre Leben,* displaying a flair for parody, heretofore not too noticeable in his work. In it a woman writes dime novels at the time of the great enthusiasm for Greece in the early nineteenth century. Her literary mission remains unfulfilled because life in its coarseness brings conflict into her home with which she is unable to cope. Hey achieves comic effects by giving his female protagonist a false pathos and want of good taste.

Claus Hubalek, also born in Berlin in 1926, began writing novels after his release as a prisoner of war in 1947. Then he wrote *Der Hauptmann und sein Held,* a tragicomedy (another play of that very popular genre) which was made into a movie and for which he received the Gerhart Hauptmann prize. His *Keine Fallen für die Füchse* was a comedy, playing on the border of East and West Berlin. The absurdity of this artificial frontier is brought out, leading the inhabitants to all kinds of trickery in order to take advantage of the separation. The incidents used by Hubalek have actually happened; only the tragicomical ending is invented, perhaps as the natural result of an unnatural reality. The scene of the plot is a street in the north of Berlin where the sectional border runs through its middle, the houses on one side being in West Berlin and on the other in the Communist East.

Another of Hubalek's plays, *Die Festung,* was first written for radio, then made into a television play, and subsequently made into a film. Finally it was staged as a play in the fall of 1958.

Leopold Ahlsen, born in Munich in 1927, has two plays to his credit, both fairly successful. As can be seen from the title, the first, *Philemon und Baucis,* is of symbolic content. Although first written for radio, it was adapted for the stage by the author. Ahlsen's second play, *Raskolnikov,* was first performed in the Berlin Schlosspark Theater in the fall of 1960. It is a dramatization of the psychological tension between Raskolnikov and his pursuer Porfiry in Dostoevski's novel *Crime and Punishment.*

One of the youngest German dramatists is Hermann Moers, born in Cologne in 1930. His first play, written in 1958, had its first performance in Saarbrücken. *Zur Zeit der Distelblüte* is a one-act play, but of two-hours duration. It shows a sinister scene in a prison yard, full of hysteria. A jailer supervises five prisoners, keeping them occupied with all kinds of chores. A thistle, blooming in one corner of the yard, is a most precious possession of the prisoners who are yearning for light, air, and freedom. This is a static play, but it derives its effectiveness from the monotony and repetition of the theme. Moers's second play, *Im Haus des Riesen,* was first performed at Oberhausen at the beginning of February, 1961. In it the author tries to show symbolically man's future difficulties in coming to terms with a new enlarged cosmos. A poor family moves from a small house into a large one, abandoned by a giant. But all the members of the family fail individually in their attempts to change the house for their own needs.

While more names could be mentioned, those discussed are at present the most representative German playwrights. In the balance, this is not too encouraging a picture. In fact, it would be quite discouraging if we could not also consider dramatists writing in German outside of Germany. Concerning Austria, Friedrich Heer says: "Es gibt nämlich kein sehr beachtenswertes österreichisches Schaffen im Raume des Dramas, der Bühnenkunst der Gegenwart." [15] We would except Fritz Hochwälder. But he has been living in Switzerland for over twenty years. And it is Switzerland which, for the first time in its literary history, has come to the fore. The London *Times* stated several years ago that Switzerland had suddenly become one of the foremost countries in the development of the drama. It has had many literary figures in the past, but no one had tried his hand with any success at the drama. This has changed within a matter of years.

Why this should be so is hard to explain. Little Switzerland had one great advantage during the turbulent years of World War II: its theaters functioned freely. They proved a haven for much that was best in the German theater before Hitler. Many stage directors and actors took up residence in Switzerland. Thus the Zurich Schauspielhaus in particular became for almost a decade the one theater where the currents of the times were reflected. Here the continuity was not broken: plays from abroad in good translations as well as those written by Germans living in exile were performed. The classics were also done without fear or hindrance. Such untrammeled theatrical activity may have had something to do with the sudden blossoming of Swiss dramatic talent. Then, too, young Swiss, while they had to serve in the Swiss army, were not decimated like their German and Austrian contemporaries.

There are three men who are responsible for the birth of a Swiss drama: Fritz Hochwälder, the Austrian expatriate, Max Frisch, and Friedrich Dürrenmatt. Frisch and Hochwälder were born in the same month and the same year, the former on May 15, 1911, in Zurich, the latter on May 28, 1911, in Vienna. Dürrenmatt is ten years younger.

Hochwälder is the least known of the three and the one who follows to a larger degree the conventional theater. His most successful play to date has been *Die Herberge,* presented several years ago by the Vienna Burgtheater and since played by many German theaters. It reminds the spectator of a Slav legend or perhaps an old Jewish tale. In an inn a box with gold has been stolen from a usurer. A thorough investigation is begun. But in Hochwälder's play the inn is only a symbol: it broadens into a place of human happenings, showing some of the ugliness of life. Hochwälder's miracle play, *Donnerstag,* was one of the highlights at the Salzburg Festivals in 1959. His comedy, *Der Unschuldige,* was first performed in the first days of January, 1959, by the Akademietheater in Vienna. *Schicksalsstunde* was first performed by the Vienna Theater in der Josefstadt during the 1960/1961 season.

According to Hochwälder, as he stated in answer to a question concerning the theater in our time, "the forward road leads back to some unchangeable values whose possession we have never relinquished, not in a reactionary but in a conservative sense. I have recently read a sentence which expresses my own opinion: 'I believe that tomorrow's play will have to be a constructed play, quite in contrast to the dissolving drama of the last few decades.' "

Max Frisch is a versatile personality of diversified background. He studied architecture and became a successful architect, continually writing at the same time. There is hardly a field of literature or journalism in which he has not excelled. He is an original thinker, a rebel against the narrowness (the

Kantönligeist) with which his country is afflicted. His aggressiveness and occasional intellectual arrogance did not make him very popular with his compatriots when he was in his literary infancy, but today he is respected and admired. In 1958 he received the annual literary award of his birthplace Zurich as well as the annual Georg Büchner Prize which the Deutsche Akademie für Sprache und Dichtung had never before granted to a foreigner.

All of Frisch's plays are original although not always successful on the stage. Two tendencies are clearly discernible in his works: a certain romantic intellectualism on the basis of egotism and a constructive demonstration of inner happenings. The "estrangement" effect, introduced in the theater by Brecht, has been transposed by Frisch into a person who thus experiences the estrangement in himself. In his play *Graf Oederland* the district attorney is also a criminal (just as in Dürrenmatt's *Die Ehe des Herrn Mississippi*); his *Don Juan* is a paramour and a mathematician. In *Santa Cruz*, where his intentions have perhaps found their crowning achievement, a couple is awakened to the life of their innermost wishes from which they had closed themselves off in reality.

Die Chinesische Mauer is an attempt to bring together history and the present: Brutus talks with a modern business executive; Cleopatra has a dialogue with the emperor of China; an intellectual of our time tries to talk Napoleon out of his old conceptions of power and victory; etc. This is a sort of literary cabaret in the form of a stage play, provocative, but not the kind of theater that is likely to survive.

In 1958, two more plays by Frisch were performed: *Biedermann und die Brandstifter* and *Die grosse Wut des Philipp Hotz*. His *Biedermann* is a comedy with the subtitle "Lehrstück ohne Lehre," clearly a travesty of Brecht's style, although there is much in his work that reminds us of Brecht.

Herr Biedermann, frightened by a country-wide wave of arson, believes he can protect himself best by asking two notorious arsonists to share his home. He eats and drinks with them until one day they burn down his house also. Biedermann knows all the time what is going on, but he is too weak and too cowardly to stave off the inevitable. In the end he even hands the arsonists the matches with which they light the fire in his attic.

This theme is treated in the best manner of Molière: the alliance of the lamb with the wolves, the complete paralysis of the coward who misses the moment when he still might have come to a positive decision. In order to emphasize the human conflict in his comedy, Frisch makes use of a chorus of firemen, standing on both sides of the stage, achieving highly comic and tragic effects almost at the same time. What happens to Biedermann is dutifully commented on by the choristers, quite in the style of an old tragedy. The play is followed by an epilogue in hell, *Biedermann in der Hölle*. Here we find Biedermann in an anteroom, just being dismissed by the devil, who is none other than one of the arsonists, because the devil himself is fed up with life in hell. Is he not forced to see how his ambitions are being frustrated by heaven where the greatest scoundrels are kept, whereas only the mediocre Biedermanns are left to the devil? So the devil returns to earth, which has become more beautiful than ever, to set new fires. And since he knows that earth has not changed essentially, he also knows that the Biedermanns will once again hand him the matches. Biedermanns never learn anything; therefore, fires might even be morally useful in making better people out of them.

Frisch pokes a great deal of fun at many people, including himself. One of the figures is a Ph.D., representing the intellectual, who is far to the left and ideologically on the side of the arsonists. But at the last moment, when the house is already in flames, he disavows all responsibility and saves his own skin.

Friedrich Dürrenmatt is today undoubtedly the strongest stage personality in the German-speaking countries and perhaps the only one known outside of Europe. He was born on January 5, 1921, in Konolfingen near Berne, the son of a Protestant minister. He studied philosophy, theology, and the history of art at Berne and Zurich, but terminated his formal education in 1946 without finishing in any of his fields of interest. After trying his

hand at painting, he became convinced that it was not his medium of expression and turned to prose writing at first, then to
the theater, in order to grapple with the clashing spiritual problems of his time. Since 1947 he has written at least nine plays[16]
and for some time was also active as a theater critic. He has written two detective stories and a number of successful radio plays.
Asked why he wrote, Dürrenmatt answered:

Ich schreibe nicht aus dem Grunde etwa, die Welt zu retten oder
zu ändern—wie wenn dies so prompt möglich wäre—oder zu war-
nen—wie wenn sie darauf hören würde, noch schreibe ich, um
irgendwelche Philosophien, Weltanschauungen oder Dramaturgien
entweder zu bestätigen oder zu überwinden, auch nicht, um Dinge
zu sagen, die ich für wahr halte oder um Ungerechtes aufzudecken,
all dies sind mehr oder weniger erfreuliche Nebenaffekte, Aus-
brüche des Temperaments, Gefühle der Verantwortung und was
sonst noch Zierde des Mannes ist; daneben jedoch freilich auch
Freude an Bedenklichem, Groteskem, Anarchistischem, Unordent-
lichem, ich gestehe, doch all dies ist nicht die Hauptsache, spielt nur
hinein, sei es störend, sei es belebend, denn der tiefste noch einzu-
gestehende Grund meines Schreibens ist der Trieb, für mich und nur
für mich—sehe ich scharf,—Welten zu erschaffen, eigene Welten,
Eigenwelten. Von hier aus, von diesem Satze aus bin ich zu verste-
hen. Ich lebe in der Welt, ich bin ein Teil von ihr, ich muss sie
bestehen, werde von ihr bedroht, bin verantwortlich, mächtig in
einer bestimmten Weise und ohnmächtig auch in einer bestimmten
Weise. Ich liebe sie, ich hasse sie, sie begeistert mich, sie erzürnt
mich, sie setzt mich in Furcht, in Bewunderung.
Dieser Welt, in der ich lebe, die vorhanden ist, setze ich Welten
gegenüber, die ich erschaffe. Nun wird man weiter fragen, wieso ich
dies tue. Allgemein kann darauf geantwortet werden, dass dies
geschieht, weil sich das Ich zu einer Welt, die es erschafft, anders
verhält, als zu einer Welt, in der es lebt: Die vorhandene Welt,
darf gesagt werden, enthält mich, sie ist unendlich mir gegenüber,
unkontrollierbar zu ihrem unermesslich grössten Teil, sie spielt mit
mir während ich mit einer Welt, die ich erschaffe, selber spiele und
sie selber kontrolliere.[17]

The Swiss consider Dürrenmatt an *enfant terrible* among
their writers. His literary style is somewhat reminiscent of
Frank Wedekind with whom he shares the grotesque and scur-
rilous in his visions as well as the passions of a moralist. This

trend becomes more noticeable with each new play. Unlike Wedekind, Dürrenmatt makes full use of the possibilities of the epic theater. Also his humor is much more genuine than that of Wedekind who is usually too aggressive to provide for laughs. But Dürrenmatt's type of humor does not necessarily please the audience. He uses it to attack his listeners. His so-called comedies are anything but that; particularly in *Der Besuch der alten Dame,* the laughs soon freeze on the spectators' faces. His language shows plasticity and strength. In intensity it excels anything that the present-day German-language drama has to offer.

Dürrenmatt's first play, the Anabaptist drama *Es steht geschrieben* was premiered in 1947. His second drama, *Der Blinde,* followed in 1948. It deals with a theme similar to that of Frisch in *Santa Cruz.* Here, too, dream becomes a double of reality. Dürrenmatt calls his spectators as witnesses for the reality shown on the stage which contrasts with the world of the blind man. To the latter the prostitute appears as a duchess to whom he shows due reverence. It should be noted that these first two plays are the only ones that Dürrenmatt labeled dramas.

Romulus der Grosse, which followed in 1949, was labeled an "unhistoric historic comedy" by the young playwright. It attacks civilization and the superstate and has a certain resemblance to Frisch's *Chinesische Mauer.* The macabre farce *Die Ehe des Herrn Mississippi,* in which Dürrenmatt assails various ideologies, appeared in 1952; it was produced in New York under the title *Fools Are Passing Through.* It depicts a doomed world without love, justice, or brotherhood, another "comedy" with many dead people at the end. The only survivor is a fool of love —a wretched creature who loves the world whether it is destined for destruction or not; he is as the world is. The room in which the entire action takes place is described in the stage directions as "ein Zimmer, dessen spätbürgerliche Pracht und Herrlichkeit zu beschreiben nicht eben leicht sein wird. . . . Der Raum stinkt zum Himmel." There is no narrator as in Wilder's *Our Town* who tells the audience only what is not revealed by the action itself. In *Die Ehe des Herrn Mississippi* the figures themselves act as narrators who now and then abandon their roles in order to tell parts of the action they are going to enact.[18] According to the New York critics who saw the off-Broadway production, Dürrenmatt handles his technique with originality and effectiveness.

Dürrenmatt's most successful "tragic comedy," *Der Besuch der alten Dame* (*The Visit*), appeared in 1956. It represents his criticism of a world in which wealth and possessions have become absolute values and is, at the same time, a paean of revenge. The author himself explains his "heroine" as follows:

Claire Zachanassian stellt weder die Gerechtigkeit dar noch den Marshallplan oder gar die Apokalypse, sie sei nur das, was sie ist, die reichste Frau der Welt, durch ihr Vermögen in der Lage, wie eine Heldin der griechischen Tragödie zu handeln, absolut, grausam, wie Medea etwa. Sie kann es sich leisten. Die Dame hat Humor, das ist nicht zu übersehen, da sie Distanz zu den Menschen besitzt als zu einer käuflichen Ware, Distanz auch zu sich selber, eine seltsame Grazie ferner, einen bösartigen Charme. Doch da sie sich ausserhalb der menschlichen Ordnung bewegt, ist sie etwas Unabänderliches, Starres geworden, ohne Entwicklung mehr, es sei denn, die, zu versteinern, ein Götzenbild zu werden. Sie ist eine dichterische Erscheinung.[19]

Claire Zachanassian (a contraction made up from the names of the three wealthiest men in the Balkans: Zacharoff, Onassis, and Gulbenkian) comes back to her home town of Güllen ("Gülle" means "puddle" in Swiss dialect). Her lover of many years ago, who had left her with a child, now must pay for his faithlessness—with his life. She has brought a coffin and a check for a billion which will make all the inhabitants of Güllen wealthy if the faithless lover dies. In the beginning the people are aghast at the idea of killing their esteemed fellow citizen Alfred Ill, the keeper of a run-down store in the impoverished town of Güllen. But there is a gradual change until Alfred Ill appears to the people of Güllen as the only obstacle on their way to wealth, luxury, and a life of ease. Having arrived at this point in their reasoning, they soon decide together that Ill must die. They speak of "justice" to justify murder. And Claire Zachanassian has shown that money can buy everything. At last, after his death, she can claim the man she had loved in her early

youth. She is a specter of revenge. Alfred Ill's corpse is placed in
the coffin and Claire calls off her wedding to husband number
nine: "Ich habe meinen Geliebten gefunden."

Eine gallenbittere Komödie, so bitter, dass sie von Sartre sein
könnte, wenn dieser die groteske Phantasie von Dürrenmatt hätte.
Natürlich geht es dem Autor in diesem Stück nicht darum, die
banale Wahrheit "Mit Geld lässt sich alles kaufen" durch eine
Bühnenparabel zu erhärten. Die makabre Automatik einer morali-
schen Pervertierung, die sich daraus ergibt, ist vielmehr das Thema
dieser drei Akte, die wahrhaft mit Entsetzen Scherz treiben: Dass
nämlich die Aussicht auf die Milliarde das "sittliche Gewissen" der
Güllener so mobilisiert, dass sie in der Tat Gerechtigkeit zu üben
glauben, wenn sie ihren Mitbürger Ill töten.[20]

In 1959, Dürrenmatt with Paul Burkhard as his collaborator
wrote a musical play.[21] It was the first attempt by Burkhard to
produce such an ambitious work. These two most prominent
Swiss, the one in music, the other in the field of the drama, had
set themselves the goal of producing a Swiss national opera in
Frank V, Opera of a Private Bank. Before it was finished, Dürrenmatt made this characteristic statement about it: "It is a
very angry and very wild play. It will be a kind of Shakespear-
ean royal tragedy, projected into the bank atmosphere. An old
generation of bankers departs and a new one takes over. The
old ones were still real scoundrels, the new ones, however, all
want to appear very decent but do not succeed since the heritage
is too strong. It is a tragic story with a great number of funny
things in it. There will also be a number of murders. A high
point develops when the gangsters have stories told to them by
decent people, just as we sometimes listen to stories by gangsters."

Frank V had its *première* during the winter of 1959 at the
Zurich Schauspielhaus and its first German performance a year
later at the Kammerspiele of Munich. Its success did not equal
that of *The Visit.* Anticipating the critics, Dürrenmatt thought
that they would compare his latest stage production with
Brecht's *Threepenny Opera.* But he pointed out that Brecht's
songs were actually satirized. He would rather consider Offen-

bach as his artistic ancestor. He also expressed the hope that, together with Burkhard, he would succeed in creating a Swiss national opera. At any rate, Dürrenmatt, who is only forty years old, is striking out in a new direction. It will have to be seen whether he will be as original in the future as he was in the nine stage productions which have led the modern German-language drama along new paths.

If our sketchy survey of the contemporary German-language drama acquires a positive note, it is due to the achievements of Friedrich Dürrenmatt. He was awarded the Schiller Prize for 1959 of the City of Mannheim, which is endowed with the sum of DM 10,000 and given every second year to the person who "has served cultural progress in Schiller's spirit in a superior manner." Dürrenmatt—and to a lesser extent Frisch, Hochwälder, and Hildesheimer—are the hope of the German-language theater.

Drama and theater are not identical. In Germany today there is a gap between them. When, anywhere, they become identical —when the development of the one matches the other—we have the rare periods of great drama. Technically the theater is far ahead of the drama today. It will take many Dürrenmatts to catch up and once more establish a German-language drama as a vital force in the world theater. At present, other countries are dramatically more creative, especially France, England, and the United States.

In his *Atlantic* article Luft evaluates the present-day German drama as follows:

We are faced with a strange and fundamentally unnatural situation. The German theater, splendidly equipped externally, gifted with versatile interpretive faculties, courted by a mass audience of all ages, has not yet really found itself. The much touted German "economic miracle" has lavishly reconstructed most of our bombed-out theaters. It has provided legions of enthusiastic consumers, beyond even the fondest dreams of earlier days. But the innermost and decisive kernel is undernourished and has remained inactive. The "miracle" has not touched it. The poetic word, the dramatic reflection of our time, the positive evaluation of the problems of the day, cannot be found anywhere. The heart of the theater barely beats, no matter how prosperous its external aspect may appear.

This in itself need not be a tragedy, many will say; every country has known periods of poetic drought. Is it not sufficient to keep up the precious instrument of the theater while we wait for new genius to appear? No harm is done—these people say—if the German theater, after the protracted period of nationalistic-egotistic narcissism which it suffered from 1933 to 1945, now feeds for a while on the classic past and the best foreign production. Perhaps they are right, but it seems to me that this period of waiting and borrowing is lasting suspiciously long. Can our writers justly claim that the days of Apocalypse are still too close to be converted objectively into drama? Should they not by now have reached a distance safe enough to enable them to deal with even the hottest subject?

The situation of the German theater seems to indicate that Western Germany is prospering and flourishing in many external ways, that admirable work has been done wherever it was a matter of coming to grips with practical problems and of clearing away the ruins. But the great malaise of the mind, the feeling of a spiritual vacuum and exhaustion, persists.[22]

In 1960, Luft ended his *Jahresring* article on a less pessimistic note: "Noch immer ist das Theater dieses Landes im Wartezustand. Intervalle solcher Art hat es immer gegeben. Ein Grund zu Ungeduld ist es nicht, vor allem ist es kein Grund, das Theater über die Schulter anzusehen und seine Funktion als Spiegel des Lebens im Spiel zu vergessen oder zu unterschätzen.—Gut, dass das Instrument in Ordnung gehalten wird. Wenn sich die Talente endlich nähern, werden sie eine Heimat haben." [23]

Erasmus Redivivus in the Mid-Twentieth Century

by
Margaret Kober Merzbach

In 1514, THE PARISIAN theologian Lefèvre d'Etaples wrote: "Quis non suspiciat, amet, colat Erasmum? Nemo non qui bonus et literatus fuerit." [1] In 1519, Martin Luther called Erasmus "decus nostrum et spes." [2] In 1522, however, Ulrich von Hutten in his *Expostulatio cum Erasmo* attacked the once revered scholar as a Proteus and a betrayer of his own ideas. Since then, a variety of shadings has arisen in the judgment of the man who least fitted Jacob Burckhardt's conception of a "Renaissance man." The tenor of judgment was rather constant: Erasmus was a great humanist, but not a great man. [3] There were exceptions: biographers pointed to the courage of a man who refused to be partisan to any group, and there was the statement of Rudolf Pfeiffer that man will be able to survive as the eternal *Antibarbarus* only if he accepts the Erasmian principle of humanism. Only the *homo humanissimus*, the man of highest erudition, integrity, and gentleness could save mankind from submersion in barbarous subhumanity. [4]

Generally, men of the twentieth century react to Erasmus as did the people of the sixteenth century. When Albrecht Dürer wished that Erasmus would offer himself for the martyr's crown, he knew that "the old mannikin" would not do so; [5] Erasmus had said before that there had been many martyrs in the history of Christendom, but only a few scholars. In 1943, A. N. White-

130

head remarked: "It is a great pity that Erasmus was not a stronger character. His ideas were the right ones and could have provided a much happier solution for the development of Christendom than the one which came. But he lacked the force." [6] Whitehead spoke further about Erasmus' view as "that of the sensible and enlightened" people and wished Erasmus had taken the role of the great Greek dramatists who transformed a crude peasants' religion into a beautiful symbolism. But Erasmus was a deeply religious searcher for the truth and not "enlightened" in the meaning of the eighteenth century. He was a man who knew a wide scale of meanings and interpretations; he was tolerant of old ideas and did not share in the crazy fear of new ones, but he did not feel the need for a new doctrine or for a complete abdication of doctrines. He was a member of an imaginary Platonic-Scipionic aristocracy of thinkers and not willing at all to be a leader of masses, of men with passions and emotions not bridled by erudition and charity. It would have made no difference to him whether these masses were a crowd in the market place, a group of soldiers on the battlefield, or an audience at the public performance of a drama. He was neither a Zwingli nor a Sophocles nor did he want to be either of them. Sophocles transformed a primitive belief in monstrous snake gods into an esthetic and elevating experience of human tragedy; Erasmus had read in the Gospels, in the letters of Paul, and in the writings of the Church Fathers the message of Jesus Christ, *Caritas,* and the only task he set for himself was the philological editing and exposition of these writings. There is no doubt that without Erasmus the historical Reformation never would have been realized or, at least, never would have taken the same aspect. His satirical attacks on a variety of abuses, his scriptural paraphrases, but above all his new edition of the Greek New Testament had prepared the way. This was acknowledged by the Reformers, themselves, and was repeated endlessly by their enemies to the distress of the scholar, who saw both humanistic scholarship and the peace of the world threatened and the endeavors of his life frustrated.

During the freewill controversy Luther stated that Erasmus

had hit the core of his cause—the adversaries of the Reformation maintained that both had played with words and that in spite of the increasing sharpness of the utterances against each other their heresy was the same. The adversaries were right; modern Protestant theology does not deny that. Paul Tillich says, "Erasmus points to that moral responsibility which makes man, man. Yet this was not denied, either by Luther or by the other representatives of the concept of the bondage of the will." [7] Karl Barth admits that Paul's parable of the potter and his clay is not adequate,[8] and Tillich confirms that the "language" of Paul and Augustine may lead to the misunderstanding that man is an object among objects. It is exactly this misleading language that had aroused Erasmus. His defense of man's liberty had been misunderstood not only by Luther, but also by the humanists of his time, by the philosophers of the eighteenth century who held to the optimistic view of Rousseau's *l'homme naît bon,* and by the theologians of the twentieth century who put the emphasis on the depravity of man. Erasmus, however, does not believe that man is good; he knows that man is a sinner and can not be saved but by the grace of God. But he stresses man's special situation which is different from that of nature. Tillich, while not retracting at all from Luther's averment, bridges the gap: "Luther's assertion that man's will is in bondage to demonic structure is meaningful only if man in his essential nature is free." [9] But Tillich fails to see in Erasmus more than the optimistic humanist.

In the light of mid-twentieth-century existentialist theology and philosophy the paradoxical position of both, Luther and Erasmus, becomes manifest. Luther, exalting the bondage of the will, depending on the grace of God alone, trusting in faith alone, and listening to no other voice but his own conscience, rushes into action without fear of the outcome. In the conviction that God wills in him, he is able to make decisions without regard to the evil which may arise from them. Erasmus, in the deep consciousness of man's moral responsibility, respects the boundaries set by environment and retreats from action listening to the voice of *his* conscience. Like the leaders of the Reformation, he chooses conscience and not the conventional moral law of society to be his guide.

What is conscience? The constant urge to be loyal to the standard to which a man has professed his allegiance. For Luther that standard was the complete surrender to the majesty of almighty God; for Erasmus, it was the unconditional allegiance to the gospel of love. Erasmus was neither a theologian nor a philosopher, but a philologist. He had arrived at his conclusion by the philological method of studying and comparing the sources of Christian wisdom. Like Luther, he was aware of the fact that the study of sacred literature means selection and interpretation as in every field of learning, and he knew also that "truth" had changed through the ages. Inspiration did not seem sufficient help for interpretation; he demanded an objective test. He found it in the Church. He did not identify "Church" with the Pope or the monastic orders, nor with the Gospels or Paul or Augustine or Thomas of Aquinas alone, but with the consensus of all. He found the consensus in the message of Charity. For that reason, Charity is for him the test of truth.

Erasmus did not insist that his interpretation of man's relation to God was right; he was willing to let himself be persuaded by the arguments of either the representatives of the Roman see or of the "younger man" (Luther) ; but violence in word and deed on both sides was not proof of truth, but of *error.* Man had to be held responsible for his decisions and for his errors. Erasmus held Luther responsible for the Peasants' War and for the religious war and disorders of the following centuries which he rightly foresaw. Deep inside he felt his own responsibility, too. He tried to deny it, but he knew that Luther's work and the incidents that led to Thomas Muenzer's death no less than those which caused the execution of his own beloved friend Thomas More had their roots in the atmosphere of those years when Erasmus' sayings were received with reverence. In the twentieth century the existentialist Sartre insists that there are no victims in the world catastrophes, that it is man's destiny to bear the responsibility for all that happens to him. In the paraphrase of the Epistle to the Romans where the controversy started, Erasmus had said, "Nemo damnatur nisi sua culpa."

Man's freedom of choice does not mean that he knows the right choice or that he knows the will of God—man is limited by the darkness of ignorance. It may be God's will that Luther, the harsh one, does the work of reformation; the world may need the burning cure. But Erasmus can not have an active part in Luther's work nor in a suppression of Luther. His conscience does not allow him to act in contradiction of the gospel of love.

The man who had been the most influential person in the early sixteenth century voluntarily abdicated his leadership in a barbarous fight over faith and resigned himself to his scholarly work. He never attained the peaceful serenity of a spectator for which he yearned throughout the later years of his life. Contrary to his wishes, he still found himself in the center of controversy when his body felt the nearness of death. His mind had been occupied by the thought of death a long time before. Death meant rescue from the tormenting pains of a frail body, rescue from the smarting sting of loneliness in a world of willful misinterpretations and fanatic dogmatism. Death meant also the end of his life's labor and the final negation of his desire to lift the veil of ignorance from his own eyes and from the eyes of his fellow men. The fear of finding his work frustrated—by death, by illness, by suspicion, by misunderstanding, by any unfavorable circumstance—hunted him through the years and caused him to be a restless worker. Neither Erasmus' contemporaries nor the following generations correctly interpreted the meaning of his signet ring.

In vain he tried to explain it as a *memento mori;*[10] people have continued to quote his *Nulli concedo* and have maintained that Erasmus did not wish to belong to anyone, to yield to anyone.[11] But Terminus, the god, the boundary stone, says, "I, Terminus, do not cede to anyone." Terminus is the symbol of the end of life or of man's striving in life; it is the symbol of the finitude of man, that which Tillich calls the threat of spacelessness.[12] How deep was Erasmus' consciousness of the limitations of man's free will! He did not share the "optimistic individualism"[13] of later humanists; he knew that man is only able to desire good, not to do it. His erudition had granted him wisdom as well as knowledge; he recognized the demonic powers of destruction hidden in a precious case. He had dreamed about the growth of man into a higher man by education to wisdom, he had been awakened roughly, but he refused to lend the power of his word and his superior knowledge to anything that might lead to greater devastation. Against the demands of two powerful groups he followed his own conscience and revealed himself as the true teacher of the Western world.

The story of the sixteenth century was the story of spiritual leaders, martyrs, heroes and the story of a man who did not want to be one of them. His gentle voice was drowned by the clamor of the great men, his call to peace by the summons to war. Still, the Erasmian voice emerged again whenever the tumult of battling forces seemed to make men deaf against their conscience. Men have stumbled from one war into another up to the middle of the twentieth century. The threat of the "last war" has arisen. A reawakened Erasmus means a reawakened conscience, a reawakened sense of responsibility, a reawakened understanding of man's fate. Man is doomed to make decisions and man alone is responsible for his failures. True to the Socratic view that ignorance is cause of failure, Erasmus wanted man to search for knowledge. But he did not want to use the power of knowledge for the ravages of the human mind or for the more efficient and faster destruction of man's world.

Erasmus demands from the Western world, from men who have professed their allegiance to the gospel of love, that they renounce everything which may cause the conflagration of man's greatest treasures and that they search for a profounder learning which will make them better servants in the realm of charity.

For Erasmus, who knew that man cannot save himself from damnation even by the most violent struggling, believed that man is free to ready himself for the acceptance of grace—by erudition and charity.

Gertrud von Le Fort and Bertolt Brecht: Counter Reformation and Atomic Bomb

by
Frank Wood

IT MAY SEEM odd to juxtapose two such different figures in modern literature as Gertrud von Le Fort (1876—) and Bertolt Brecht (1898–1956)—the Catholic author of *Der Kranz der Engel* and other distinguished novels and tales, on the one hand; and on the other, the Communist sympathizer and exponent of the most original "realistic" theater since the Expressionist movement. At least once, however, their respective literary orbits intersected in the treatment of a unique theme that has had, and will continue to have, far-reaching consequences for the precarious world of today. My discussion of this theme is not primarily concerned, if at all, with esthetic and literary criteria as such (problems of structure, form, style, etc.) nor does it entail any value judgments as to the literary excellence or status of the two writers concerned. What is intended is a closer ideological examination of another chapter in the history of ideas, so critical in twentieth-century thinking, as reflected by two German writers who have also felt the need to reconcile historical circumstance with their own quite different interpretations of that circumstance's bearing on Western society today.

Gertrud von Le Fort's novella, *Am Tore des Himmels* (1954) and Brecht's *Das Leben des Galilei* (1938–1955) have at least

136

this in common: besides the main protagonist, they both present the struggle for truth (here "scientific") in the face of authoritarian restrictions (here "religious orthodoxy"). The dialectics of this struggle are presented from the Christian and the Communist viewpoints respectively. The seventeenth-century Counter Reformation is the natural and obvious milieu for the staging of this drama, but the implications of these two works far transcend the mere historical clash between a fanatical and perturbed Inquisition and the representatives of the "new" scientific discoveries in seventeenth-century astronomy and cosmology. To be sure, the immediate plots of the two works bear directly on the relationship between secular science and religious orthodoxy in respect to the tensions set up between two kinds of "truth" in a certain period of Western history; but they also point quite clearly to what happens, in the effect, when bigotry and pusillanimity fail to resolve a conflict which has led to the divorce of science from morality in so many instances and which has eventuated in the recent tragedies of Hiroshima and Nagasaki.

I

In Le Fort's framing-story *Am Tore des Himmels,* the author-narrator reveals the existence in the family archives of a certain "Galileo document" and relates her attempt to rescue it from the family's city residence before it is destroyed by the accelerated bombing of the last war. Upon her arrival in town she is received by a distant cousin, a brilliant young doctor of science currently employed in the war laboratories (*Das war die Mördergrube,* he was to say later). Despite her first instinctive dislike for what she considers to be an arrogant and typical example of the "new" education of the Third Reich, she is persuaded to listen as the young scientist reads aloud from the seventeenth-century manuscript that neither of them had read before. Here the framing-story is interrupted to recount the destiny of a celebrated German astronomer, the "physicist" of today, as told

by his most promising disciple. The *Meister* is clearly patterned
after the model of Galileo, although the author maintains a free
hand in calling it *ein typisches Gelehrtenschicksal jener Tage;*
and by not giving her character a local habitation and a name,
she intends to lend him a more universal and international significance. The features of this destiny are familiar enough to us:
the astronomer's summons to Rome to answer for his heretical
Copernican theories before the Holy Office of the Inquisition
where, despite numerous sympathizers with his new views even
among the clergy, his experiments are condemned and he is
forced to recant.

The recantation scene in the forbidding atmosphere of the
Inquisition is the climax of the story, as we view it through the
eyes of the loyal young disciple who has followed his master to
Rome and secretly witnessed the humiliating ceremony behind
closed doors. The novelist has constructed her story with such
care for motivation that, up to this point, there is hardly a
doubt that this German Galileo will not betray his obligation
to uphold the truths of science when they are so clearly manifest
and, accordingly, will refuse to capitulate to his enemies. Was
not the presiding Cardinal himself a friend of and sympathizer
with the new trends? Yet the anathema is delivered univocally
while the distressed witness offers an explanation upon which
the story's theme basically hinges. He is careful to emphasize
that the recantation was not the result of mere fear or cowardice, as it is to a considerable degree in the case of Brecht's
Galileo:

Sondern der Meister hat abgeschworen im Triumph, und im ganzen
Saal ist niemand gewesen, der nicht verstanden hätte, dass da ein
Mensch seinen Richtern nicht die Ehre antun wollte, sie zu wider-
legen, sondern dass er ihnen gleichsam ihren Verrat der Wahrheit
mit dem seinen zurückzahlte. . . . Es war etwas unglaublich Gross-
artiges in seinem Widerruf: die absolute Verachtung seiner Richter
war darinnen, aber auch die Verachtung seiner selbst, und eben sie
gab seinem Widerruf die erschütternde, ja schauerliche Grösse. O
dieser Hohn über die eigene Selbst-Vernichtung! Er liess den Menschen in sich restlos fallen, aber über dem gefallenen Menschen
erhob sich der Stolz des Wissenschaftlers, masslos bis zur wahrhaft

glorreichen Vermessenheit. Sprach er es aus? O nein, er sprach nichts aus, aber man verstand nur zu gut, was er sagen wollte. Er wollte sagen: ja, ich tue jetzt dasselbe, was ihr tatet, ich verrate, was ich für wahr halte, ich verrate meine Wissenschaft, aber ihr gebt mir die Freiheit, dass ich sie getrost verraten kann! Ich weiss, ich bin in diesem Augenblick unsäglich klein, aber meine Wissenschaft ist gross und herrlich! Ob ihr sie verurteilt und ob ich sie widerrufe, das ist eins so gleichgültig wie das andere—diese Wissenschaft ist unantastbar und unaufhaltsam. Erstickt mich hier in meiner Schmach—ich will gern an ihr ersticken, denn meine Wissenschaft wird Siegerin der Zukunft sein! . . .[1]

The formidable final sentence is more than a mere recapitulation of the historical Galileo's *eppur si muove*. For Gertrud von Le Fort it amounts to a declaration of war on the part of one humanistic discipline against another, of science against theology, daughter against mother, a fateful parting of the ways between one kind of truth and another, one system of beliefs and another, a cleavage fatal to the realization of the image of *homo humanus* in the centuries to come. "Zwei Tore," the diarist concludes his manuscript, "die bisher einander offen standen, schlossen sich, zwei Geistesräume bebten auseinander —für immer—auch in meinem Innern. Ich habe damals den Palast der Inquisition fluchtartig verlassen, von Schmerz und Abscheu überwältigt, vernichtet in allem, was für mich Vertrauen und Verehrung hiess. . . ."[2] In turning his back on Rome to seek a more tolerant climate for his scientific pursuits, he not only abandons his teacher who had failed him but also the religious faith of his youth: "In dem ungeheuren Sturz meiner bisherigen jugendlichen Welt stand nur eines unerschüttert: die verstossene Wahrheit. Ich liebte sie mit Trotz und Jubel, gerade um ihrer Verstossenheit willen."[3] Henceforth he will forge ahead on his own, unlike his master a "free" scientist, but, alas, the ancestor of the "pure" scientist as well, indifferent so frequently to the perils of an increasingly immoral technocracy.

The framing-story picks up as the manuscript ends. Just as the young doctor lays aside the handwritten sheets, there is a sudden air raid alert. The author and her young relative seek

shelter in the cellar from which they barely escape with their
lives. The "Galileo document" is left behind to perish in the
flames. "Der Feuersturm wirbelte die Blätter empor," writes
the author, "ich sah sie aufflammen—was kümmerte es mich?
. . . Meine eigene Zeit war untergegangen. Wohin gehörte ich
nun?" [4]

The postlude to this adventure resolves both the issues raised
in the seventeenth-century diary as well as those resulting from
the twentieth-century bombing. The war has just ended and, as
an expert atomic scientist, the young doctor's services have been
sought for abroad. He visits his author-cousin at her country
home to bid her farewell. Her opinion of him has changed considerably for the better since the reading of the manuscript and
the air raid; she understands him now as the inevitable result
of historical circumstances and forces. Their brief conversation
contains Le Fort's interpretation of her own tale in its ethico-
religious bearing on the position of science today:

"Aber wenn ihr doch in eurer Wissenschaft alles neu seht, kommt
euch denn niemals der Gedanke, dass es auch einen Gott geben
könnte?", rief ich verzweifelt.
"Doch," erwiderte er gelassen, "der Gedanke kommt uns tatsächlich, nach langer, langer Zeit kommt er uns wieder. Est ist nämlich
etwas schwierig geworden, das Universum ohne einen Schöpfer zu
erklären, aber er geht uns etwas schwer ein, wir sind zu lange ohne
ihn ausgekommen—wir mussten es ja—siehe das verlorene Doku-
ment!" [5]

And when his companion adds that perhaps he was afraid,
like a certain character in the document (here the Cardinal is
meant) that he might actually find God again, the young man
frankly replies: "Ja, vielleicht ist es so: wir fürchten uns, denn
wir stehen überall an den äussersten Grenzen, und wenn wir
wieder zu Gott fänden, dann könnten wir ihn nicht mehr in
unsere Kausalitätsgesetze einschliessen—dann würde es ein Gott
sein, der wirklich etwas zu sagen hätte. Aber einstweilen ist es
noch nicht soweit, also nützen wir unsere Freiheit!" [6]

The doctor's car vanishes down the road and the author
leaves the reader with the challenge: "Ja, Gott musste wieder

etwas zu sagen haben, auch bei mir. Wir standen im Grunde vor der gleichen Entscheidung. Wie würde sie ausfallen?" [7]

Gertrud von Le Fort is a master of the historical novel as it develops out of her triad of themes—*die Kirche, die Frau, das Reich*—not only because her sympathies enable her to reconstruct the past so faithfully and warmly in the spirit but equally because this very historical past, beneath the skillful reproduction of costume and setting, serves indirectly to throw a baleful light on the physical horrors and mental confusions of recent times. From her point of view, as revealed in this story, the tragic fissure between science and faith was not at all inevitable. If the seventeenth-century Church had only been willing and ready to acknowledge that the new science in no way impinged on the domain of faith ("Two truths cannot stand in contradiction to each other," the young disciple is made to say with true Thomistic fervor), science might not have developed in the direction of the unconscionable entity which is with us today. But both the Cardinal and the Galileo of the document allowed themselves to be forced into a position where their respective depositions ran counter to what they actually believed and what inner conviction persuaded them was the truth. The betrayal was mutual, for if the position of seventeenth-century orthodoxy was wrong, so was that of the practitioner of the "new" science in throwing overboard a tradition of moral control for the uncontrolled freedoms of a research which, for all its benefits, has become today a Janus-faced blessing. We hear much in our time of the *deus absconditus* in existential literature, and Le Fort's novella, for all its weaknesses in character-drawing and contrived situations (due in large measure to the baroque landscaping of her story) is a forthrightly honest commentary on the urgency of this timely theme.

II

Brecht's drama or *Schauspiel, Das Leben des Galilei,* is concerned with the same historical subject matter but treats it from a different point of view. The emphasis is radically shifted. What is at issue is no longer the historical split between science and Christian orthodoxy as such. Here the issue is the social responsibility of the scientist, then as well as now, who for personal, selfish reasons fails society (i.e., society in the Marxist sense) by withholding from it the scientific fruits of his pursuits. Out of this debacle, of course, develops the same type of "pure" scientist that fires the apprehensions of Gertrud von Le Fort.

In thirteen scenes of epic theater Brecht deals with an historical Galileo (also with certain autobiographical aspects of his own personality) rather than with an anonymous German surrogate (although the variant is of little significance for our present purpose).[8] A series of vignettes unfolds Galileo's life from his impoverished days in Padua where, at the age of forty-six, he still gives private lessons, for which he is poorly paid, to support himself and his research. We trace the vicissitudes of his Florentine fame, his condemnation and recantation in Rome, all culminating in his final days in Florence where, half-blind, under scrutiny by the Church and his own pious daughter, he is able to finish on the sly his revolutionary *Discorsi*. In Le Fort's story what happens up to and through the recantation scene is important; with Brecht the important section is what follows. The difference is a natural outgrowth of two different writing techniques, two different literary genres and, most important of all, two conflicting views of the world.

There are several versions of the work: the first (1938/39), written in Denmark, then the American version (1945/46) and, finally, a German re-working of the American version for the Schiffbauerdamm Theater (1955).[9] Since Brecht is dealing closely with modern theater, the critic is fortunate in having considerable firsthand material to fall back on, not only the dramatist's prose appendices to the play but also numerous observations and statements made during the German rehearsals.

If the condemnation scene provided the fulcrum of Le Fort's story, this function is taken over in the play by the fourteenth scene, or *Schluszszene* (thirteenth scene in the stage version). It derives organically, as a kind of *replique,* from the play's open-ing scene (*Begrüssungsszene*) in which Galileo heralds the dawn of a new era, *die neue Zeit,* and it follows by several years the interdict of the Inquisition. Brecht presents a series of intimate vignettes of Galileo's life and not a cloak-and-dagger plot such as Le Fort's prose tale so often threatens to become. The main events of the fourteenth scene are as follows: old, blind, spied on by the Inquisition, Galileo is visited by his former disciple, Andrea Sarti, the young apprentice of the first scene, who is now a promising scientist himself. (It is important that there is a "favorite disciple" assigned to Galileo in both works. Their reaction to the recantation is in both cases one of disappoint-ment and disgust but, more to the point, they represent the "new" science, the *avant-garde* of the future.) Thus the meeting between master and disciple is cold until Galileo reveals that he has secretly been working on his *Discorsi,* which he now entrusts to Sarti to be smuggled over the border of the *Kirchenstaat.* Sarti's great joy, however, is considerably dampened when Gali-leo delivers his own condemnation—the core of the play—as a scientist who has failed:

. . . Der Kampf um die Messbarkeit des Himmels ist gewonnen durch Zweifel; durch Gläubigkeit muss der Kampf der römischen Hausfrau um Milch immer aufs neue verlorengehen. Die Wissen-schaft, Sarti, hat mit beiden Kämpfen zu tun. Eine Menschheit, stol-pernd in diesem tausendjährigen Perlmutterdunst von Aberglauben und alten Worten, zu unwissend, ihre eigenen Kräfte voll zu entfal-ten, wird nicht fähig sein, die Kräfte der Natur zu entfalten, die ihr enthüllt. Wofür arbeitet ihr? Ich halte dafur, dass das einzige Ziel der Wissenschaft darin besteht, die Mühseligkeit der menschlichen Existenz zu erleichtern. Wenn Wissenschaftler, eingeschüchtert durch selbstsüchtige Machthaber, sich damit begnügen, Wissen um des Wissens willen aufzuhäufen, kann die Wissenschaft zum Krüppel gemacht werden, und eure neuen Maschinen mögen nur neue Drangsale bedeuten. Ihr mögt mit der Zeit alles entdecken, was es zu entdecken gibt, und euer Fortschritt wird doch nur ein Fortschrei-ten von der Menschheit weg sein. Die Kluft zwischen euch und ihr kann eines Tages so gross werden, dass euer Jubelschrei über irgen-deine neue Errungenschaft von einem universalen Entsetzensschrei beantwortet werden könnte. . . .

This startingly realistic appraisal of the impasse of our atomic
century is immediately followed by his pronouncement of judgment on himself:

Ich hatte als Wissenschaftler eine einzigartige Möglichkeit. In
meiner Zeit erreichte die Astronomie die Marktplätze. Unter diesen
ganz besonderen Umständen hätte die Standhaftigkeit eines Mannes grosse Erschütterungen hervorrufen können. Hätte ich wider-
standen, hätten die Naturwissenschaftler etwas wie den hypokrati-
schen Eid der Ärzte entwickeln können, das Gelöbnis, ihr Wissen
einzig zum Wohle der Menschheit anzuwenden! Wie es nun steht, ist
das Höchste, was man erhoffen kann, ein Geschlecht erfinderischer
Zwerge, die für alles gemietet werden können. Ich habe zudem die
Überzeugung gewonnen, Sarti, dass ich niemals in wirklicher Gefahr
schwebte. Einige Jahre lang war ich ebenso stark wie die Obrigkeit.
Und ich überlieferte mein Wissen den Machthabern, es zu gebrauchen, es nicht zu gebrauchen, es zu missbrauchen, ganz wie es ihren
Zwecken diente. Ich habe meinen Beruf verraten. Ein Mensch, der
das tut, was ich getan habe, kann in den Reihen der Wissenschaft
nicht geduldet werden.[10]

It is not Galileo's character that is important for Brecht but
his social attitude (at rehearsals he rarely spoke of a subject's
character, but of his reaction to the social context).[11] The important thing is what a person *does,* not what he *is.* Thus one of
Brecht's directions for the German rehearsals reads as follows:

Er ist sechsundvierzig Jahre alt und hatte noch nicht die Zeit, etwas
Richtiges zu schaffen. Er ist etwas bitter. Er ist im allgemeinen
physiologisch nicht in der Lage, Fragen unbeantwortet zu lassen. Er
unterliegt der Versuchung der Wissenschaft.—Zum Schluss ist er ein
Förderer der Wissenschaften und ein sozialer Verbrecher.—Im
Grunde zwingt er seinem so schwachen Körper eine ungeheure Hel-
dentat ab, indem er die "Discorsi" schreibt und, in der Realität, den
Komfort risquiert, wenn auch aus Eitelkeit, aber er unterliegt der
Versuchung der Wissenschaft. . . .[12]

And the temptation of "pure" science, we might add! Here is
the situation that Gertrud von Le Fort had predicted would
arise, and actually did arise, from the premises of her own story:
ein Geschlecht erfinderischer Zwerge. From that fatal moment
of recantation the scientist henceforth was clothed with full
authority to endanger, without moral control over his purpose,

the future of civilization and, in Brecht's language, he pursues science "without obvious purpose, like a vice." [13] Hence in this specifically Brechtian *Entlegendarisierung* of the historical figure, Galileo "must be shown as a social criminal, a complete rogue." [14]

But Brecht's Galileo is not entirely a criminal, of course, as we have seen from the above quotation; he shares again the duality of the Brechtian character, both hero and criminal in one.

Galileo becomes a criminal [writes a recent Brecht critic] because by his cowardice he has established the tradition of the scientist's subservience to the State—the tradition that, according to Brecht, reached its culmination in the production of the atomic bomb, which science put at the disposal of ordinary, non-scientific men, to serve their power politics. Galileo, the hero of science, thus becomes the embodiment of reason in all its splendour, ruined once more by its inability to overcome the base, instinctive, inarticulate side of human nature. The greatest of intellects, the personification of science itself, is thus as helplessly tied to the blind instincts of his subconscious nature, as poor Mazeppa is tied to the wild steed that carried him to his doom.[15]

It is this conflict between hero and criminal, between reason and instinct which accounts for the dramatist's shifting conception of his character in the course of creation:

In the earlier version of the play Galileo's action was made to appear excusable as a deliberate act of calculation and cunning: by recanting he saved his life and gained time to complete his treatise which was then smuggled out into the free world. But shortly before Brecht died . . . he had changed his mind—(as he put the final touches to the revised version of the play and conducted rehearsals of the Berliner Ensemble)—he insisted that Galilei "must be shown as a social criminal and rogue". . . .[16]

We have seen how Gertrud von Le Fort established a connection between the Galileo controversy and the atomic bomb by introducing in her story, toward the end, the air raid episode followed by her parting conversation with a representative of the new science. She is writing, of course, with full knowledge of the events that terminated World War II. Brecht's interpretation is all the more remarkable in that it anticipates the course of things long before they took place. In Denmark, at the time of the first writing, he stood close to Niels Bohr, then an assistant researcher in atomic energy; newspapers already carried news of the fracture of the uranium atom by German physicists; later, during his collaboration with Charles Laughton on the American version, he was able to sum up his experience as follows:

Das "atomarische Zeitalter" machte sein Debut in Hiroshima in der Mitte unserer Arbeit. Der infernalische Effekt der Grossen Bombe stellte den Konflikt des Galilei mit der Obrigkeit seiner Zeit in ein neues, schärferes Licht. Wir hatten nur wenige Änderungen zu machen, keine einzige in der Struktur.[17]

Brecht's condemnation of the "pure" scientist (i.e., the scientist for whom knowledge is an end in itself and not the welfare of a "classless" society) is as positive as Le Fort's. But where she sees salvation in the restoration of the orthodox relationship between God and man, Brecht warns against the acceptance of any "new religious" dogma as *Ersatz* for the old. "Unter keinen Umständen aber darf man dem aus dem Bankrott alten Glaubens kommenden Wunsch nach neuem Glauben nachgeben, dem schrecklichen Wunsch nach Blindheit." [18] At the same time Brecht makes it quite clear that the Catholic church in his play simply performs the role of authority (*Obrigkeit*). Modern science, after all, is a legitimate daughter of the Church, once a branch of theology and only recently emancipated from the mother. Science has its spiritual as well as its worldly aspect, and Brecht is concerned primarily with the victory of the worldly and not the spiritual factor.[19]

The real opposition between the two authors can be nicely summed up in Galileo's trenchant words in the fourteenth scene: "Der Kampf um die Messbarkeit des Himmels ist gewonnen durch Zweifel; durch Gläubigkeit muss der Kampf der römischen Hausfrau um Milch aufs neue verlorengehen. Die Wissenschaft hat mit beiden Kämpfen zu tun." Summing up, in Le Fort's narrative it is the scientist's relation to the higher supranatural principle that is the crux of the argument; with

Brecht what matters is the scientist's relation to a socialist society and its welfare. In both of their central characters there is
a conflict between reason and instinct, to use Martin Esslin's
language, but the instinct in each is of a different nature: pusillanimity and clerical inertia in Le Fort's work; cowardice and
sensuousness in Brecht's.

Regardless of their merits or defects as pieces of literature,
scarcely two other works in modern times have succeeded so
well in removing the study of history from the arid professional
archives and making of it a living force (as Nietzsche conceived
it in *Vom Nutzen und Nachteil der Historie für das Leben*)
with which to confront one of the most baffling dilemmas of our
era. Whether they interpret the "historical" Galileo correctly or
not is beside the point. The decisive factor is the acute rele-
vance to our critical *condition humaine* of what the artistic and
ethical conscience of each of these two writers has selected for
emphasis. They make the reader only too uncomfortably aware
of the immediate challenge in Gertrud von Le Fort's closing
paragraph: "Wir standen im Grunde vor der gleichen Entscheidung. Wie würde sie ausfallen?" [20]

Notes

ARTHUR BURKHARD

1 John R. Frey, "The Schiller Bicentennial in German-speaking Countries," *The American-German Review*, XXVI, 3, 15–18; it seems appropriate to call attention to the well-documented and illuminating article of Dmitrij Tschiżewskij, "Schiller in Russland," *Ruperto-Carola, Mitteilungen der Vereinigung der Freunde der Studentenschaft der Universität Heidelberg*, Bd. XXVII (Juni, 1960), 111–20.

2 Karl-Heinz Planitz, "The Schiller Bicentennial in America," *The American-German Review*, XXVI, 6, 6–9.

3 *Schiller, Bicentenary Lectures*, ed. F. Norman ("Institute of Germanic Languages and Literatures" [University of London, 1960]); reviewed in *Times Literary Supplement* (London), December 2, 1960, No. 3066, p. 780 f.; the *Times Literary Supplement* is hereinafter cited as *LTLS*. *Schiller 1759–1959: Commemorative American Studies*, ed. John R. Frey ("Illinois Studies in Language and Literature," Vol. XLVI [Urbana, Ill., 1959]); reviewed in *The German Quarterly*, XXXIII, No. 4 (Nov., 1960), 375–76; and also in the *Modern Language Review*, LVI (1961), 314–15; the *Modern Language Review* is hereinafter abbreviated as *MLR*. *A Schiller Symposium*, ed. and with an introduction by A. Leslie Willson (Austin, Tex., 1960).

4 William Witte, *Schiller* ("Modern Language Studies," Vol. VI [Oxford, 1949]); Schiller, *Wallenstein, Ein dramatisches Gedicht*, ed. William Witte (Oxford, 1952); William Witte, *Schiller and Burns, and Other Essays* (Oxford, 1959); H. B. Garland, *Schiller Revisited, Some Bicentennial Reflections* (London, 1959); *Friedrich Schiller, Ausgewählte Briefe*, ed. H. B. Garland (Manchester, 1959); reviewed in *MLR*, LVI (1961), 290–91; Walter Silz, "Schiller After Two Centuries," *The American-German Review*, XXVI, 1, 3, 36.

5 Frederick Ungar (ed.), *Friedrich Schiller: An Anthology for Our Time* (New York, 1959); reviewed in *The German Quarterly*, XXXIII, No. 4 (Nov., 1960), 372–73.

6 *Wallenstein, Don Carlos, Mary Stuart, The Maid of Orleans*, trans. Charles E. Passage (New York, 1959 ff.); *The Maiden of Orleans*, trans. John T. Krumpelmann (Chapel Hill, N.C., 1959). Passage, *Don Carlos, Infante of Spain* and Krumpelmann, *The Maiden of Orleans*, reviewed in *The German Quarterly*, XXXIII, No. 4 (Nov., 1960) 370–72;

149

Krumpelmann, *The Maiden of Orleans,* reviewed also in *Études Anglaises,* XIII, No. 3 (1960), 405; *Morning Advocate* (Baton Rouge, La.), October 11, 1959; *The South-Central Bulletin,* XIX, No. 3 (Oct., 1959), 5–6.

7 Cf. the convenient and comprehensive summary in Planitz, "The Schiller Bicentennial in America," *loc. cit.;* for *Maria Stuart,* cf. Knepler's article, note 8, *infra.*

8 Henry W. Knepler, "Maria Stuart in America," *The Theatre Annual,* XVI (1959), 30–50, gives an historical account of the various vicissitudes of this play on the American stage from its earliest performance to the present day. Among recent performances Knepler cites the following: October 8, 1957, Phoenix Theater, New York and July 28, 1959, Vancouver Festival (both of these in the translation of Jean Stock Goldstone and John Reich); September 2, 1958, Edinburgh Festival and September 17, 1958, London (both by the Old Vic Company in the translation of Stephen Spender). Knepler calls attention also to a performance in German by the Düsseldorf Company in London, September 29, 1958.

9 Knepler's second article, "Schiller's Maria Stuart on the Stage in England and America," in *Anglo-German and American-German Cross Currents,* ed. Philip A. Shelley with Arthur O. Lewis, Jr. (2 vols.; Chapel Hill, N.C., 1962), II, treats the various English translations; among others, the following: *Mary Stuart, Derived from Friedrich Schiller's Maria Stuart. A Play in Six Scenes,* trans. Jean Stock Goldstone and John Reich (New York: Dramatists Play Service, Inc., 1958), originally copyrighted in 1957 as an unpublished work under the title "Elizabeth and Mary"; *Schiller's Mary Stuart,* freely translated and adapted by Stephen Spender, with a preface by Peter Wood (London, 1959); *Mary Stuart, A Tragedy,* trans. by Joseph Mellish and adapted by Eric Bentley in Bentley's *Five German Plays* (Garden City, 1959), Volume II of *The Classic Theatre.*

10 Camillo von Klenze, *Charles Timothy Brooks, Translator from the German, and the Genteel Tradition* (Boston, 1937). Von Klenze knew what he calls the most important biography of Brooks (1813–1883), the Memoir by Charles W. Wendte, published in *Poems, Original and Translated, by Charles Timothy Brooks. With a Memoir by Charles W. Wendte,* ed. W. P. Andrews (Boston, 1885). Indeed, he comments (p. 100): "Wendte (p. 235) under the caption *Unpublished Works,* lists the following translations: 1) Schiller's Dramas, *Mary Stuart* and *Joan of Arc."* Von Klenze questions the existence of a complete *Joan of Arc,* but, although he asserts categorically, "There can be no doubt as to the *Mary Stuart,"* he makes no attempt to discover or inspect the manuscript. On the same page he makes a cavalier-like disposal of Franz Grillparzer's drama, *The Ancestress (Die Ahnfrau):* "I have not seen the MS." An attempt to compensate for this neglect and to call attention to Brooks's *Ancestress* will be found in Arthur Burkhard, *Franz Grillparzer in England and America* ("Österreich-Reihe, Band 134/136" [Wien, 1961]), 42 ff. and Plates XIV–XIX. Cf. also Arthur

Burkhard, "Grillparzer in English Translation," in *Österreich und die angelsächsische Welt,* ed. Otto Hietsch (Wien, 1961).

11 Herewith thanks to Mrs. A. Alexander Robey of South Lincoln, Massachusetts, a descendant of Brooks; also to John R. Turner Ettlinger, John Hay Library, Brown University; Hilda E. Conlon, Richard De Gennaro, Foster M. Palmer, Widener Library and Carolyn E. Jakeman, Houghton Library, Harvard University. My thanks also for help to the following friends and colleagues: F. E. Coenen, Carl Hammer, Jr., John A. Herbert, Ernst Hölzl, Henry W. Knepler, John T. Krumpelmann, Winfred Lehmann, Karl-Heinz Planitz, Leroy R. Shaw, Philip A. Shelley, Frederick Ungar, John J. Weisert, Kathleen Cunningham, Maria Jensen, Dorothea May Moore, and Esther Whitmarsh Phillips.

12 Excerpts quoted are usually cited by reference to the page numbers in Arabic numerals of Brooks's manuscript; some important passages are further identified by act and scene, the act in Roman numerals, the scene in Arabic; only rarely was it deemed necessary to clutter the text with the line numbers of Schiller's German text.

13 Although in no way an excuse for Brooks's mistake, an even more primitive error, made as late as 1956 by a man who indulges in translation from the German and has tried his hand also at an English version of *Maria Stuart,* makes us charitable. Stephen Spender, translating Heinrich Heine's *Lorelei,* renders the last two lines: "And this, they with their singing, The Lorelei had done." Cf. *LTLS,* February 17, 1956, No. 2816, p. 94, for the translation and *LTLS,* February 24, 1956, No. 2817, p. 117, for a correction and Spender's lame apology "for the howler." Cf. also in this connection, *MLR,* LVI (1961), 316.

14 Cf. Burkhard, "Grillparzer in English Translation," 51 ff.; for inversions in Gustav Pollak's translation of Grillparzer's dramas in Gustav Pollak, *Franz Grillparzer and the Austrian Drama* (New York: Dodd, Mead, 1907), xxi, 440 pp.; and Burkhard, "Grillparzer in English Translation," 62–63, for precious turns of phrase in translations of German dramas by Ellen Frothingham.

15 A picture of Brooks in later years is reproduced as the frontispiece of the volume of Brooks's poems and also in the article of the Hietsch Festschrift, both cited in note 10, *supra.*

16 Recent translations of the dramas of Grillparzer by Henry Harmon Stevens and Arthur Burkhard, conveniently listed in Burkhard, *Franz Grillparzer in England and America,* 80, n. 44 and 81–82, n. 55, aim to render the German original line for line.

17 The volume of Brooks's poems (cited note 10, *supra*) prints one speech from Schiller's *Jungfrau,* entitled *Joan of Arc,* 188. Joan of Arc's Farewell to her Home (from the German of Schiller):

> "Farewell ye mountains, ye beloved pastures,
> And peaceful friendly valleys, fare ye well." (1. 383 f.)

A complete manuscript translation of the play apparently does not exist.

HORST OPPEL

1 R. LeConte, "Les Allemands à la Louisiane au XVIIIe siècle," *Journal de la Société des Américanistes,* N.S. 16 (Paris, 1924), S. 1–17.

2 F. de Chaville, "Le Voyage en Louisiane, 1720–1724," *Journal de la Société des Américanistes,* IV (Paris, 1903), S. 98–143, bes. S. 134.

3 Helmut Blume, *Die Entwicklung der Kulturlandschaft des Mississippideltas in kolonialer Zeit unter besonderer Berücksichtigung der deutschen Siedlung* ("Schriften des Geographischen Instituts der Universität Kiel," Bd. XVI, Heft 3 [Kiel, 1956]), S. 11.

4 Tab. 1 in *ibid.*

5 Wiedergabe der Zählung von 1724 in englischer Übersetzung durch J. H. Deiler, *The Settlement of the German Coast of Louisiana and the Creoles of German Descent* ("Americana Germanica," N.S. 8 [Philadelphia, 1909]), S. 80 ff. Ergänzung und Berichtigung durch H. Blume, *op. cit.,* S. 15 ff.

6 A. Franz, *Die erste deutsche Einwanderung in das Mississippital* ("Deutsch-amerikanische Geschichtsblätter," 12 [Chicago, 1912]), S. 190–282, bes. S. 267.

7 H. Blume, *op. cit.,* S. 102 f.

8 J. H. Deiler, "Die ersten Deutschen am unteren Mississippi," in *Das Buch der Deutschen in Amerika* (Philadelphia, 1909), S. 195–210, bes. S. 207.

9 R. LeConte, "Les Allemands à la Louisiane," S. 13.

10 L. Voss, *The German Coast of Louisiana* ("The Concord Society Historical Bulletin," No. 9 [Hoboken, N.J., 1928]).

11 Harold Jantz, "Amerika im deutschen Dichten und Denken," in *Deutsche Philologie im Aufriss,* ed. W. Stammler (2. Aufl.; Berlin, 1960), Bd. III, S. 333.

12 Hauptwerke: *Anweisung für Schullehrer auf dem Lande* (1799); *Historische Denkwürdigkeiten der schweizerischen Staatsumwälzung,* 3 Bde. (1803–1805); *Die Alpenwälder* (1804); *Stunden der Andacht,* 8 Bde. (1809–1816); *Des Schweizerlandes Geschichte für das Schweizervolk* (1822); *Bilder aus der Schweiz* (historische Novellen, 1825–1826); *Gesammelte Schriften,* 35 Bde. (1851–1854).

13 *Eine Selbstschau* (2. Aufl.; Aarau, 1842), S. 277.

14 *Ibid.,* S. 278.

15 *Ibid.,* S. 281.

16 *Ibid.,* S. 278.

17 *Ibid.,* S. 48; vgl. auch S. 63 f.

18 Montague Summers, *The Gothic Quest* (London, 1938), S. 144.

19 Über Zschokkes Popularität in Amerika im Zeitraum von 1810 bis 1864 vgl. Henry A. Pochmann, *German Culture in America,* 1600–1900 (Madison: University of Wisconsin Press, 1957), S. 329. Zschokkes Drama *Abellino* gehört in der Fassung von William Dunlap zu den Erfolgsstücken auf der New Yorker Bühne um die Wende vom 18. zum 19. Jahrhundert (Pochmann, *op. cit.,* S. 351). Der erste Teil der

Selbstschau in der Übersetzung von Parke Godwin hat Whitman beeindruckt. Vgl. Pochmann, *op. cit.,* S. 466; "Whitman's memoranda indicate that what impressed him most was Zschokke's simple, honest, straightforward account of himself. Already provided by Goethe's *Dichtung und Wahrheit* with one notable model of autobiography, he saw in Zschokke's book another."

20   Philip Allen, "Lewis and Zschokke," *Modern Languages Notes,* XVII (1902), 61–62.

21   Karl S. Guthke, "Englische Vorromantik und deutscher Sturm und Drang," *Palaestra* (Göttingen, 1958), Bd. CCXXIII, S. 201–11.

22   Merton M. Sealts, "Melville's Reading: A Check-list of Books Owned and Borrowed," *Harvard Library Bulletin,* II (1948), S. 387 und VI (1952), S. 243.

23   Rudolf Majut, *Der deutsche Roman vom Biedermeier bis zur Gegenwart,* in *Deutsche Philologie im Aufriss,* ed. W. Stammler (2. Aufl.; Berlin, 1960), Bd. II, Sp. 1361.

24   Walter Wadepuhl, *Goethe's Interest in the New World* (Jena, 1934), S. 24 ff.

25   Ida G. Everson, "Goethe's American Visitors," *American Literature,* IX (1937), S. 356–57.

26   John T. Krumpelmann, "Young Southern Scholars in Goethe's Germany," *Jahrbuch für Amerikastudien,* Bd. IV (Heidelberg, 1959), S. 220–35, bes. S. 225.

27   Hanno Beck, *Alexander von Humboldt,* Bd. I (Wiesbaden, 1959), S. 228.

28   Brief Alexanders an Wilhelm v. Humboldt vom 21.9.1801.

29   *Heinrich Zschokkes Gesammelte Schriften, Zweite vermehrte Ausgabe* (Aarau, 1859), Siebenter Teil, S. 235.

30   *Eine Selbstschau,* S. 303.

31   *Gesammelte Schriften* (2. Ausg.; Aarau, 1851–1854), 7. Teil, S. 5.

32   Es müsste heissen: M. Bossu, *Nouveaux Voyages dans l'Amérique Septentrionale, contenant une collection de lettres écrites sur les lieux par l'auteur, à son ami M. Douin* (Amsterdam und Paris, 1778). Dieses Werk führt die Berichterstattung weiter, die Bossu schon ein Jahrzehnt früher begonnen hatte: *Nouveaux Voyages aux Indes Occidentales: contenant une relation des différens peuples qui habitent les environs du grand fleuve Saint-Louis, appellé vulgairement le Mississippi* (3 Bde.; Paris, 1768).

33   Durand Echeverria, *Mirage in the West: A History of the French Image of American Society to 1815* (Princeton, N.J.: Princeton University Press, 1957), S. 20.

34   *Ibid.,* S. 21.

35   Howard Mumford Jones, *America and French Culture, 1750–1848* (Chapel Hill, N.C.: University of North Carolina Press, 1927), S. 114.

36   *Nouveaux voyages aux Indes Occidentales,* Bd. I, S. 39.

37   J. A. Robertson, *Louisiana under the Rule of Spain, France and the United States, 1785–1807* (Cleveland, 1911), Bd. II, S. 29–59.

38   Echeverria, *op. cit.,* S. 228.

39 *Voyages dans l'intérieur de la Louisiane* (Paris, 1807).

40 *Voyage dans les deux Louisianes* (Paris, 1805).

41 *Vue de la colonie espagnole du Mississippi ou des provinces de la Louisiane et Floride occidentale, en l'année 1802* (Paris, 1803).

42 Zschokke, *Gesammelte Schriften*, S. 57.

43 *Ibid.*, S. 74.

44 *Ibid.*, S. 75.

45 *Ibid.*, S. 124.

46 *Ibid.*, S. 133.

47 *Ibid.*, S. 145.

48 *Ibid.*, S. 146.

49 *Ibid.*, S. 147.

50 *Ibid.*, S. 149–50.

51 *Ibid.*, S. 150.

52 *Ibid.*

53 *Ibid.*, S. 151.

54 *Ibid.*, S. 153.

55 *Ibid.*, S. 174.

56 *Ibid.*, S. 182.

57 *Ibid.*, S. 151.

58 Pochmann, *op. cit.*, S. 3.

59 F. de Chaville, "Le Voyage en Louisiane, 1720–1724," S. 134.

60 Blume, *op. cit.*, S. 8.

61 *Die Prinzessin von Wolfenbüttel, in Gesammelte Schriften, op. cit.*, S. 148.

62 *Ausführliche Historische und Geographische Beschreibung des an dem grossen Flusse Mississippi in Nord-Amerika gelegenen herrlichen Landes Louisiana; In welches die neu-aufgerichtete Frantzösische grosse Indianische Compagnie Colonien zu schicken angefangen . . .* (Leipzig: J. F. Gleditschens seel. Sohn, 1720), S. 29; Blume, *op. cit.*, S. 6.

63 *Die Prinzessin von Wolfenbüttel, op. cit.*, S. 149–50.

64 Blume, *op. cit.*, S. 5.

65 Helmut Blume, "Deutsche Kolonisten im Mississippidelta," *Jahrbuch für Amerikastudien* (Heidelberg, 1956), Bd. 1, S. 177–83, bes. S. 180.

66 *Die Prinzessin von Wolfenbüttel, op. cit.*, S. 124.

67 J. H. Deiler, *Die ersten Deutschen am unteren Mississippi und die Creolen deutscher Abstammung* (New Orleans, 1904).

68 *Die Prinzessin von Wolfenbüttel, op. cit.*, S. 8.

69 R. LeConte, "Les Allemands à la Louisiane au XVIIIe siècle," S. 8–9.

70 Blume, *op. cit.*, S. 98.

71 Jones, *op. cit.*, S. 113; Grace King, *Creole Families of New Orleans* (New York, 1921).

72 Vgl. Harold Jantz, "Amerika im deutschen Dichten und Denken," Sp. 332.

73 *Die Prinzessin von Wolfenbüttel, op. cit.*, S. 143.

74 *Ibid.*, S. 190.

75 *Das Blüthenalter der Empfindung* (Gotha, 1794), S. 146.

76 Friedrich v. Schlegel, *Sämmtliche Werke* (2. Aufl.; Wien, 1846), Bd. XI, S. 167.
77 *Ibid.,* Bd. VIII, S. 142–43. Vgl. Harold von Hofe, "Friedrich Schlegel and the New World," *PMLA,* LXXVI (1961), S. 63–67.
78 *Wilhelm Meisters Wanderjahre,* in *Goethes Sämtliche Werke* ("Jub.-Ausg."), Bd. 20, S. 202.
79 Karl J. R. Arndt, "The Harmony Society and *Wilhelm Meisters Wanderjahre,*" *Comparative Literature,* X (1958), S. 193–202.

W. A. WILLIBRAND

1 Cf. my paper, "When German was King: a FLES program around 1900," *The German Quarterly,* XXX (1957), 254–61.
2 A lady of sixty-five recalls having memorized these lines for the wedding of her aunt: "Begrüsst das junge Hochzeitspaar/zu ihrem Eh'stands-Bunde!/Sie knieten heute vorm Altar/Gott segnet' diese Stunde./Liebet ihr euch treu und gleich/So ist die Ehe ein Himmelreich."
3 His name was O. M. Sankey. Out of respect for his learning, which was probably superior to that of all other schoolmasters in the tri-county German-speaking area, people called him "Professor" Sankey. He contributed both prose and verse to weekly papers in the area. In its New Year's edition of 1904 the Osage County *Volksblatt* printed his "1904," a greeting in verse to the readers of the weekly. Here is the first stanza: "Du liebe Neunzehnhundert-Drei/Auch Du bist wieder mal vorbei:/Hast wie der Mohr Dein' Pflicht getan/ Und jetztund kannst Du scheiden!/Erst heiss ersehnt—ein eitler Wahn,/Mag nun Dich niemand leiden./Adieu dann, 1903,/Goodbye, goodbye." This piece was printed on pink paper as a sort of festive supplement to the *Volksblatt.*
4 In the issue of May 23, 1883, p. 2, the *Glockenweihe* having taken place on May 14, of the previous week.
5 Reichbronn has been anglicized as Richfountain.
6 The pages of this booklet are, unfortunately, not numbered. On the outside cover, in large to medium type, is this description: "Souvenir of the Centennial Celebration of St. Joseph's Parish, Westphalia, Missouri, August 6, 1935." The title page has these words: "History of the Founding of the Parish and Town of Westphalia, Missouri from August 6, 1835 to August 6, 1935, by Rev. J. C. Melies, S.T.L., Pastor." On the last page there is a box of three words which indicate that the printing was done in the *Home Adviser* plant at Vienna, Missouri.
7 This pastor was Father *Nicholas* Schlechter. Cf. Gilbert J. Garraghan, S.J., *The Jesuits of the Middle United States* (3 vols.; New York, 1938), I, 455, 463, 655, and III, 538.
8 *Amerika,* June 27, 1883, p. 2.
9 In the issue of September 16, 1888, p. 2.

10 Many of the early-day Westphalians no doubt experienced all the implications of extreme poverty. See Garraghan, *The Jesuits in Middle America,* I, 455. Cf. also my article, "A Forgotten Pioneer of West-phalia, Missouri," in *The American-German Review,* IX (April, 1943), 7–9 and 25. Its subject is Nicholas Hesse, a German pioneer who lived in the Westphalia community from the summer of 1835 until April 12, 1837. After his return to Germany Hesse published a book entitled, *Das westliche Nordamerika, in besonderer Beziehung auf die deutschen Einwanderer in ihren landwirtschaftlichen Handels- und Gewerbeverhältnissen* (Paderborn, 1838). It deals mainly with the hardships of pioneering in those northern foothills of the Ozarks.

ERICH A. ALBRECHT

1 "Laporte (l'abbé Jos. de), ex-jésuite, compilateur infatigable; né à Bedford, en 1713, mort à Paris, le 19 Décembre 1779." (Entry from J.-M. Quérard, *La France Littéraire* [Paris: Didot, 1830], IV, 549.)— "Cependant dans tout ce qu'il écrivoit, on remarquoit toujours un jugement droit, un goût sain, un style naturel, et pardessus tout le tact analytique, moins commun et plus estimable qu'on ne pense. Feu M. Fréron lui rendoit cette justice, et M. le Président de Montesquieu disoit, que le seul de ses critiques qui l'eut entendu, étoit l'Abbé de la Porte." (From *L'Année Littéraire* [Paris: Merigot, 1780], I, 108–109.)

2 *Le Voyageur François, ou la connoissance de l'Ancien et du Nouveau Monde,* mis au jour par M. L'Abbé Delaporte (Paris: L. Cellot, 1777), XXIII, 424–37.

3 *Reisen eines Franzosen, oder Beschreibung der vornehmsten Reiche in der Welt,* etc., vom Herrn Abte Delaporte (Leipzig: J. G. I. Breitkopf, 1782), XXVII, 164–86.

4 *Journal Encyclopédique* (Paris: Bouillon, 1766), V, 143 and *Zugabe zu den Goettingischen Anzeigen von Gelehrten Sachen* (Göttingen: J. A. Barmeier, 1774), XXXI, 261; both should be consulted for reviews of the *Voyageur François.*

5 J.-M. Querard (*op. cit.,* p. 551) credits him with the editing of the works of Massillon, L'Attaignant, Rousseau, Legrand, Regnard, Diderot, Crébillon, Sainte-Foix, and Pope. Heinsius, *Allgem. Buecherlexikon* (Leipzig: J. F. Gleditsch, 1812), III, 227, lists, in translation, *Hausmanns Vernunft, eine Sprachtabelle für Reisende,* and others like them.

6 M. Tourneux, *Correspondance Littéraire, Philosophique et Critique par Grimm, Diderot, Raynal, Meister, etc.* (Paris: Garnier, 1882), XVI, 269–87 (First letter: Aug. 4, 1750; second: Nov. 20, 1750).

7 Heinsius, *op. cit.,* p. 227.

8 *Zugabe zu den Goettingischen Anzeigen,* XXI, 174.

9 Tourneux, *op. cit.,* XVI, 269–87.

10 Michael Huber, *Choix de Poésies Allemandes* (Paris: Humblot, 1766), Vols. I–IV. Authors represented in Huber's book can be found in the *Journal Encyclopédique* (1766), V, 134–35.

11   *Mercure de France,* Oct., 1750, and Tourneux, *op. cit.,* XVI, 269.
12   *Le Voyageur François,* XXIII, 424.
13   *Ibid.,* 427–37.
14   J. R. Smiley, *Diderot's Relations with Grimm* ("University of Illinois Studies in Language and Literature," XXXIV, No. 4 [Urbana, 1950]), 116.
15   Anne C. Jones sides with Danzel in her dissertation ("F. M. Grimm as a Critic of the 18th Century French Drama" [Bryn Mawr, Pa., 1926], 30) in assuming that Grimm wrote reviews for Mylius' *Beyträge zur Historie und Aufnahme des Theaters.* See also: J. R. Smiley, "Grimm's Alleged Authorship of Certain Parisian Articles on the Theater in Paris," *Modern Language Notes,* LXIII (1948), 248–51.
16   Smiley, *Diderot's Relations with Grimm,* 6, discusses the question of Grimm's Gottschedian ties and credits A. C. Jones, "In Defense of Melchior Grimm," *PMLA,* XLIII (1928), 210–19, with a convincing refutation of the opinion that Grimm had been sent to Paris by Gottsched.
17   *Deutsches Anonymen-Lexikon* (Weimar: Holzmann u. Bohatta, 1905) erroneously names Gustav von Bergmann the "Verfasser" of the "Reisen . . ."
18   *Reisen eines Franzosen,* XXVII, 164.
19   F. W. Zachariä, in *Auserlesene Gedichte der Besten Deutschen Dichter von Martin Opitz bis auf die Gegenwaertige Zeit* (Braunschweig: Waisenhaus, 1766).
20   Viktor Hehn, *Goethe und das Publikum, eine Literaturgeschichte im kleinen* (Gütersloh: Bertelsmann, 1949) deals extensively with the problem of the inability of the eighteenth-century poets to appreciate their contemporaries, but fails to consider the lesser poets and the general reader.

G. WALDO DUNNINGTON

1   Über sie vgl. Leopold von Schlözer, *Dorothea von Schlözer, ein deutsches Frauenleben um die Jahrhundertwende 1770–1825* (Göttingen, 1937).
2   Vgl. *Polyanthea, ein Taschenbuch für das Jahr 1807,* hrsg. von Karl Reinhard (Münster).
3   Vgl. E. Eggli *L'Erotique comparée de Charles de Villers* (Paris, 1927).
4   Darüber, in Christian Otto und Ernst Förster, *Wahrheit aus Jean Pauls Leben,* 7. Heftlein (Breslau, 1833), S. 127 ff.
5   Ebda. S. 162 ff., hier auch die drei Antwortschreiben des Herzogs, S. 164–178.
6   Vgl. *le Spectateur du Nord,* IX, S. 238.
7   Als Fussnote gelegentlich der Behandlung der deutschen Universitäten, deutsche Ausgabe (Reutlingen, 1815), Bd. I, S. 133.
8   In späteren Jahren hat man pietätlos auf diesem ehrwürdigen Gottesacker der Göttinger Gelehrtenwelt "aufgeräumt." Besonders hat man in den Zeiten des Nazismus die kunstvollen alten schmiedeeisernen

Grabkreuze mit allen übrigen grausam fortgerissen, um sie zu Kriegs-
material einzuschmelzen.

ALFRED R. NEUMANN

1   *Goethes Gespräche,* ed. by Flodoard Freiherr von Biedermann (5
    vols.; Leipzig: F. W. Biedermann, 1909–11), IV, 219.
2   Alfred Einstein, *Gluck* (New York: E. P. Dutton, 1936), 114 f.
3   *Teutscher Merkur,* XI (1775, Drittes Vierteljahr), 68.

HELLMUT A. HARTWIG

1   *Wilhelm Tell, Schauspiel von Friedrich Schiller,* hrsg. v. Arthur H.
    Palmer (New York: Henry Holt and Co., 1898; Neuauflage, 1931); vgl.
    Einleitung Palmers, S. lxvii, Fussnote. Alle Schillerzitate sind aus
    dieser Ausgabe.
2   Karl Schmid, "Schiller und die Schweiz," in *Schiller, Reden im
    Gedenkjahr 1955* (Stuttgart: Ernst Klett Verlag, 1955). Schmid meint
    u.a.: "Ein Goethischer *Tell,* ein richtigerer ganz ohne Zweifel, weil
    ein dumpferes, schwerkräftiges Bild des Ursprungs dieses Volkes, es
    hätte diesem Volke nicht sein können was der Schillersche." (Auf
    Seite 13 dieser Sammlung von Gedenkreden sagt Thomas Mann in
    seinem Vortrag, den er schlicht und souverän "Schiller" betitelte:
    "Man findet in den Äusserungen dieses Freiheitsideologen zur Politik
    und zum sozialen Problem eine realistische Unverschwärmtheit, die
    verblüfft. Es bleibt nicht bei dem berühmten 'Die Mehrheit ist der
    Unsinn,' womit er die Demokratie vor den Kopf stösst. Er konnte es
    mit dem Worte so grob treiben wie in dem Distichon von der 'Würde
    des Menschen': 'Nichts mehr davon, ich bitt' euch. Zu essen gebt
    ihm, zu wohnen; habt ihr die Blösze bedeckt, gibt sich die Würde
    von selbst.' " Eben diese "realistische Unverschwärmtheit" in Schiller,
    scheint mir, verkörpert seine Tellgestalt mehr als seine Schwärmereien
    für alles Ideale, die in seinen anderen Gestalten und Dramen so zum
    Ausdruck kommen.)
3   "Meister Anton" in Friedrich Hebbels *Maria Magdalena.*
4   Lily Hohenstein, *Schiller, der Kämpfer, der Dichter* (Berlin: Paul Neff
    Verlag, 1940)—Dazu vergleiche man folgenden Auszug aus diesem
    Buche (S. 369): ". . . Tell, der auf seinen Knaben schiessen muss, und
    der doch, ein schlichtes Kind des Volkes, mit ganz derselben Unter-
    würfigkeit für seinen 'gnädigen Herrn,' wie sie einst Hauptmann
    Schiller erfüllte, unmöglich auf die dem denkenden Menschen so
    einfache Lösung verfallen kann, sofort aufs Herz des Peinigers zu
    zielen." Hierzu kann ich nur sagen, dass der "denkende" Mensch
    eben nicht auf Gessler geschossen hätte, denn er konnte sich "den-
    ken," was gleich darauf von der Übermacht der bewaffneten Knechte
    Gesslers zu erwarten gewesen wäre. Wenn die Verfasserin mit "den-
    kender Mensch" aber den überverfeinerten Idealisten, der sich bewusst

opfert, meint, warum dann der Ausdruck "so einfache Lösung"? Bewusster Opfertod ist doch nicht eine *"einfache* Lösung"?

5 Vgl. *Friedrich Schiller, Wilhelm Tell,* hrsg. v. Robert Waller Deering (Orig. Ausg., 1894; Boston: D. C. Heath and Co., 1961). Auf S. xxxiii der Einleitung schreibt Deering: "It (die Ermordung Gesslers aus dem Hinterhalt) is as necessary as the apple-shot, for without it Tell is no longer Tell; it is, moreover, justified by the logic of the monologue and the Parricida scene, as well as by every human instinct." Auf S. xxxii sagt Deering betreffs "des ersten Pfeils": ". . . to shoot Gessler instead would have meant the wholesale slaughter of himself, his boy, and his friends by the body-guard."

6 Vgl. Fritz Strich, *Schiller. Sein Leben und Werk,* "Tempel Klassiker" (Leipzig: Tempel-Verlag, 1912), *Schillers Sämtliche Werke,* 13ter Bd. ("Ergänzungsband"), S. 424 schreibt Strich: "Er (Tell) muss allein stehen und seiner eigenen Kraft, nicht dem Bunde vertrauen." Tell ist der Helfer für alle, ihm hilft sein Volk nicht; er muss sich selbst helfen. Wie heldenhaft ist also das Volk "als Held"? Tells Einstellung zum Volk ist aus seinem: "Ich helfe mir schon selbst. Geht, gute Leute!" zu erkennen. Allerdings, hätte ihm das Volk bei der Gelegenheit geholfen, den Hutwächtern zu entkommen, wäre es nicht zum Apfelschuss gekommen, und ein *Tell*-Drama ohne Apfelschuss wäre undenkbar. Also musste das Volk *im Vergleich zu Tell* schwach und unheroisch bleiben.

7 Melitta Gerhard, *Schiller* (Bern: A. Francke A. G. Verlag, 1950), S. 409.

8 Hans Rudolf Hilty, *Friedrich Schiller, Abriss seines Lebens, Umriss seines Werkes* (Bern: Gute Schriften, 1955), S. 63.

9 Arthur Böhtlingk, *Shakespeare und unsere Klassiker* (Leipzig: Fritz Eckardt Verlag, 1910), S. 417 ff. (des Dritten Bandes: "Schiller und Shakespeare").

10 *Ibid.,* S. 420.

11 Ludwig Bellermann, *Schillers Dramen, Beiträge zu ihrem Verständnis,* zweiter Teil, zweite Aufl. (Berlin: Weidmannsche Buchhandlung, 1898), S. 460.

12 *Ibid.,* S. 452.

13 Reinhard Buchwald, *Schiller—Leben und Werk* (4. u. neu bearbeitete Auflage; Wiesbaden: Insel-Verlag, 1959), S. 782.

14 Hohenstein, *op. cit.,* S. 369.

15 Hoxie Neale Fairchild, *The Noble Savage. An Inquiry into a Phase of Romantic Naturalism* (New York: Columbia University Press, 1929).

16 In *Archiv für das Studium der neueren Sprachen und Literaturen,* CLVII (1930), 93–98.

17 Vgl. Johann Gottfried Herder, *Sämtlichte Werke,* hrsg. v. Bernhard Suphan (32 Bde.; Berlin: Weidmannsche Buchhandlung, 1877–1913), Bd. XVIII, S. 221, 222, 226, 229 ff.

18 Fairchild, *op. cit.,* S. 507.

19 Wer sich mit der Symbolik in *Faust II* befasst hat, weiss was ich meine.

20 Robert T. Clark, Jr., "The Noble Savage and the Idea of Tolerance in Herder's *Briefe zu Beförderung der Humanität," JEGP,* XXXIII (1934), 46–56.
21 Bellermann, *op. cit.,* S. 461.
22 *Ibid.*
23 Buchwald, *op. cit.,* S. 780 ff.
24 *Ibid.,* S. 776. Vgl. auch William Witte, *Schiller* ("Modern Language Studies," VI [Oxford: Basil Blackwell, 1949]), S. 193 ff.
25 Herder, *Werke,* Bd. XIII, S. 250.
26 Bellermann, *op. cit.,* S. 462.
27 Vgl. *Friedrich Schiller, Briefe,* hrsg. v. Gerhard Fricke (München: Carl Hanser Verlag, o.j.), S. 614, Brief No. 569 (An Wilhelm von Wolzogen, Weimar, 4. Sept. 1803). Mit Bezug auf einen "brillant'nen Ring," den Schiller vom König von Schweden erhalten hatte (für sein Werk über den Dreissigjährigen Krieg), schrieb der Dichter: "Ihr Herren Staats- und Geschäftsleute habt eine grosse Affinität zu diesen Kostbarkeiten; aber unser Reich ist nicht von dieser Welt . . ." Vgl. *supra,* Fussnote 2, Thomas Manns Bemerkung über Schillers "realistische Unverschwärmtheit." Damit hätten wir in Schiller selbst die zwei Typen, die in "einer Brust wohnen."

WALTER SILZ

1 *Hölderlin, Sämtliche Werke,* ed. Friedrich Beissner (Stuttgart, 1943–), II, 539 f.
2 Wilhelm Böhm, *Hölderlin* (Halle, 1928–30), II, 509 f., does find the Ganymede reference "verwirrend" and the "sharpening" of the language in B overdone to the point of impairing oral delivery and strophic structure. But he has no major fault to find.
3 Alfred Romain, *"Ganymed,"* in *Hölderlin-Jahrbuch 1952* (Tübingen), 51–84; the passages quoted are on p. 81 f.
4 Richard M. Müller, *Die deutsche Klassik.* Wesen und Geschichte im Spiegel des Strommotivs (Bonn, 1959), 114.
5 Ernst Müller, *Hölderlin.* Studien zur Geschichte seines Geistes (Stuttgart [1944]), 453.
6 Robert Ulshöfer, "Hölderlin, *Des Morgens* und *Der gefesselte Strom,"* in *Der Deutschunterricht,* 1948–49, Heft 2/3, p. 52.
7 Romain, *op. cit.,* 77, bases on "Stromgeist" (B 19) a contrived explanation that permits the "spirit" of the river to rise like Ganymede to heaven while its "irdisch-zeitliche Daseinsform" flows on! Conveniently for this explanation, Hölderlin has refrained, "mit künstlerischem Takt," from bringing in Jove's eagle!
8 E.g., in *Heidelberg,* youth is an essential trait of the river, and not an attribute of age, for by this criterion the Neckar would be a "Greis" by the time it reaches Heidelberg.
9 It might also suggest the unhappy private individual Hölderlin. There are other features in B: the "gewanderter Mann," the "Linki-

sche," the "Schlacken" and need of "Reinigung," the sense of "Irrge-
hen" and "nicht mehr dabei sein," and even the wish for a Ganyme-
dian translation, that could conceivably be read as constituents of
another poem, one of personal tragedy, superimposed on A with a sort
of double-exposure effect. But such conjecture would soon go beyond
the evidence of the texts before us.

10   Beissner's note on A 8, "wohl der Aether," is not as definite as it
might be (II, 546), and the referral to his note on *Der blinde Sänger*,
line 8 (II, 508, and the reverse reference there) is misleading, for
the "Boten" in *Der gefesselte Strom*, line 5, are *not* messengers from
Aether.

11   Norbert von Hellingrath, however (*Hölderlin, Sämtliche Werke*
[Berlin, 1923], IV, 309), persuades himself *"der Linkische* ebenso
Gegensatz zu *eilt* wie früher *Zauderer."*

12   Hellingrath, *ibid.:* "die minder gebräuchliche Stellung nötigt uns
dort und da viel sinnlicher aufzufassen (auch: näher kommend) als
früher in gewohnter Folge."—It is surely pedantic to impute to Hölderlin a concern over the hiatus "da/und" (Liegler).

13   The MS. shows in turn "Zitternden," "Bebenden," "Schütternden";
"Schallenden," "Stürzenden" [already questionable], and "Schauenden"—see Beissner, *op. cit.,* II, 541, 545.

14   Romain, *op. cit.,* 73, reasons that since the hills are already shaken
up (according to his "Bergdurchbruch" theory), it is no longer necessary for them to "awake"! The getting up of the cattle, on the other
hand, means "Das hereinbrechende Getöse wirkt wie Alarmruf, der
dem geschichtslosen Hirtendasein ein Ende macht"—but no "Hir-
ten" have been mentioned, and the "Dasein" of the cattle is presumably
unchanged!

15   Of late years there has been much criticism (some of it occasioned
by my article on Goethe's *Tasso* in *GR* [1956], 243 ff.) of the biographical approach to poetry. Such criticism is justified where it is
levelled against a naïve paralleling of work and life and an "explain-
ing" of poetry as the "expression" of the poet's private experiences.
But there is an area where the personal reference is valid, and where
to ignore it would be as unscholarly as to overemphasize it. If we
approach a work of literature with a prejudice derived from biographical information, we are guilty of unscientific procedure; if,
having observed flaws in a work of literature—in the present case
the objectively verifiable inferiority of one text to another—we
disregard biographical facts that explain and corroborate our observations, then we are failing to make use of one of the tools of our
discipline; and as a humane discipline it can never forego human
considerations altogether. If Hölderlin scholarship would mercifully
recognize the human fact that many of the later poems were written
under the awful impediment of insanity, we should be spared a great
deal of unfruitful construction and rationalization.

GILBERT J. JORDAN

1 Vgl. hierzu Nietzsches *Zarathustra*, "Mittags," 4. Teil: "Und Zarathu- stra lief und fand niemanden mehr und war allein und fand immer wieder sich und genoss und schlürfte seine Einsamkeit und dachte an gute Dinge—stundenlang."

2 Die Seitenangaben zu den Zitaten aus dem *Stundenbuch* beziehen sich auf *Rainer Maria Rilkes Ausgewählte Werke* (Leipzig: Insel-Verlag, 1942).

F. E. COENEN

1 Cf. Otto Zoff, *The German Theater Today* (Milwaukee: Marquette University Press, 1960), 6.

2 Friedrich Luft, "Theaterfülle—Dramenleere," *Jahresring 1956/57* (Stuttgart, 1956).

3 Friedrich Luft, "Bühnenkonjunktur—Theaterlethargie," *Jahresring 1957/58* (Stuttgart, 1957).

4 Friedrich Luft, "Dreissig Millionen suchen einen Autor," *Jahresring 1959/60* (Stuttgart, 1959).

5 Friedrich Luft, "Das multiplizierte Theater," *Jahresring 1960/61* (Stuttgart, 1960).

6 Gerhart Hauptmann, the last of the great German dramatists, re- mained almost silent during those years; in one instance he prevented the performance of a play, *Magnus Garbe,* because in it he showed an anti-Catholic line and he did not want it to appear as if he were sharing the Nazi régime's anti-clerical attitude.

7 Cf. also Fritz Martini, "Das Theater der Gegenwart," in *Deutsche Literatur in unserer Zeit* (Göttingen, 1959), 80–104, and the bibliog- raphy, p. 104. Further: Hans Schweikart, "Zum Theater der Gegen- wart," *Welt und Wort*, XVI (Jan., 1961), 1–4.

8 Friedrich Luft, "Postwar Theater. A Crowded Vacuum," *Atlantic*, CXCIX, No. 3 (March, 1957), 185.

9 *Ibid.*, 186.

10 Mordecai Gorelik, "Brecht. 'I am the Einstein of the New Stage Form . . . '," *Theater Arts*, XLI, No. 3 (March, 1957), 72–73, 86–87, 73.

11 *Ibid.*, 86.

12 Cf. also Klaus Lazarowicz, "Bertolt Brecht," in *Lexikon der Weltlitera- tur* (Freiburg, Basel, Wien, 1960), I, 247–54.

13 Zoff, *op. cit.*, 2.

14 Cf. also Zoff, *op. cit.*, 10.

15 Friedrich Heer, "Perspektiven österreichischer Gegenwartsdichtung," *Deutsche Literatur in unserer Zeit* (Göttingen, 1959), 149.

16 *Es steht geschrieben* (1947), *Der Blinde* (1948), *Romulus der Grosse* (1949), *Die Ehe des Herrn Mississippi* (1952), *Nächtlicher Besuch* (1953), *Ein Engel kommt nach Babylon* (1954), *Der Besuch der alten*

Dame (1956), and (an opera together with Paul Burkhard) *Frank V. —Oper einer Privatbank* (1959).

17 Claus Helmut Drese (ed.), *Das neue Nationaltheater* (Mainz, 1955), 75–76.

18 Another form of the epic theater is used by Anouilh in his *Antigone* where the speaker details the action in the beginning, telling the audience about the characters of the stage figures, thus diminishing the dramatic tension.

19 Friedrich Dürrenmatt, *Komödien* (Zurich, 1957), 358.

20 Otto C. A. Zur Nedden and Karl H. Ruppel (eds.), *Reclams Schauspielführer* (5th ed.; Stuttgart, 1958), 841–42. Cf. also Ian C. Loram, " 'Der Besuch der alten Dame' and 'The Visit,' " *Monatshefte,* LIII, No. 1 (Jan., 1961), 15–21; and Eugene E. Reed, "Dürrenmatt's 'Der Besuch der alten Dame': A Study in the Grotesque," *Monatshefte,* LIII, No. 1 (Jan., 1961), 9–14.

21 Paul Burkhard is a Swiss composer, born in Zurich in 1911. Mainly self-taught, he has written a number of operetta scores. His most successful is *Fireworks* with the hit "Oh My Papa," probably the most frequently sung number in Europe between 1950 and 1955. Introduced in New York by Eddie Fisher, it is said to have sold more than four million records.

22 Luft, "Postwar Theater," 186–87.

23 Luft, "Das multiplizierte Theater," 365. Cf. also F. E. Coenen's articles titled "German Literature" in the *Annuals* of the *Encyclopedia Americana* for the years 1956, 1957, 1958, 1959, 1960, 1961, 1962, and 1963.

MARGARET KOBER MERZBACH

1 *Opus Epistolarum De. Erasmi Roterodami,* ed. P. S. Allen (Oxford, 1906 ff.), II, 37.

2 *Ibid.,* III, 517.

3 Robert H. Murray, *Erasmus and Luther* (London, 1920), 87.

4 Rudolf Pfeiffer, *Humanitas Erasmiana* (Leipzig and Berlin, 1931).

5 Johan Huizinga, *Erasmus and the Age of Reformation,* trans. F. Hopman (New York, 1957), 148.

6 Lucien Price, *Dialogues of Alfred North Whitehead* (Boston, 1945), 236.

7 Paul Tillich, *Systematic Theology* (Chicago, 1951 ff.), II, 78–79.

8 Karl Barth, *The Epistle to the Romans,* trans. E. C. Hopkins (London, 1960), 357.

9 Paul Tillich, *The Protestant Era,* trans. James Luther Adler (Chicago, 1947), 129.

10 Allen, *op. cit.,* VII, 430–32.

11 Stefan Zweig, *Triumph und Tragik des Erasmus von Rotterdam* (Vienna, 1935), 22.

12 Tillich, *Systematic Theology,* I, 195.

13 Tillich, *The Protestant Era,* 168.

FRANK WOOD

1   Gertrud von Le Fort, *Am Tore des Himmels. Novelle* (Wiesbaden: Insel-Verlag, 1954), 66–68.
2   *Ibid.*
3   *Ibid.*
4   *Ibid.*, 78.
5   *Ibid.*, 84–85.
6   *Ibid.*, 87.
7   *Ibid.*
8   Cf. Martin Esslin, *Brecht: A Choice of Evils, A Critical Study of the Man, his Work and his Opinions* (London, 1959), 227.
9   For more complete details on the various versions, see Käthe Rülicke, "*Leben des Galilei*—Bemerkungen zur Schlussszene," in *Sinn und Form, Beiträge zur Literatur. Zweites Sonderheft Bertolt Brecht* (Berlin: Rütten & Loening, 1958), 269 ff.
10 Brecht, *Leben des Galilei, Versuche, 19* (Berlin: Suhrkamp-Verlag, 1955), 97 ff.
11 Rülicke, *op. cit.*, 282.
12 *Ibid.*
13 *Ibid.*, 275.
14 *Ibid.*, 292.
15 Esslin, *op. cit.*, 227.
16 *Ibid.*, 226.
17 Rülicke, *op. cit.*, 272.
18 Brecht, *op. cit.*, 92.
19 *Ibid.*, 98.
20 Further interesting variations on the theme discussed may be found in the chapter in Thomas Mann's *Zauberberg*, "Vom Gottesstaat und von übler Erlösung." The dialectical duel between Naphta and Settembrini regarding the role of science in Western society forms a rather ironical commentary on the arguments of Le Fort and Brecht. For example, in a passage in which Galileo's name occurs, Naphta attacks Settembrini's conception of a "voraussetzungslose Wissenschaft": Guter Freund, es gibt keine reine Erkenntnis . . . Der Glaube ist das Organ der Erkenntnis und der Intellekt sekundär. Ihre voraussetzungslose Wissenschaft ist eine Mythe." Finally, Naphta's conception of a "staats-und klassenlose Gotteskindschaft" sets up in paradoxical, not to mention contradictory, relief the argument so far presented. See *Der Zauberberg* (Berlin: S. Fischer-Verlag, 1930), 519.

Publications of
John T. Krumpelmann

Compiled by
Carl Hammer, Jr.

TRANSLATIONS

Hans Sachs. *Brooding Calves, Shrovetide Play in Four Acts* (verse), *Poet Lore,* XXXVIII (1927), 435–46.

Andreas Gryphius. *The Beloved Hedgerose, A Play in Four Acts* (prose), *Poet Lore,* XXXIX (1928), 544–72.

Heinrich von Kleist. *The Broken Jug, A Comedy* (verse), *Poet Lore,* XLV (1939), 146–209.

Friedrich Schiller. *The Maiden of Orleans, A Romantic Tragedy,* translated into English in the verse forms of the original German. ("University of North Carolina Studies in the Germanic Languages and Literatures," ed. F. E. Coenen, No. 24.) Chapel Hill, 1959; revised edition, in "University of North Carolina Studies in the Germanic Languages and Literatures," No. 37. 1962.

MONOGRAPHS

Mark Twain and the German Language ("Louisiana State University Studies, Humanities Series," No. 3.) Baton Rouge, 1953.

Bayard Taylor and German Letters ("Britannica et Americana," eds. Ludwig Borinski and Horst Oppel, Band IV.) Hamburg: Cram, de Gruyter & Co., 1959.

ARTICLES AND ESSAYS

(Abbreviations: *AGR* = *American-German Review; Archiv* = *Archiv für das Studium der neueren Sprachen; GQ* = *German Quarterly; GR* = *Germanic Review; JEGP* = *Journal of English and Germanic Philology; MLJ* = *Modern Language Journal; MLN* = *Modern Language Notes; MLQ* = *Modern Language Quarterly.*)

165

"Why Study German?" *North Carolina High School Journal*, IV (1921), 147–49.

"Carnival in Munich," New Orleans *Times-Picayune*, Jan. 31, 1926, p. 3.

"Goethe's *Faust*, 4203–4205," *MLN*, XLI (1926), 107–14.

"Longfellow's *Golden Legend* and the 'Armer Heinrich' Theme in Modern German Literature," *JEGP*, XXV (1926), 173–92.

"George Eliot's *The Mill on the Floss* and Theodor Storm's *Immensee*," *MLJ*, XI (1926), 41–43.

" 'Studio,' " *American Speech*, II (1926), 158.

"A Survival?" *American Speech*, II (1926), 158.

"Schiller's *Hoffnung* and Pope's *Essay on Man*," *GR*, III (1928), 128–33.

"Hoodlum," *MLN, L* (1935), 93–95.

"Some West Virginia Peculiarities," *American Speech*, XIV (1939), 155 f.

"Some Observations on Storm's *Von Jenseit des Meeres*," *GR*, XV (1940), 46–49.

"American Speech and Foreign Listeners," *American Speech*, XV (1940), 448 f.

"Charles Sealsfield's Americanisms," *American Speech*, XVI (1941), 26–31.

"Charles Sealsfield's Americanisms," II, *American Speech*, XVI (1941), 104–11.

"For the DAE Supplement," *American Speech*, XVII (1942), 69 f.

" 'Chicken Feed,' 'Rascal,' 'Rowel,' " *American Speech*, XVII (1942), 76 f.

"Schiller and Saint Joan of Arc," *Monatshefte*, XXXIV (1942), 159–68.

"Gleanings from Parker's Trip to the West," *American Speech*, XVIII (1943), 52.

"Ingraham's *South-West* as a Source of Americanisms," *American Speech*, XVIII (1943), 157 f.

"The Genesis of Bayard Taylor's Translation of Goethe's *Faust*," *JEGP*, XLII (1943), 551–62.

"A Re-examination of Vocabulary of *A Stray Yankee in Texas*," *American Speech*, XIX (1944), 43–46.

"Some Americanisms from Texas in 1848," *American Speech*, XIX (1944), 69 f.

"Charles Sealsfield's Americanisms," III, *American Speech*, XIX (1944), 196–99.

"A Source for Local Color in Sealsfield's *Cajütenbuch*," *JEGP*, XLIII (1944), 429–33.

"Giving the Keys of the City," *American Notes and Queries*, III (1944), 174.

"Du Pratz's *History of Louisiana* (1763), A Source of Americanisms, Especially of Those Attributed to Imlay," *American Speech*, XX (1945), 45–50.

"Gerstäcker's *Germelshausen* and Lerner's *Brigadoon*," *Monatshefte*, XL (1948), 396–400.

"Madness or Method?" *American Speech*, XXIII (1948), 316 f.

"Supplementing the DAE," *American Speech*, XXIV (1949), 149–51.

"Lessing's *Faust Fragment* and *Romeo and Juliet*," *MLN*, LXIV (1949), 395–97.

"Kibitzer," *American Speech,* XXV (1950), 154.

"Sealsfield's 'China Trees,'" *Monatshefte,* XLIII (1951), 44 f.

"Kleist's *Krug* and Shakespeare's *Measure for Measure,*" GR, XXVI (1951), 13–21.

"Shakespeare's Falstaff Dramas and Kleist's *Zerbrochener Krug,*" MLQ, XII (1951), 462–72.

"The Renaming of Berlin Street and Berlin Streets," *American Speech,* XXVI (1951), 156 f.

"Sealsfield and Sources," *Monatshefte,* XLIII (1951), 324–26.

"Hoodlum," MLN, LXVII (1952), 255.

"This Was Goethe" (popular discourse), in *Goethe After Two Centuries,* ed. Carl Hammer, Jr. ("Louisiana State University Studies, Humanities Series," No. 1.) Baton Rouge, 1952.

"The Goethe Bicentennial in Frankfurt am Main," in *Goethe After Two Centuries,* ed. Carl Hammer, Jr. ("Louisiana State University Studies, Humanities Series," No. 1.) Baton Rouge, 1952.

"Sealsfield's Inebriated Robbins," *Monatshefte,* XLVI (1954), 225 f.

"Midsummer Night's Dreams," *Monatshefte,* XLVI (1954), 281 f.

"More Americanisms from C. F. Hoffman," *American Speech,* XXIX (1954), 119–21.

"Bayard Taylor and Schiller," in *Contributions to the Humanities* ("Louisiana State University Studies, Humanities Series," No. 5.) Baton Rouge, 1954.

"Spoon-Löffel," *Archiv,* 191. Band, 106. Jahrgang (1955), 321–23.

"Bayard Taylor as a Literary Mediator between Germany and the South Atlantic States," *Die neueren Sprachen, Neue Folge* (Jahrgang 1955), 115–18.

"Americanisms in Poinsett's *Notes on Mexico,*" *American Speech,* XXX (1955), 256–59.

"Revealing the Source of Irving's *Rip van Winkle,*" *Monatshefte,* XLVII (1955), 361 f.; *Archiv,* 193. Band, 108. Jahrgang (1956), 39 f.

"Germany: Tragedy or Miracle?" *Louisiana State University Alumni News,* XXXII (1956), 6–11.

"Hawthorne's *Young Goodman Brown* and Goethe's *Faust,*" *Die neueren Sprachen, Neue Folge* (Jahrgang 1956), 516–21.

"New Orleans of 1826 to a German," New Orleans *Times-Picayune,* Dec. 23, 1956, Sec. 3, p. 2.

"In Memoriam, Robert Clark," *South-Central Bulletin,* XVII, No. 3 (Oct., 1957), 2–3.

"More Words from Mexico," *American Speech,* XXXII (1957), 176–79.

"Charles Sealsfield and the College of Orleans," *Louisiana State University Alumni News,* XXXIV (1958), 22 f.

"Sealsfield Vindicated," *Monatshefte,* L (1958), 257–59.

"Duponceau and Weimar," *Die neueren Sprachen, Neue Folge* (Jahrgang 1959), 57–61.

"Notes on American Lexicography and Joel R. Poinsett's *Notes on Mexico,*" *Archiv,* 195. Band, 110. Jahrgang (1959), 325–30.

"Americanisms Recorded by Duke Bernhard of Saxe-Weimar," in *Festschrift für Walther Fischer,* hrsg. von Horst Oppel. Heidelberg: Carl Winter Universitätsverlag, 1959.

"Young Southern Scholars in Goethe's Germany," *Jahrbuch für Amerikastudien,* IV (Heidelberg: Carl Winter Universitätsverlag, 1959), 220–35.

"Schiller: Two Hundred Years After," *The Bridge* (Hamburg), III, No. 2 (Nov., 1959), 4 f.

"Schiller's Rehabilitation of Jeanne d'Arc," *AGR,* XXVI (Dec., 1959–Jan., 1960), 8–9, 38.

"A More Genteel David Crockett?" *American Speech,* XXV (1960), 309.

"Basil Lanneau Gildersleeve, Classicist and Germanist," *AGR,* XXVII (1961), 25–27.

"Goethe's *Faust* and Marc Connelly's *Green Pastures,*" in *Studies in Comparative Literature* ("Louisiana State University Studies, Humanities Series," No. 11.) Baton Rouge, 1962.

REVIEWS

Kuno, Francke. *Weltbürgertum in der deutschen Literatur von Herder bis Nietzsche* (= *Die Kulturwerte der deutschen Literatur in ihrer geschichtlichen Entwicklung,* Dritter Band, Erste Abteilung [Berlin: Weidmannsche Buchhandlung, 1928]), in *Harvard Graduates' Magazine,* June, 1929, pp. 527 f.

Walter Silz. *Early German Romanticism: Its Founders and Heinrich von Kleist,* Cambridge: Harvard University Press, 1929, in *Harvard Graduates' Magazine,* September, 1929, pp. 137–39.

E. L. Stahl. *Heinrich von Kleist's Dramas* ("Modern Language Studies," ed. James Boyd, *et al.,* IV), Oxford: Blackwell, 1948, in *JEGP,* L (1951), 269–71.

L. H. Woodson. *American Negro Slavery in the Works of Friedrich Strubberg, Friedrich Gerstäcker and Otto Ruppius,* Washington: The Catholic University of America Press, 1949, in *Monatshefte,* XLIII (1951), 243.

Eduard Castle. *Der grosse Unbekannte, das Leben von Charles Sealsfield,* Wien: Manutiuspresse, 1952, in *GR,* XXVIII (1953), 303–305.

Hans Plischke. *Von Cooper bis Karl May: Eine Geschichte des völkerkundlichen Reise-und Abenteuerromans,* Düsseldorf: Droste Verlag, 1951, in *JEGP,* LII (1953), 432 f.

Horst Oppel. *Der Einfluss der englischen Literatur auf die deutsche* (Sonderdruck aus *Deutsche Philologie,* hrsg. von Wolfgang Stammler [Berlin, etc.: Erich Schmidt Verlag, n.d.], in *Archiv,* 192. Band, 107. Jahrgang (1955), 73.

Walther Fischer (ed.). *Jahrbuch für Amerikastudien,* I, Heidelberg: Carl Winter Universitätsverlag, 1956, in *AGR,* XXIII (April–May, 1957), 30 and in *Monatshefte,* XLIX (1957), 215–17.

Max Freund (tr. and ed.). *Gustav Dresel's Houston Diary, Adventures in North America and Texas, 1837–1841,* Austin: University of Texas Press, 1955, in *South-Central Bulletin,* XVIII (1958), 22.

Eduard Castle, *Der grosse Unbekannte, das Leben von Charles Sealsfield:*

Briefe und Aktenstücke, Wien: Verlag Karl Werner, 1955, in *GQ,* XXXI (1958), 247 f.

John R. Frey (ed.). *Schiller 1759–1959: Commemorative American Studies,* Urbana: University of Illinois Press, 1959, in *JEGP,* LIX (1960), 188 f.

A. Leslie Willson (ed.). *A Schiller Symposium,* Austin: Department of Germanic Languages, University of Texas, 1960, in *South-Central Bulletin,* XXI (1961), 33.

Karl J. R. Arndt and May E. Olson. *German American Newspapers and Periodicals: History and Bibliography,* Heidelberg: Quelle & Meyer, 1961, in *The Library Quarterly,* XXXII (1962), 255.

Contributors

ERICH A. ALBRECHT

Professor and Chairman of the Department of German, Tulane University.

ARTHUR BURKHARD

Formerly of the German Department of Harvard University; later Visiting Professor at the universities of Pennsylvania and Texas, and recently at the universities of Graz and Bologna.

F. E. COENEN

Professor of German, University of North Carolina, and Editor, "University of North Carolina Studies in the Germanic Languages and Literatures."

G. WALDO DUNNINGTON

Professor of English and German, Northwestern State College of Louisiana.

HELLMUT A. HARTWIG

Professor of German, Southern Illinois University.

GILBERT J. JORDAN

Professor and Head of Department of German, Southern Methodist University.

MARGARET KOBER MERZBACH

Visiting Professor of German, Louisiana State University.

171

ALFRED R. NEUMANN

Professor of German and Dean, College of Arts and Sciences, University of Houston.

HORST OPPEL

Director, Englisches Seminar, University of Marburg.

WALTER SILZ

Gebhard Professor of Germanic Languages and Literatures, Columbia University.

W. A. WILLIBRAND

Professor Emeritus of Modern Languages, University of Oklahoma.

FRANK WOOD

Professor of German, University of Minnesota.